Praise *for*

The Underground Railroad

"An engrossing and harrowing novel."
—*The Sunday Times* (London)

"[A] triumph. . . . The canon of essential novels about America's peculiar institution just grew by one."　—*The Washington Post*

"Lovely and rare, dark and imaginative. . . . Whitehead's best work and an important American novel."　—*The Boston Globe*

"Whitehead's achievement is truly remarkable: by giving the Underground Railroad a new mythology, he has found a way of confronting other myths, older and persistent, about the United States. His book cannot have enough readers."　—*The Telegraph* (London)

"[Whitehead] is the best living American novelist."
—*Chicago Tribune*

"An extraordinary novel, a rich, confident work that will deservedly win—on the basis of literary merit as well as moral purpose. . . . A virtuoso novel that should be read by every American as well as readers across the world. And it will be, it should be."
—*The Irish Times*

"Masterful, urgent. . . . One of the finest novels written about our country's still unabsolved original sin."　—*USA Today*

"Whitehead's novel unflinchingly turns our attention to the foundations of the America we know now."　—*Elle*

COLSON WHITEHEAD

The Underground Railroad

Colson Whitehead is the *New York Times* bestselling author of *The Underground Railroad*, winner of the National Book Award; *The Noble Hustle*; *Zone One*; *Sag Harbor*; *The Intuitionist*; *John Henry Days*, a finalist for the Pulitzer Prize; *Apex Hides the Hurt*; and one collection of essays, *The Colossus of New York*. A recipient of MacArthur and Guggenheim fellowships, he lives in New York City.

www.colsonwhitehead.com

Colson Whitehead is available for select speaking engagements. To inquire about a possible appearance, please contact Penguin Random House Speakers Bureau at speakers@penguinrandomhouse.com or visit www.prhspeakers.com.

ALSO BY COLSON WHITEHEAD

The Noble Hustle

Zone One

Sag Harbor

Apex Hides the Hurt

The Colossus of New York

John Henry Days

The Intuitionist

The
Underground
Railroad

A NOVEL

Colson
Whitehead

ANCHOR BOOKS

A Division of Penguin Random House LLC

New York

FIRST ANCHOR BOOKS OPEN-MARKET EDITION, JULY 2017

The Library of Congress has cataloged the Doubleday edition as follows:
Names: Whitehead, Colson, 1969– author.
Title: The underground railroad : a novel / Colson Whitehead.
Description: New York : Doubleday, 2016.
Subjects: LCSH: Underground Railroad—Fiction. | Fugitive slaves—United States—Fiction. | United States—History—19th century—Fiction.
BISAC: FICTION / Literary. | FICTION / Historical. | FICTION / African American / General. | GSAFD: Historical fiction.
Classification: LCC PS3573.H4768 U53 2016 | DDC 813/.54—dc23
LC record available at http://lccn.loc.gov/2016000643

**Anchor Books Open-Market ISBN: 978-0-525-43570-9
eBook ISBN: 978-0-385-53704-9**

Book design by Maria Carella

www.anchorbooks.com

Printed in the United States of America
10 9 8 7 6 5 4

For
Julie

CONTENTS

Ajarry   1

Georgia   9

Ridgeway   71

South Carolina   83

Stevens   133

North Carolina   141

Ethel   189

Tennessee   197

Caesar   229

Indiana   237

Mabel   289

The North   297

Ajarry

THE first time Caesar approached Cora about running north, she said no.

This was her grandmother talking. Cora's grandmother had never seen the ocean before that bright afternoon in the port of Ouidah and the water dazzled after her time in the fort's dungeon. The dungeon stored them until the ships arrived. Dahomeyan raiders kidnapped the men first, then returned to her village the next moon for the women and children, marching them in chains to the sea two by two. As she stared into the black doorway, Ajarry thought she'd be reunited with her father, down there in the dark. The survivors from her village told her that when her father couldn't keep the pace of the long march, the slavers stove in his head and left his body by the trail. Her mother had died years before.

Cora's grandmother was sold a few times on the trek to the fort, passed between slavers for cowrie shells and glass beads. It was hard to say how much they paid for her in Ouidah as she was part of a bulk purchase, eighty-eight human souls for sixty crates of rum and gunpowder, the price arrived upon after the standard haggling in Coast English. Able-bodied men and child-bearing women fetched more than juveniles, making an individual accounting difficult.

The *Nanny* was out of Liverpool and had made two previous stops along the Gold Coast. The captain staggered his purchases, rather than find himself with cargo of singular culture and disposition. Who knew what brand of mutiny his captives might cook up if they shared a common tongue. This was the ship's final port of call before they crossed the Atlantic. Two yellow-haired sailors rowed Ajarry out to the ship, humming. White skin like bone.

The noxious air of the hold, the gloom of confinement, and the screams of those shackled to her contrived to drive Ajarry to madness. Because of her tender age, her captors did not immediately force their urges upon her, but eventually some of the more seasoned mates dragged her from the hold six weeks into the passage. She twice tried to kill herself on the voyage to America, once by denying herself food and then again by drowning. The sailors stymied her both times, versed in the schemes and inclinations of chattel. Ajarry didn't even make it to the gunwale when she tried to jump overboard. Her simpering posture and piteous aspect, recognizable from thousands of slaves before her, betrayed her intentions. Chained head to toe, head to toe, in exponential misery.

Although they had tried not to get separated at the auction in Ouidah, the rest of her family was purchased by Portuguese traders from the frigate *Vivilia*, next seen four months later drifting ten miles off Bermuda. Plague had claimed all on board. Authorities lit the ship on fire and watched her crackle and sink. Cora's grandmother knew nothing about the ship's fate. For the rest of her life she imagined her cousins worked for kind and generous masters up north, engaged in more forgiving trades than her own, weaving or spinning, nothing in the fields. In her stories, Isay and Sidoo and the rest somehow bought their way out of bondage and lived as free men and women in the City of Pennsylvania, a place she had overheard two white men discuss once. These fantasies gave Ajarry comfort when her burdens were such to splinter her into a thousand pieces.

The next time Cora's grandmother was sold was after a month in the pest house on Sullivan's Island, once the physicians certified her and the rest of the *Nanny*'s cargo clear of illness. Another busy day on the Exchange. A big auction always drew a colorful crowd. Traders and procurers from up and down the coast converged on Charleston, checking the merchandise's eyes and joints and spines, wary of venereal distemper and other afflictions. Onlookers chewed fresh oysters and hot corn as the auctioneers shouted into the air. The slaves stood naked on the platform. There was a bidding war over a group of Ashanti studs, those Africans of renowned industry and musculature, and the foreman of a limestone quarry bought a bunch of pickaninnies in an astounding bargain. Cora's grandmother saw a little boy among the gawkers eating rock candy and wondered what he was putting in his mouth.

Just before sunset an agent bought her for two hundred and twenty-six dollars. She would have fetched more but for that season's glut of young girls. His suit was made of the whitest cloth she had ever seen. Rings set with colored stone flashed on his fingers. When he pinched her breasts to see if she was in flower, the metal was cool on her skin. She was branded, not for the first or last time, and fettered to the rest of the day's acquisitions. The coffle began their long march south that night, staggering behind the trader's buggy. The *Nanny* by that time was en route back to Liverpool, full of sugar and tobacco. There were fewer screams belowdecks.

You would have thought Cora's grandmother cursed, so many times was she sold and swapped and resold over the next few years. Her owners came to ruin with startling frequency. Her first master got swindled by a man who sold a device that cleaned cotton twice as fast as Whitney's gin. The diagrams were convincing, but in the end Ajarry was another asset liquidated by order of the magistrate. She went for two hundred and eighteen dollars in a hasty exchange, a drop in price occasioned by the realities of the local market. Another owner expired from dropsy, whereupon his widow held an estate sale to fund a return to her native Europe, where it was clean. Ajarry spent three months as the property of a Welshman who eventually lost her, three other slaves, and two hogs in a game of whist. And so on.

Her price fluctuated. When you are sold that many times, the world is teaching you to pay attention. She learned to quickly adjust to the new plantations, sorting the nigger breakers from the merely cruel, the layabouts from the hardworking, the informers from the secret-keepers. Masters and mistresses in degrees of wickedness, estates of disparate means and ambition. Sometimes the planters wanted nothing more than to make a humble living, and then there were men and women who wanted to own the world, as if it were a matter of the proper acreage. Two hundred and forty-eight, two hundred and sixty, two hundred and seventy dollars. Wherever she went it was sugar and indigo, except for a stint folding tobacco leaves for one week before she was sold again. The trader called upon the tobacco plantation looking for slaves of breeding age, preferably with all their teeth and of pliable disposition. She was a woman now. Off she went.

She knew that the white man's scientists peered beneath things to understand how they worked. The movement of the stars across the night, the cooperation of humors in the blood. The temperature requirements for a healthy cotton harvest. Ajarry made a science of her own black body and accumulated observations. Each thing had a value and as the value changed, everything else changed also. A broken calabash was worth less than one that held its water, a hook that kept its catfish more prized than one that relinquished its bait. In America the quirk was that people were things. Best to cut your losses on an old man who won't survive a trip across the ocean. A young buck from strong tribal stock got customers into a froth. A slave girl squeezing out pups was like a mint, money that bred money. If you were a thing—a cart or a horse or a slave—your value determined your possibilities. She minded her place.

Finally, Georgia. A representative of the Randall plantation bought her for two hundred and ninety-two dollars, in spite of the new blankness behind her eyes, which made her look simpleminded. She never drew a breath off Randall land for the rest of her life. She was home, on this island in sight of nothing.

Cora's grandmother took a husband three times. She had a predilection for broad shoulders and big hands, as did Old Randall, although the master and his slave had different sorts of labor in mind. The two plantations were well-stocked, ninety head of nigger on the northern half and eighty-five head on the southern half. Ajarry generally had her pick. When she didn't, she was patient.

Her first husband developed a hankering for corn whiskey and started using his big hands to make big fists. Ajarry wasn't sad to see him disappear down the road when they sold him to a sugarcane estate in Florida. She next took up with one of the sweet boys from the southern half. Before he passed from cholera he liked to share stories from the Bible, his former master being more liberalminded when it came to slaves and religion. She enjoyed the stories and parables and supposed that white men had a point: Talk of salvation could give an African ideas. Poor sons of Ham. Her last husband had his ears bored for stealing honey. The wounds gave up pus until he wasted away.

Ajarry bore five children by those men, each delivered in the same spot on the planks of the cabin, which she pointed to when they misstepped. That's where you came from and where I'll put you back if you don't listen. Teach them to obey her and maybe they'll obey all the masters to come and they will survive. Two died miserably of fever. One boy cut his foot while playing on a rusted plow, which poisoned his blood. Her youngest never woke up after a boss hit him in the head with a wooden block. One after another. At least they were never sold off, an older woman told Ajarry. Which was true—back then Randall rarely sold the little ones. You knew where and how your children would die. The child that lived past the age of ten was Cora's mother, Mabel.

Ajarry died in the cotton, the bolls bobbing around her like whitecaps on the brute ocean. The last of her village, keeled over in the rows from a knot in her brain, blood pouring from her nose and white froth covering her lips. As if it could have been anywhere else. Liberty was reserved for other people, for the citizens of the City of Pennsylvania bustling a thousand miles to the north. Since the night she was kidnapped she had been appraised and reappraised, each day waking upon the pan of a new scale. Know your value and you know your place in the order. To escape the boundary of the plantation was to escape the fundamental principles of your existence: impossible.

It was her grandmother talking that Sunday evening when Caesar approached Cora about the underground railroad, and she said no.

Three weeks later she said yes.

This time it was her mother talking.

Georgia

THIRTY DOLLAR REWARD

Ran away from the subscriber, living in Salisbury, on the 5th instant, a negro girl by the name of LIZZIE. It is supposed that said girl is in the vicinity of Mrs. Steel's plantation. I will give the above reward on the delivery of the girl, or for information on her being lodged in any Gaol in this state. All persons are forewarned of harboring said girl, under penalty of law prescribed.

W. M. DIXON
JULY 18, 1820

JOCKEY'S birthday only came once or twice a year. They tried to make a proper celebration. It was always Sunday, their half day. At three o'clock the bosses signaled the end of work and the northern plantation scurried to prepare, rushing through chores. Mending, scavenging moss, patching the leak in the roof. The feast took precedence, unless you had a pass to go into town to sell crafts or had hired yourself out for day labor. Even if you were inclined to forgo the extra wages—and no one was so inclined—impossible was the slave impudent enough to tell a white man he couldn't work because it was a slave's birthday. Everybody knew niggers didn't have birthdays.

Cora sat by the edge of her plot on her block of sugar maple and worked dirt from under her fingernails. When she could, Cora contributed turnips or greens to the birthday feasts, but nothing was coming in today. Someone shouted down the alley, one of the new boys most likely, not completely broken in by Connelly yet, and the shouts cracked open into a dispute. The voices more crotchety than angry, but loud. It was going to be a memorable birthday if folks were already this riled.

"If you could pick your birthday, what would it be?" Lovey asked.

Cora couldn't see Lovey's face for the sun behind her, but she knew her friend's expression. Lovey was uncomplicated, and there was going to be a celebration that night. Lovey gloried in these rare escapes, whether it was Jockey's birthday, Christmas, or one of the harvest nights when everyone with two hands stayed up picking and the Randalls had the bosses distribute corn whiskey to keep them happy. It was work, but the moon made it okay. The girl was the first to tell the fiddler to get busy and the first to dance. She'd try to pull Cora from the sidelines, ignoring her protestations. As if they'd twirl in circles, arm in arm, with Lovey catching a boy's eyes for a second on every revolution and Cora following suit. But Cora never joined her, tugging her arm away. She watched.

"Told you when I was born," Cora said. She was born in winter. Her mother, Mabel, had complained enough about her hard delivery, the rare frost that morning, the wind howling between the seams in the cabin. How her mother bled for days and Connelly didn't bother to call the doctor until she looked half a ghost. Occasionally Cora's mind tricked her and she'd turn the story into one of her memories, inserting the faces of ghosts, all the slave dead, who looked down at her with love and indulgence. Even people she hated, the ones who kicked her or stole her food once her mother was gone.

"If you could pick," Lovey said.

"Can't pick," Cora said. "It's decided for you."

"You best fix your mood," Lovey said. She sped off.

Cora kneaded her calves, grateful for the time off her feet. Feast or no feast, this was where Cora ended up every Sunday when their half day of work was done: perched on her seat, looking for things to fix. She owned herself for a few hours every week was how she looked at it, to tug weeds, pluck caterpillars, thin out the sour greens, and glare at anyone planning incursions on her territory. Tending to her bed was necessary maintenance but also a message that she had not lost her resolve since the day of the hatchet.

The dirt at her feet had a story, the oldest story Cora knew. When Ajarry planted there, soon after her long march to the plantation, the plot was a rumble of dirt and scrub behind her cabin, at the end of the line of slave quarters. Beyond that lay fields and after that the swamp. Then Randall had a dream one night about a white sea that ranged as far as the eye could see and switched his crop from dependable indigo to Sea Island cotton. He made new contacts in New Orleans, shook hands with speculators backed by the Bank of England. The money came in as never before. Europe was famished for cotton and needed to be fed, bale by bale. One day the bucks cleared the trees and at night when they returned from the fields they got in chopping logs for the new row of cabins.

Looking at them now as folks chased in and out, getting ready, it was hard for Cora to imagine a time when the fourteen cabins hadn't been there. For all the wear, the complaints from deep in the wood at every step, the cabins had the always-quality of the hills to the west, of the creek that bisected the property. The cabins radiated permanence and in turn summoned timeless feelings in those who lived and died in them: envy and spite. If they'd left more space between the old cabins and the new cabins it would have spared a lot of grief over the years.

White men squabbled before judges over claims to this or that tract hundreds of miles away that had been carved up on a map. Slaves fought with equal fervor over their tiny parcels at their feet. The strip between the cabins was a place to tie a goat, build a chicken coop, a spot to grow food to fill your belly on top of the mash doled out by the kitchen every morning. If you got there first. When Randall, and later his sons, got a notion to sell you, the contract wasn't dry before someone had snatched up your plot. Seeing you out there in the evening calm, smiling or humming, might give your neighbor an idea to coerce you from your claim using methods of intimidation, various provocations. Who would hear your appeal? There were no judges here.

"But my mother wouldn't let them touch her field," Mabel

told her daughter. Field in jest, as Ajarry's stake was scarcely three yards square. "Said she'd dig a hammer in they heads if they so much as looked at it."

The image of her grandmother assaulting another slave didn't jibe with Cora's recollections of the woman, but once she started tending to the plot she understood the truth of the portrait. Ajarry kept watch over her garden through prosperity's transformations. The Randalls bought out the Spencer spread to the north, once that family decided to try their luck out west. They bought the next plantation south and switched the crop from rice to cotton, adding two more cabins to each row, but Ajarry's plot remained in the middle of it all, immovable, like a stump that reached down too deep. After Ajarry's death, Mabel assumed care of the yams and okra, whatever struck her fancy. The fuss started when Cora took it over.

WHEN Mabel vanished Cora became a stray. Eleven years old, ten years, thereabouts—there was no one now to tell for sure. In Cora's shock, the world drained to gray impressions. The first color to return was the simmering brown-red of the soil in her family's plot. It reawakened her to people and things, and she decided to hold on to her stake, even though she was young and small and had nobody to look after her anymore. Mabel was too quiet and stubborn to be popular but people had respected Ajarry. Her shadow had provided protection. Most of the original Randall slaves were in the ground now or sold, some variety of gone. Was there anyone left who was loyal to her grandmother? Cora made a canvass of the village: Not a soul. They were all dead.

She fought for the dirt. There were the small pests, the ones too young for real work. Cora shooed off those children trampling her sprouts and yelled at them for digging up her yam slips, using the same tone she used at Jockey's feasts to corral them into footraces and games. She handled them with good nature.

But pretenders stepped from the wings. Ava. Cora's mother and Ava grew up on the plantation at the same time. They were treated to the same Randall hospitality, the travesties so routine and familiar that they were a kind of weather, and the ones so imaginative in their monstrousness that the mind refused to accommodate them. Sometimes such an experience bound one person to another; just as often the shame of one's powerlessness made all witnesses into enemies. Ava and Mabel did not get along.

Ava was wiry and strong, with hands as quick as a cotton-mouth. Speed that was good for picking and for clopping her little ones across the face for idleness and other sins. She cherished her chickens more than those children and coveted Cora's land to expand her coop. "It's a waste," Ava said, ticking her tongue against her teeth. "All that for her." Ava and Cora slept next to each other every night in the loft and even though they were crammed up there with eight other people Cora could distinguish Ava's every frustration as it moved through the wood. The woman's breath was humid with rage, sour. She made a point of knocking Cora whenever she got up to make water.

"You in Hob now," Moses told Cora one afternoon when she came in from helping with the baling. Moses had made a deal with Ava, using some form of currency. Ever since Connelly had promoted the field hand to boss, to one of the overseer's enforcers, Moses had set himself up as a broker of cabin intrigues. Order in the rows, such as it was, needed to be preserved, and there were things a white man could not do. Moses accepted his role with enthusiasm. Cora thought he had a mean face, like a burl sprouting from a squat, sweaty trunk. She wasn't surprised when his character revealed itself—if you waited long enough, it always did.

Like the dawn. Cora slunk over to Hob, where they banished the wretched. There was no recourse, were no laws but the ones rewritten every day. Someone had already moved her things over.

No one remembered the unfortunate who had lent his name to the cabin. He lived long enough to embody qualities before being undone by them. Off to Hob with those who had been crippled by the overseers' punishments, off to Hob with those who had been broken by the labor in ways you could see and in ways you could not see, off to Hob with those who had lost their wits. Off to Hob with strays.

The damaged men, the half men, lived in Hob first. Then the women took up residence. White men and brown men had used the women's bodies violently, their babies came out stunted and shrunken, beatings had knocked the sense out of their heads, and they repeated the names of their dead children in the darkness: Eve, Elizabeth, N'thaniel, Tom. Cora curled on the floor of the main room, too afraid to sleep up there with them, those abject creatures. Cursing herself for her small-mindedness even as she was powerless before it. She stared at dark shapes. The fireplace, the beams undergirding the loft, the tools dangling off nails on the walls. The first time she had spent a night outside the cabin she'd been born in. A hundred paces and as many miles.

It was only a matter of time before Ava implemented the next stage of her scheme. And there was Old Abraham to contend with. Old Abraham, who was not old at all but who had comported himself in the manner of an elderly misanthrope since he first learned to sit up. He had no designs but wanted the plot gone on principle. Why should he and everyone else respect this little girl's claim just because her grandmother had kicked the dirt over once? Old Abraham was not one for tradition. He'd been sold too many times for the proposition to have much weight. On numerous occasions as she passed on errands, Cora overheard him lobby for the redistribution of her parcel. "All that for her." All three square yards of it.

THEN Blake arrived. That summer young Terrance Randall assumed duties to prepare for the day he and his brother took over the plantation. He bought a bunch of niggers out of the Carolinas. Six of them, Fanti and Mandingo if the broker was to be believed, their bodies and temperament honed for labor by nature. Blake, Pot, Edward, and the rest made a tribe of themselves on Randall land and were not above helping themselves to that which was not theirs. Terrance Randall made it known they were his new favorites, and Connelly made sure that everyone remembered it. You learned to step aside when the men were in a mood, or on a Saturday night once they'd emptied all the cider.

Blake was a big oak, a double-ration man who quickly proved a testament to Terrance Randall's investment acumen. The price they'd get for the offspring of such a stud alone. Blake wrassled his buddies and any other comers in a frequent spectacle, kicking up the dust, inevitably emerging the conqueror. His voice boomed through the rows as he worked and even those who despised him couldn't help but sing along. The man had a miserable personality but the sounds that came from his body made the labor fly.

After a few weeks of sniffing around and assessing the northern half, Blake decided that Cora's spread would be a nice place to tie up his dog. Sun, breeze, proximity. Blake had coaxed the mutt to his side during a trip to town. The dog stayed, lingering around the smokehouse when Blake worked and barking at every noise in the busy Georgia night. Blake knew some carpentry—it was not, as was often the case, a lie put out by the trader to bump up his price. He built a little house for his mutt and tried to induce compliments. The kind words were genuine, for the doghouse was a handsome piece of work, of nice proportion, with clean angles.

There was a door on a hinge and sun and moon cutouts along the back wall.

"Ain't this a nice mansion?" Blake asked Old Abraham. Blake had come to value the man's sometimes bracing candor since his arrival.

"Mighty fine work. That a little bed in there?"

Blake had sewn a pillowcase and stuffed it with moss. He decided that the patch outside his cabin was the most appropriate spot for his dog's home. Cora had been invisible to him but now he sought her eyes when she was close, to warn her that she was invisible no more.

She tried to call in a few debts owed her mother, the ones she knew about. They rebuffed her. Like Beau, the seamstress Mabel had nursed back to health when she was struck with fever. Mabel had given the girl her own supper portion and spooned potlikker and roots into her trembling lips until she opened her eyes again. Beau said she had paid that debt and then some and told Cora to get back to Hob. Cora remembered that Mabel had extended an alibi to Calvin when some planting tools went missing. Connelly, who had an aptitude for the cat-o'-nine-tails, would have stripped the meat off Calvin's back if she hadn't concocted his defense. Would have done the same to Mabel if he'd found she was lying. Cora crept on Calvin after supper: I need help. He waved her away. Mabel had said that she never discovered to what purpose he used those instruments.

Not soon after Blake made his intentions known, Cora woke one morning to the violation. She left Hob to check her garden. It had been a cool dawn. Wisps of white moisture hovered over the ground. There she saw it—the remains of what would have been her first cabbages. Heaped by the steps of Blake's cabin, the tangled vines already drying out. The ground had been turned and tamped to make a nice yard for the mutt's house, which sat in the center of her plot like a grand mansion in the heart of a plantation.

The dog poked his head out of the door as if it knew it had been her land and wanted to signal his indifference.

Blake stepped out of the cabin and crossed his arms. He spat.

People moved in the corners of Cora's vision: shadows of gossips and scolds. Watching her. Her mother was gone. She'd been moved into the wretch house and no one had come to her aid. Now this man three times her size, a bruiser, had taken her stake.

Cora had been mulling strategy. In later years she could have turned to the Hob women, or Lovey, but this was then. Her grandmother had warned that she would knock open the head of anyone who messed with her land. That seemed out of proportion to Cora. In a spell, she walked back to Hob and plucked a hatchet off the wall, the hatchet she stared at when she could not sleep. Left by one of the previous residents who came to one bad end or another, lung sickness or peeled open by a whip or shitting their insides out on the floor.

By now word had spread and bystanders lingered outside the cabins, heads tilted in anticipation. Cora marched past them, bent as if burrowing her body into a gale. No one moved to stop her, so strange was this display. Her first blow brought down the roof of the doghouse, and a squeal from the dog, who had just had his tail half severed. He scrambled to a hidey-hole beneath his owner's cabin. Her second blow wounded the left side of the doghouse gravely and her last put it out of its misery.

She stood there, heaving. Both hands on the hatchet. The hatchet wavered in the air, in a tug-of-war with a ghost, but the girl did not falter.

Blake made fists and stepped toward Cora. His boys behind him, tensing. Then he stopped. What happened between those two figures in that moment—the burly young man and the slender girl in white shift—became a matter of vantage. To those watching by the first line of cabins Blake's face distorted in surprise and worry, that of a man stumbling into a kingdom of hornets. Those standing by the new cabins saw Cora's eyes dart to and fro, as if she took the measure of an advancing host, not just one man. An army she was nonetheless prepared to meet. Regardless of perspective, what was important was the message imparted by one through posture and expression and interpreted by the other: You may get the better of me, but it will cost you.

They stood a few moments until Alice sounded the bell for breakfast. Nobody was going to forgo their mash. When they came in from the fields, Cora cleaned up the mess that had been made of her plot. She rolled over the block of sugar maple, a cast-off from someone's construction project, and it became her perch whenever she had a spare moment.

If Cora didn't belong in Hob before Ava's maneuvering, she did now. Its most infamous occupant, and the most long-term. Eventually the work broke the crippled—it always did—and those in a state of unreason were sold off cheap or took a knife to their own throats. Vacancies were brief. Cora remained. Hob was her home.

She used the doghouse for firewood. It kept her and the rest of Hob warm one night, but its legend marked her for the rest of her time on the Randall plantation. Blake and his friends started telling tales. Blake recounted how he woke from a nap behind the stables to find Cora standing over him with her hatchet, blubbering. He was a natural mimic and his gestures sold the story. Once Cora's chest started to sprout, Edward, the most wicked of Blake's gang, bragged of how Cora flapped her dress at him while she made lascivious suggestions and threatened to scalp him when he refused her. Young women whispered how they watched her slink away from the cabins on the full moon, to the woods, where she fornicated with donkeys and goats. Those who found this last story less than credible nonetheless recognized the usefulness of keeping the strange girl outside the circle of respectability.

Not long after it became known that Cora's womanhood had come into flower, Edward, Pot, and two hands from the southern half dragged her behind the smokehouse. If anyone heard or saw, they did not intervene. The Hob women sewed her up. Blake was gone by then. Perhaps having looked into her face that day, he had counseled his companions against revenge: It will cost you. But he was gone. He ran off three years after she busted up the doghouse, hiding in the swamp for weeks. It was his mutt's barking that gave away his location to the patrollers. Cora would have said it served him right, had his punishment not made her shiver to think about.

———

They had already dragged the big table from the kitchen and covered it with food for Jockey's celebration. At one end a trapper skinned his raccoons and at the other Florence scraped dirt from a mound of sweet potatoes. The fire under the big cauldron cracked and whistled. The soup roiled within the black pot, bits of cabbage chasing around the hog's head that bobbed up and down, the eye roving in the gray foam. Little Chester ran up and tried to grab a handful of cowpeas, but Alice swatted him away with her ladle.

"Nothing today, Cora?" Alice said.

"Too early," Cora said.

Alice made a brief show of disappointment and returned to supper.

That's what a lie looks like, Cora thought, and marked it. It was just as well her garden had refused. On Jockey's last birthday she had donated two heads of cabbage, which were graciously received. Cora made the mistake of turning back as she departed the kitchen and caught Alice tossing the heads into the slop bucket. She staggered into the sunlight. Did the woman think her food tainted? Is that how Alice had got rid of everything Cora had contributed these past five years, treated every turnip knob and bunch of sour greens? Had it started with Cora, or Mabel, or her grandmother? There was no point in confronting the woman. Alice had been beloved of Randall, and now James Randall, who had grown tall on her mincemeat pies. There was an order of misery, misery tucked inside miseries, and you were meant to keep track.

The Randall brothers. Since he was a young boy, James could be placated by a treat from Alice's kitchen, the sugar apple that cut short a fit or tantrum. His younger brother, Terrance, was a different sort. The cook still had a knot next to her ear where Master Terrance expressed his displeasure over one of her broths. He had been ten years old. The signs had been there since he could walk, and he perfected the more distasteful aspects of his personality as he lurched into manhood and assumed his responsibilities. James had a nautilus disposition, burrowing into his private appetites, but Terrance inflicted every fleeting and deep-seated fancy on all in his power. As was his right.

Around Cora, pots clanged and pickaninnies squealed over the delights to come. From the southern half: nothing. The Randall brothers had flipped a coin years ago to determine stewardship of each half of the plantation and in doing so made this day possible. Feasts like this didn't happen in Terrance's domain, for the younger brother was stingy with slave amusements. The Randall sons managed their inheritances according to their temperaments. James contented himself with the security of a fashionable crop, the slow, inevitable accumulations of his estate. Land and niggers to tend it were a surety beyond what any bank could offer. Terrance took a more active hand, ever scheming for ways to increase the loads sent to New Orleans. He wrung out every possible dollar. When black blood was money, the savvy businessman knew to open the vein.

The boy Chester and his friends grabbed Cora, startling her. But it was only children. Time for the races. Cora always arranged the children at the starting line, aiming their feet, calming the skittish ones, and graduating some to the older kids' race if need be. This year she kicked up Chester one slot. He was a stray, like her, his parents sold off before he could walk. Cora looked after him. Burr-headed and red-eyed. He'd shot up the last six months, the rows triggering something in his lithe body. Connelly said he had the makings of a top picker, a rare compliment from him.

"You run fast," Cora said.

He crossed his arms and cocked his head: You don't need to tell me anything. Chester was half a man, even if he didn't know it. He wouldn't race next year, Cora saw, but loll at the sidelines, joking with his friends, devising mischief.

The young slaves and the old slaves gathered on the sidelines of the horse path. Women who had lost their children drifted over little by little, to mortify themselves with possibilities and never-would-bes. Huddles of men swapped cider jugs and felt their humiliations slip away. Hob women rarely participated in the feasts, but Nag hustled about in her helpful way, rounding up little ones from their distractions.

Lovey stood at the finish as the judge. Everyone but the children knew that she always proclaimed her darlings the winner, when she could get away with it. Jockey also presided at the finish, in his rickety maple armchair, the one he used to watch the stars most nights. On his birthdays he dragged it up and down the alley, to give proper attention to the amusements held in his name. The runners went to Jockey after they were done with their races, and he dropped a piece of ginger cake onto their palms, no matter what they placed.

Chester panted, hands on his knees. He had flagged at the end.

"Almost had it," Cora said.

The boy said, "Almost," and went for his piece of ginger cake.

Cora patted the old man's arm after the last race. You never could tell how much he saw with those milky eyes of his. "How old are you, Jockey?"

"Oh, let me see." He drifted off.

She was sure he had claimed a hundred and one years at his last party. He was only half that, which meant he was the oldest slave anyone on the two Randall plantations had ever met. Once you got that old, you might as well be ninety-eight or a hundred and eight. Nothing left for the world to show you but the latest incarnations of cruelty.

Sixteen or seventeen. That's where Cora put her age. One year since Connelly ordered her to take a husband. Two years since Pot and his friends had seasoned her. They had not repeated their violation, and no worthy man paid her notice after that day, given the cabin she called home and the stories of her lunacy. Six years since her mother left.

Jockey had a good birthday plan, Cora thought. Jockey awoke on a surprise Sunday to announce his celebration and that was that. Sometimes it was in the midst of the spring rains, other times after harvest. He skipped some years or forgot or decided according to some personal accounting of grievance that the plantation was undeserving. No one minded his caprices. It was enough that he was the oldest colored man they had ever met, that he had survived every torment big and small white men had concocted and implemented. His eyes were clouded, his leg lame, his ruined hand permanently curled as if still clenched around a spade, but he was alive.

The white men left him alone now. Old man Randall said nothing about his birthdays, and neither did James when he took over. Connelly, the overseer, made himself scarce every Sunday, when he summoned whatever slave gal he'd made his wife that month. The white men were silent. As if they'd given up or decided that a small freedom was the worst punishment of all, presenting the bounty of true freedom into painful relief.

One day Jockey was bound to choose the correct day of his birth. If he lived long enough. If that was true, then if Cora picked a day for her birthday every now and then she might hit upon hers as well. In fact, today might be her birthday. What did you get for that, for knowing the day you were born into the white man's world? It didn't seem like the thing to remember. More like to forget.

"Cora."

Most of the northern half had moved to the kitchen to get fed but Caesar dallied. Here he was. She'd never had occasion to speak to the man since he arrived at the plantation. New slaves were quickly warned against the Hob women. It saved time.

"Can I talk with you?" he asked.

James Randall had bought him and three other slaves from a traveling agent after the fever deaths a year and a half ago. Two women to work the laundry, and Caesar and Prince to join the field gangs. She had seen him whittling, worrying blocks of pine with his curved carving knives. He didn't mix with the more bothersome element on the plantation, and she knew that he sometimes went off with Frances, one of the housemaids. Were they still laying together? Lovey would know. She was a girl, but Lovey kept track of man-and-woman business, the impending arrangements.

Cora felt proper. "What can I do for you, Caesar?"

He didn't bother to see if anyone was in earshot. He knew there was no one because he had planned. "I'm going back north," he said. "Soon. Running away. I want you to come."

Cora tried to think of who put him up to this prank. "You going north and I'm going to eat," she said.

Caesar held her arm, gently and insistent. His body was lean and strong, like any field hand his age, but he carried his strength lightly. His face was round, with a flat button nose—she had a quick memory of dimples when he laughed. Why had she kept that in her head?

"I don't want you to tell on me," he said. "Have to trust you on that. But I'm going soon, and I want you. For good luck."

Then she understood him. It was not a trick being played on

her. It was a trick he was playing on himself. The boy was simple. The smell of the raccoon meat brought her back to the celebration and she pulled her arm away. "I ain't trying to get killed by Connelly, or patrollers, or snakes."

Cora was still squinting over his idiocy when she got her first bowl of the soup. White man trying to kill you slow every day, and sometimes trying to kill you fast. Why make it easy for him? That was one kind of work you could say no to.

She found Lovey, but did not ask her what the girls whispered about Caesar and Frances. If he was serious about his plan, Frances was a widow.

It was the most any young man had talked to her since she moved to Hob.

They lit the torches for the wrestling matches. Someone had unearthed a stash of corn whiskey and cider, which circulated in due course and fed the spectators' enthusiasm. By now, the husbands who lived on other plantations had come for their Sunday-night visits. Walking miles, time enough to fantasize. Some wives were happier at the prospect of marital relations than others.

Lovey giggled. "I'd wrestle with him," she said, nodding at Major.

Major looked up as if he heard her. He was turning out to be a prime buck. Worked hard and rarely forced the bosses to raise the whip. He was respectful to Lovey because of her age and it wouldn't surprise if Connelly arranged a match one day. The young man and his opponent twisted in the grass. Take it out on each other if you cannot take it out on the ones who deserve it. The children peeked between their elders, making bets they had nothing to back up with. They pulled weeds and worked in trash gangs now, but one day the field work would make them as big as the men grappling and pinning each other to the grass. Get him, get that boy, teach him what he needs to learn.

When the music started and the dancing commenced, they appreciated the extent of their gratitude for Jockey. Once again he picked the right day for a birthday. He had been attuned to a shared tension, a communal apprehension beyond the routine facts of their bondage. It had built up. The last few hours had dispelled much of the ill feeling. They could face the morning toil and the following mornings and the long days with their spirits replenished, however meagerly, by a fond night to look back on and the next birthday feast to look forward to. By making a circle of themselves that separated the human spirits within from the degradation without.

Noble picked up a tambourine and tapped it. He was a fast picker in the rows and a joyful instigator outside of them; he brought both kinds of dexterity to this night. Clap hands, crook elbows, shake hips. There are instruments and human players but sometimes a fiddle or a drum makes instruments of those who play them, and all are put in servitude to the song. So it was when George and Wesley picked up their fiddle and banjo on days of carousing. Jockey sat in his maple chair, tapping his bare feet on the dirt. The slaves moved forward and danced.

Cora did not move. She was wary of how sometimes when the music tugged, you might suddenly be next to a man and you didn't know what he might do. All the bodies in motion, given license. To pull on you, take both of your hands, even if they were doing it with a nice thought. One time on Jockey's birthday, Wesley treated them to a song he knew from his days up north, a new sound none of them had heard before. Cora had dared to step out among the dancers and close her eyes and twirl and when she opened them Edward was there, his eyes alight. Even with Edward and Pot dead—Edward strung up after shorting the scale by loading his sack with stones and Pot in the ground after a rat bite turned him black and purple—she shrank from the idea of loosening her leash on herself. George sawed with his fiddle, the notes swirling up into night like sparks gusted from a fire. No one approached to pull her into the lively madness.

THE music stopped. The circle broke. Sometimes a slave will be lost in a brief eddy of liberation. In the sway of a sudden reverie among the furrows or while untangling the mysteries of an early-morning dream. In the middle of a song on a warm Sunday night. Then it comes, always—the overseer's cry, the call to work, the shadow of the master, the reminder that she is only a human being for a tiny moment across the eternity of her servitude.

The Randall brothers had emerged from the great house and were among them.

The slaves stepped aside, making calculations of what distance represented the right proportion of fear and respect. Godfrey, James's houseboy, held up a lantern. According to Old Abraham, James favored the mother, stout as a barrel and just as firm in countenance, and Terrance took after the father, tall and owl-faced, perpetually on the verge of swooping down on prey. In addition to the land, they inherited their father's tailor, who arrived once a month in his rickety carriage with his samples of linen and cotton. The brothers dressed alike when they were children and continued to do so in manhood. Their white trousers and shirts were as clean as the laundry girls' hands could make them, and the orange glow made the men look like ghosts emerging from the dark.

"Master James," Jockey said. His good hand gripped the arm of his chair as if to rise, but he did not stir. "Master Terrance."

"Don't let us disturb you," Terrance said. "My brother and I were discussing business and heard the music. I told him, Now that is the most god-awful racket I'd ever heard."

The Randalls were drinking wine out of goblets of cut glass and looked as if they had drained a few bottles. Cora searched for Caesar's face in the crowd. She did not find him. He hadn't been present the last time the brothers appeared together on the northern half. You did well to remember the different lessons of those occasions. Something always happened when the Randalls ventured into the quarter. Sooner or later. A new thing coming that you couldn't predict until it was upon you.

James left the daily operations to his man Connelly and rarely visited. He might grant a tour to a visitor, a distinguished neighbor or curious planter from another neck of the woods, but it was rare. James rarely addressed his niggers, who had been taught by the lash to keep working and ignore his presence. When Terrance appeared on his brother's plantation, he usually appraised each slave and made a note of which men were the most able and which women the most appealing. Content to leer at his brother's women, he grazed heartily upon the women of his own half. "I like to taste my plums," Terrance said, prowling the rows of cabins to see what struck his fancy. He violated the bonds of affection, sometimes visiting slaves on their wedding night to show the husband the proper way to discharge his marital duty. He tasted his plums, and broke the skin, and left his mark.

It was accepted that James was of a different orientation. Unlike his father and brother, James did not use his property to gratify himself. Occasionally he had women from the county to dine, and Alice was always sure to make the most sumptuous, seductive supper at her means. Mrs. Randall had passed many years before, and it was Alice's thought that a woman would be a civilizing presence on the plantation. For months at a time, James entertained these pale creatures, their white buggies traversing the mud tracks that led to the great house. The kitchen girls giggled and speculated. And then a new woman would appear.

To hear his valet Prideful tell it, James confined his erotic energies to specialized rooms in a New Orleans establishment. The madam was broad-minded and modern, adept in the trajectories of human desire. Prideful's stories were hard to believe, despite assurances that he received his reports from the staff of the place, with whom he'd grown close over the years. What kind of white man would willingly submit to the whip?

Terrance scratched his cane in the dirt. It had been his father's cane, topped with a silver wolf's head. Many remembered its bite on their flesh. "Then I recollected James telling me about a nigger he had down here," Terrance said, "could recite the Declaration of Independence. I can't bring myself to believe him. I thought perhaps tonight he can show me, since everyone is out and about, from the sound of it."

"We'll settle it," James said. "Where is that boy? Michael."

No one said anything. Godfrey waved the lantern around pathetically. Moses was the boss unfortunate enough to stand closest to the Randall brothers. He cleared his throat. "Michael dead, Master James."

Moses instructed one of the pickaninnies to fetch Connelly, even if it meant interrupting the overseer from his Sunday-evening concubinage. The expression on James's face told Moses to start explaining.

Michael, the slave in question, had indeed possessed the ability to recite long passages. According to Connelly, who heard the story from the nigger trader, Michael's former master was fascinated by the abilities of South American parrots and reasoned that if a bird could be taught limericks, a slave might be taught to remember as well. Merely glancing at the size of the skulls told you that a nigger possessed a bigger brain than a bird.

Michael had been the son of his master's coachman. Had a brand of animal cleverness, the kind you see in pigs sometimes. The master and his unlikely pupil started with simple rhymes and short passages from popular British versifiers. They went slow over the words the nigger didn't understand and, if truth be told, the master only half understood, as his tutor had been a reprobate who had been chased from every decent position he had ever held and who decided to make his final posting the canvas for his secret revenge. They made miracles, the tobacco farmer and the coachman's son. The Declaration of Independence was their masterpiece. "A history of repeated injuries and usurpations."

Michael's ability never amounted to more than a parlor trick, delighting visitors before the discussion turned as it always did to the diminished faculties of niggers. His owner grew bored and sold the boy south. By the time Michael got to Randall, some torture or punishment had addled his senses. He was a mediocre worker. He complained of noises and black spells that blotted his memory. In exasperation Connelly beat out what little brains he had left. It was a scourging that Michael was not intended to survive, and it achieved its purpose.

"I should have been told," James said, his displeasure plain. Michael's recitation had been a novel diversion the two times he trotted the nigger out for guests.

Terrance liked to tease his brother. "James," he said, "you need to keep better account of your property."

"Don't meddle."

"I knew you let your slaves have revels, but I had no idea they were so extravagant. Are you trying to make me look bad?"

"Don't pretend you care what a nigger thinks of you, Terrance." James's glass was empty. He turned to go.

"One more song, James. These sounds have grown on me."

George and Wesley were forlorn. Noble and his tambourine were nowhere to be seen. James pressed his lips into a slit. He gestured and the men started playing.

Terrance tapped his cane. His face sank as he took in the crowd. "You're not going to dance? I have to insist. You and you."

They didn't wait for their master's signal. The slaves of the northern half converged on the alley, haltingly, trying to insinuate themselves into their previous rhythm and put on a show. Crooked Ava had not lost her power to dissemble since her days of harassing Cora—she hooted and stomped as if it were the height of the Christmas celebrations. Putting on a show for the master was a familiar skill, the small angles and advantages of the mask, and they shook off their fear as they settled into the performance. Oh, how they capered and hollered, shouted and hopped! Certainly this was the most lively song they had ever heard, the musicians the most accomplished players the colored race had to offer. Cora dragged herself into the circle, checking the Randall brothers' reactions on every turn like everyone else. Jockey tumbled his hands in his lap to keep time. Cora found Caesar's face. He stood in the shadow of the kitchen, his expression flat. Then he withdrew.

"You!"

It was Terrance. He held his hand before him as if it were covered in some eternal stain that only he could see. Then Cora caught sight of it—the single drop of wine staining the cuff of his lovely white shirt. Chester had bumped him.

Chester simpered and bowed down before the white man. "Sorry, master! Sorry, master!" The cane crashed across his shoulder and head, again and again. The boy screamed and shrank to the dirt as the blows continued. Terrance's arm rose and fell. James looked tired.

One drop. A feeling settled over Cora. She had not been under its spell in years, since she brought the hatchet down on Blake's doghouse and sent the splinters into the air. She had seen men hung from trees and left for buzzards and crows. Women carved open to the bones with the cat-o'-nine-tails. Bodies alive and dead roasted on pyres. Feet cut off to prevent escape and hands cut off to stop theft. She had seen boys and girls younger than this beaten and had done nothing. This night the feeling settled on her heart again. It grabbed hold of her and before the slave part of her caught up with the human part of her, she was bent over the boy's body as a shield. She held the cane in her hand like a swamp man handling a snake and saw the ornament at its tip. The silver wolf bared its silver teeth. Then the cane was out of her hand. It came down on her head. It crashed down again and this time the silver teeth ripped across her eyes and her blood splattered the dirt.

The Hob women were seven that year. Mary was the oldest. She was in Hob because she was prone to fits. Foaming at the mouth like a mad dog, writhing in the dirt with wild eyes. She had feuded for years with another picker named Bertha, who finally put a curse on her. Old Abraham complained that Mary's affliction dated back to when she was a pickaninny, but no one listened to him. By any reckoning these fits were nothing like those she had suffered in her youth. She woke from them battered and confused and listless, which led to punishments for lost work, and recuperation from punishments led to more lost work. Once the bosses' mood turned against you, anyone might be swept up in it. Mary moved her things to Hob to avoid the scorn of her cabin mates. She dragged her feet all the way as if someone might intervene.

Mary worked in the milk house with Margaret and Rida. Before their purchase by James Randall these two had been so tangled by sufferings that they could not weave themselves into the fabric of the plantation. Margaret produced awful sounds from her throat at inopportune moments, animal sounds, the most miserable keenings and vulgar oaths. When the master made his rounds, she kept her hand over her mouth, lest she call attention to her affliction. Rida was indifferent to hygiene and no inducement or threat could sway her. She stank.

Lucy and Titania never spoke, the former because she chose not to and the latter because her tongue had been hacked out by a previous owner. They worked in the kitchen under Alice, who preferred assistants who were disinclined to natter all day, to better hear her own voice.

Two other women took their own lives that spring, more than usual but nothing remarkable. No one with a name that would be remembered come winter, so shallow was their mark. That left Nag and Cora. They tended to the cotton in all of its phases.

At the end of the workday Cora staggered and Nag rushed to steady her. She led Cora back to Hob. The boss glared at their slow progress out of the rows but said nothing. Cora's obvious madness had removed her from casual rebuke. They passed Caesar, who loitered by one of the work sheds with a group of young hands, carving a piece of wood with his knife. Cora averted her eyes and made her face into slate for him, as she had ever since his proposal.

It was two weeks after Jockey's birthday and Cora was still on the mend. The blows to her face had left one eye swollen shut and performed a gross injury to her temple. The swelling disappeared but where the silver wolf had kissed was now a rueful scar shaped like an X. It seeped for days. That was her tally for the night of feast. Far worse was the lashing Connelly gave her the next morning under the pitiless boughs of the whipping tree.

Connelly was one of Old Randall's first hires. James preserved the man's appointment under his stewardship. When Cora was young, the overseer's hair was a livid Irish red that curled from his straw hat like the wings of a cardinal. In those days he patrolled with a black umbrella but eventually surrendered and now his white blouses were stark against his tanned flesh. His hair had gone white and his belly overflowed his belt, but apart from that he was the same man who had whipped her grandmother and mother, stalking the village with a lopsided gait that reminded her of an old ox. There was no rushing him if he chose not to be rushed. The only time he exhibited speed was when he reached for his cat-o'-nine-tails. Then he demonstrated the energy and rambunctiousness of a child at a new pastime.

The overseer was not pleased by what had transpired during the Randall brothers' surprise visit. First, Connelly had been interrupted while taking his pleasure with Gloria, his current wench. He flogged the messenger and roused himself from bed. Second, there was the matter of Michael. Connelly hadn't informed James about Michael's loss as his employer never bothered over routine fluctuations in the hands, but Terrance's curiosity had made it a problem.

Then there was the matter of Chester's clumsiness and Cora's incomprehensible action. Connelly peeled them open the following sunrise. He started with Chester, to follow the order in which the transgressions had occurred, and called for their bloody backs to be scrubbed out with pepper water afterward. It was Chester's first proper licking, and Cora's first in half a year. Connelly repeated the whippings the next two mornings. According to the house slaves, Master James was more upset that his brother had touched his property, and before so many witnesses, than with Chester and Cora. Thus was the brunt of one brother's ire toward another borne by property. Chester never said a word to Cora again.

Nag helped Cora up the steps to Hob. Cora collapsed once they entered the cabin and were out of sight of the rest of the village. "Let me get you some supper," Nag said.

Like Cora, Nag had been relocated to Hob over politics. For years she had been Connelly's preferred, spending most nights in his bed. Nag was haughty for a nigger gal even before the overseer bestowed his slim favors upon her, with her pale gray eyes and roiling hips. She became insufferable. Preening, gloating over the ill treatment that she alone escaped. Her mother had consorted

frequently with white men and tutored Nag in licentious practices. She bent in dedication to the task even as he swapped their
offspring. The northern and southern halves of the great Randall
plantation exchanged slaves all the time, unloading beat niggers,
skulky workers, and rascals on each other in a desultory game.
Nag's children were tokens. Connelly could not countenance his
mulatto bastards when their curls glowed his Irish red in the sunlight.

One morning Connelly made it clear that he no longer
required Nag in his bed. It was the day her enemies had waited
for. Everyone saw it coming except for her. She returned from the
fields to find her possessions had been moved to Hob, announcing
her loss in status to the village. Her shame nourished them as no
food could. Hob hardened her, as was its way. The cabin tended to
set one's personality.

Nag had never been close to Cora's mother but that didn't stop
her from befriending the girl when she became a stray. After the
night of the feast and in the following bloody days she and Mary
ministered to Cora, applying brine and poultices to her ravaged
skin and making sure she ate. They cradled her head and sang lullabies to their lost children through her. Lovey visited her friend as
well, but the young girl was not immune to Hob's reputation and
got skittish in the presence of Nag and Mary and the others. She
stayed until her nerves gave out.

Cora lay on the floor and moaned. Two weeks after her beating, she endured dizzy spells and a pounding in her skull. For the
most part she was able to keep it at bay and work the row, but
sometimes it was all she could do to stay upright until the sun
sank. Every hour when the water girl brought the ladle she licked
it clean and felt the metal on her teeth. Now she had nothing left.

Mary appeared. "Sick again," she said. She had a wet cloth

ready and placed it on Cora's brow. She still maintained a reservoir of maternal feeling after the loss of her five children—three dead before they could walk and the others sold off when they were old enough to carry water and grab weeds around the great house. Mary descended from pure Ashanti stock, as did her two husbands. Pups like that, it didn't take much salesmanship. Cora moved her mouth in silent thanks. The cabin walls pressed on her. Up in the loft one of the other women—Rida by the stench—rummaged and banged. Nag rubbed out the knots in Cora's hands. "I don't know what's worse," she said. "You sick and out of sight or you up and outside when Master Terrance come tomorrow."

The prospect of his visit depleted Cora. James Randall was bedridden. He'd fallen ill after a trip to New Orleans to negotiate with a delegation of trading agents from Liverpool and to visit his disgraceful haven. He fainted in his buggy on his return and had been out of sight since. Now whispers came from the house staff that Terrance was going to take over while his brother was on the mend. In the morning he would inspect the northern half to bring the operation in harmony with how things were done in the southern half.

No one doubted that it would be a bloody sort of harmony.

Her friends' hands slipped away and the walls relinquished their pressure and she passed out. Cora woke in the pit of the night, her head resting on a rolled-up linsey blanket. Everyone asleep above. She rubbed the scar on her temple. It felt like it was seeping. She knew why she had rushed to protect Chester. But she was stymied when she tried to recall the urgency of that moment, the grain of the feeling that possessed her. It had retreated to that obscure corner in herself from where it came and couldn't be coaxed. To ease her restlessness she crept out to her plot and sat on her maple and smelled the air and listened. Things in the swamp whistled and splashed, hunting in the living darkness. To walk in there at night, heading north to the Free States. Have to take leave of your senses to do that.

But her mother had.

AS if to reflect Ajarry, who did not step off Randall land once she arrived on it, Mabel never left the plantation until the day of her escape. She gave no indication of her intentions, at least to no one who admitted to that knowledge under subsequent interrogations. No mean feat in a village teeming with treacherous natures and informers who would sell out their dearest to escape the bite of the cat-o'-nine-tails.

Cora fell asleep nestled against her mother's stomach and never saw her again. Old Randall raised the alarm and summoned the patrollers. Within an hour the hunting party tromped into the swamp, chasing after Nate Ketchum's dogs. The latest in a long line of specializers, Ketchum had slave-catching in his blood. The hounds had been bred for generations to detect nigger scent across whole counties, chewing and mangling many a wayward hand. When the creatures strained against their leather straps and pawed at the air, their barking made every soul in the quarters want to run to their cabins. But the day's picking lay before the slaves foremost and they stooped to their orders, enduring the dogs' terrible noise and the visions of blood to come.

The bills and fliers circulated for hundreds of miles. Free negroes who supplemented their living catching runaways combed through the woods and wormed information from likely accomplices. Patrollers and posses of low whites harassed and bullied. The quarters of all the nearby plantations were thoroughly searched and no small number of slaves beaten on principle. But the hounds came up empty, as did their masters.

Randall retained the services of a witch to goofer his property so that no one with African blood could escape without being stricken with hideous palsy. The witch woman buried fetishes in secret places, took her payment, and departed in her mule cart. There was a hearty debate in the village over the spirit of the goofer. Did the conjure apply only to those who had an intention to run or to all colored persons who stepped over the line? A week passed before the slaves hunted and scavenged in the swamp again. That's where the food was.

Of Mabel there was no sign. No one had escaped the Randall plantation before. The fugitives were always clawed back, betrayed by friends, they misinterpreted the stars and ran deeper into the labyrinth of bondage. On their return they were abused mightily before being permitted to die and those they left behind were forced to observe the grisly increments of their demise.

The infamous slave catcher Ridgeway paid a call on the plantation one week later. He rode up on his horses with his associates, five men of disreputable mien, led by a fearsome Indian scout who wore a necklace of shriveled ears. Ridgeway was six and a half feet tall, with the square face and thick neck of a hammer. He maintained a serene comportment at all times but generated a threatening atmosphere, like a thunderhead that seems far away but then is suddenly overhead with loud violence.

Ridgeway's audience lasted half an hour. He took notes in a small diary and to hear the house speak of it was a man of intense concentration and flowery manner of speech. He did not return for two years, not long before Old Randall's death, to apologize in person for his failure. The Indian was gone, but there was a young rider with long black hair who wore a similar ring of trophies over his hide vest. Ridgeway was in the vicinity to visit a neighboring planter, offering as proof of capture the heads of two runaways in a leather sack. Crossing the state line was a capital offense in Georgia; sometimes a master preferred an example over the return of his property.

The slave catcher shared rumors of a new branch of the underground railroad said to be operating in the southern part of the state, as impossible as it sounded. Old Randall scoffed. The sympathizers would be rooted out and tarred and feathered, Ridgeway assured his host. Or whatever satisfied local custom. Ridgeway apologized once again and took his leave and soon his gang crashed to the county road toward their next mission. There was no end to their work, the river of slaves that needed to be driven from their hidey-holes and brought to the white man's proper accounting.

Mabel had packed for her adventure. A machete. Flint and tinder. She stole a cabin mate's shoes, which were in better shape. For weeks, her empty garden testified to her miracle. Before she lit out she dug up every yam from their plot, a cumbersome load and ill-advised for a journey that required a fleet foot. The lumps and burrows in the dirt were a reminder to all who walked by. Then one morning they were smoothed over. Cora got on her knees and planted anew. It was her inheritance.

NOW in the thin moonlight, her head throbbing, Cora appraised her tiny garden. Weeds, weevils, the ragged footprints of critters. She had neglected her land since the feast. Time to return to it.

Terrance's visit the next day was uneventful save for one disturbing moment. Connelly took him through his brother's operation, as it had been some years since Terrance had made a proper tour. His manner was unexpectedly civil from all accounts, absent his standard sardonic remarks. They discussed the numbers from last year's haul and examined the ledgers that contained the weigh-ins from the previous September. Terrance expressed annoyance at the overseer's lamentable handwriting but apart from that the men got along amiably. They did not inspect the slaves or the village.

On horses they circumnavigated the fields, comparing the progress of the harvest on the two halves. Where Terrance and Connelly made their crossings through the cotton, the nearby slaves redoubled their efforts in a furious wave. The hands had been chopping the weeds for weeks, slashing hoes into the furrows. The stalks were up to Cora's shoulders now, bending and tottering, sprouting leaves and squares that were bigger every morning. Next month the bolls would explode into whiteness. She prayed the plants were tall enough to hide her when the white men passed. She saw their backs as they proceeded from her. Then Terrance turned. He nodded, tipped his cane at her, and continued on.

James died two days later. His kidneys, the doctor said.

Longtime residents of the Randall plantation couldn't help but compare the funerals of the father and the son. The elder Randall had been a revered member of planter society. The western riders commanded all the attention now but it was Randall and his brethren who were the true pioneers, carving out a life in this humid Georgia hell all those years ago. His fellow planters cherished him as a visionary for being the first in the region to switch to cotton, leading the profitable charge. Many was the young farmer suffocating in credit who came to Randall for advice—advice freely and generously given—and in his time came to master an enviable spread.

The slaves got time off to attend Old Randall's funeral. They stood in a quiet huddle while all the fine white men and women paid their respects to the beloved father. The house niggers acted as pallbearers, which everyone thought scandalous at first but on further consideration took as an indicator of genuine affection, one they had indeed enjoyed with their own slaves, with the mammy whose titties they suckled in more innocent times and the attendant who slipped a hand under soapy water at bath time. At the end of the service it began to rain. It put an end to the memorial but everyone was relieved because the drought had gone on too long. The cotton was thirsty.

By the time of James's passing, the Randall sons had cut off social ties with their father's peers and protégés. James had many business partners on paper, some of whom he had met in person, but he had few friends. To the point, Terrance's brother had never received his human portion of sentimentality. His funeral was sparsely attended. The slaves worked the rows—with the harvest approaching there was no question. It was all spelled out in his will, Terrance said. James was buried near his parents in a quiet corner of their abundant acreage, next to his father's mastiffs Plato and Demosthenes, who had been beloved by all, man and nigger alike, even if they couldn't keep away from the chickens.

Terrance traveled to New Orleans to straighten his brother's affairs with the cotton trade. Although there was never a good time to run, Terrance's stewardship of both halves provided a good argument. The northern half had always relished their easier climate. James was as ruthless and brutal as any white man but he was the portrait of moderation compared to his younger brother. The stories from the southern half were chilling, in magnitude if not in particulars.

Big Anthony took his opportunity. Big Anthony was not the most clever buck in the village, but no one could say he lacked a sense for opportunity. It was the first escape attempt since Mabel. He braved the witch woman's goofer without incident and made it twenty-six miles before he was discovered snoozing in a hayloft. The constables returned him in an iron cage made by one of their cousins. "Take flight like a bird, you deserve a birdcage." The front of the cage had a slot for the name of the inhabitant, but no one had bothered to use it. They took the cage with them when they left.

On the eve of Big Anthony's punishment—whenever white men put off punishment some theater was bound to be involved—Caesar visited Hob. Mary let him in. She was puzzled. Few visitors ever came to call, and men only when it was a boss with bad news. Cora hadn't told anyone of the young man's proposition.

The loft was full of women either sleeping or listening. Cora put her mending to the floor and took him outside.

OLD Randall built the schoolhouse for his sons and the grandchildren he had hoped to have one day. The lonesome hulk was unlikely to fulfill its purpose anytime soon. Since Randall's sons had finished their education it was used only for assignations and all those different lessons. Lovey saw Caesar and Cora walk to it, and Cora shook her head at her friend's amusement.

The rotting schoolhouse smelled rank. Small animals made regular habitation. The chairs and tables had been removed a long time before, making room for dead leaves and spiderwebs. She wondered if he had brought Frances here when they were together, and what they did. Caesar had seen Cora stripped naked for her whippings, the blood pouring over her skin.

Caesar checked the window and said, "I'm sorry that happened to you."

"That's what they do," Cora said.

Two weeks ago she had judged him a fool. This night he carried himself as one beyond his years, like one of those wise old hands who tell you a story whose true message you only understand days or weeks later, when their facts are impossible to avoid.

"Will you come with me now?" Caesar said. "Been thinking it's past time to go."

She could not figure him. On the mornings of her three whippings, Caesar had stood in the front of the pack. It was customary for slaves to witness the abuse of their brethren as moral instruction. At some point during the show everyone had to turn away, if only for a moment, as they considered the slave's pain and the day sooner or later when it would be their turn at the foul end of the lash. That was you up there even when it was not. But Caesar did not flinch. He didn't seek her eyes but looked at something beyond her, something great and difficult to make out.

She said, "You think I'm a lucky charm because Mabel got away. But I ain't. You saw me. You saw what happens when you get a thought in your head."

Caesar was unmoved. "It's going to be bad when he gets back."

"It's bad now," Cora said. "Ever has been." She left him there.

The new stocks Terrance ordered explained the delay in Big Anthony's justice. The woodworkers toiled all through the night to complete the restraints, furnishing them with ambitious if crude engravings. Minotaurs, busty mermaids, and other fantastic creatures frolicked in the wood. The stocks were installed on the front lawn in the lush grass. Two bosses secured Big Anthony and there he dangled the first day.

On the second day a band of visitors arrived in a carriage, august souls from Atlanta and Savannah. Swell ladies and gentlemen that Terrance had met on his travels, as well as a newspaperman from London come to report on the American scene. They ate at a table set up on the lawn, savoring Alice's turtle soup and mutton and devising compliments for the cook, who would never receive them. Big Anthony was whipped for the duration of their meal, and they ate slow. The newspaperman scribbled on paper between bites. Dessert came and the revelers moved inside to be free of the mosquitoes while Big Anthony's punishment continued.

On the third day, just after lunch, the hands were recalled from the fields, the washwomen and cooks and stable hands interrupted from their tasks, the house staff diverted from its maintenance. They gathered on the front lawn. Randall's visitors sipped spiced rum as Big Anthony was doused with oil and roasted. The witnesses were spared his screams, as his manhood had been cut off on the first day, stuffed in his mouth, and sewn in. The stocks smoked, charred, and burned, the figures in the wood twisting in the flames as if alive.

Terrance addressed the slaves of the northern and southern halves. There is one plantation now, united in purpose and method, he said. He expressed his grief over his brother's death and his consolation in the knowledge that James was in heaven united with their mother and father. He walked among his slaves as he talked, tapping his cane, rubbing the heads of pickaninnies and petting some of the older worthies from the southern half. He checked the teeth of a young buck he had never seen before, wrenching the boy's jaw to get a good look, and nodded in approval. In order to feed the world's insatiable demand for cotton goods, he said, every picker's daily quota will be increased by a percentage determined by their numbers from the previous harvest. The fields will be reorganized to accommodate a more efficient number of rows. He walked. He slapped a man across the face for weeping at the sight of his friend thrashing against the stocks.

When Terrance got to Cora, he slipped his hand into her shift and cupped her breast. He squeezed. She did not move. No one had moved since the beginning of his address, not even to pinch their noses to keep out the smell of Big Anthony's roasting flesh. No more feasts outside of Christmas and Easter, he said. He will arrange and approve all marriages personally to ensure the appropriateness of the match and the promise of the offspring. A new tax on Sunday labor off the plantation. He nodded at Cora and continued his stroll among his Africans as he shared his improvements.

Terrance concluded his address. It was understood that the slaves were to remain there until Connelly dismissed them. The Savannah ladies refreshed their drinks from the pitcher. The newspaperman opened a fresh diary and resumed his note-taking. Master Terrance joined his guests and they departed for a tour of the cotton.

She had not been his and now she was his. Or she had always been his and just now knew it. Cora's attention detached itself. It floated someplace past the burning slave and the great house and the lines that defined the Randall domain. She tried to fill in its details from stories, sifting through the accounts of slaves who had seen it. Each time she caught hold of something—buildings of polished white stone, an ocean so vast there wasn't a tree in sight, the shop of a colored blacksmith who served no master but himself—it wriggled free like a fish and raced away. She would have to see it for herself if she were to keep it.

⊷ ⊷⋇⊷ ⊷

Who could she tell? Lovey and Nag would keep her confidence, but she feared Terrance's revenge. Better that their ignorance be sincere. No, the only person she could discuss the plan with was its architect.

She approached him the night of Terrance's address and he acted as if she had agreed long before. Caesar was like no colored man she had ever met. He had been born on a small farm in Virginia owned by a petite old widow. Mrs. Garner enjoyed baking, the daily complications of her flower bed, and concerned herself with little else. Caesar and his father took care of the planting and the stables, his mother the domestic affairs. They grew a modest crop of vegetables to sell in town. His family lived in their own two-room cottage at the rear of the property. They painted it white with robin's egg trim, just like a white person's house his mother had seen once.

Mrs. Garner desired nothing more than to spend her final years in comfort. She didn't agree with the popular arguments for slavery but saw it as a necessary evil given the obvious intellectual deficiencies of the African tribe. To free them from bondage all at once would be disastrous—how would they manage their affairs without a careful and patient eye to guide them? Mrs. Garner helped in her own way, teaching her slaves their letters so they could receive the word of God with their own eyes. She was liberal with passes, allowing Caesar and his family to range across the county as they pleased. It rankled her neighbors. In her degrees, she prepared them for the liberation that awaited them, for she had pledged to set them free upon her death.

When Mrs. Garner passed, Caesar and his family mourned and tended to the farm, awaiting official word of their manumission. She left no will. Her only relative was a niece in Boston, who arranged for a local lawyer to liquidate Mrs. Garner's property. It was a terrible day when he arrived with constables and informed Caesar and his parents that they were to be sold. Worse—sold south, with its fearsome legends of cruelty and abomination. Caesar and his family joined the march of coffles, his father going one way, his mother another, and Caesar to his own destiny. Theirs was a pathetic goodbye, cut short by the whip of the trader. So bored was the trader with the display, one he had witnessed countless times before, that he only halfheartedly beat the distraught family. Caesar, in turn, took this weak licking as a sign that he could weather the blows to come. An auction in Savannah led him to the Randall plantation and his gruesome awakening.

"You can read?" Cora asked.

"Yes." A demonstration was impossible of course, but if they made it off the plantation they would depend on this rare gift.

They met at the schoolhouse, by the milk house after the work there was done, wherever they could. Now that she had cast her lot with him and his scheme, she bristled with ideas. Cora suggested they wait for the full moon. Caesar countered that after Big Anthony's escape the overseers and bosses had increased their scrutiny and would be extra vigilant on the full moon, the white beacon that so often agitated the slave with a mind to run. No, he said. He wanted to go as soon as possible. The following night. The waxing moon would have to suffice. Agents of the underground railroad would be waiting.

The underground railroad—Caesar had been very busy. Did

they really operate this deep in Georgia? The idea of escape over-whelmed her. Apart from her own preparations, how would they alert the railroad in time? Caesar had no pretext on which to leave the grounds until Sunday. He told her that their escape would cause such a ruckus that there would be no need to alert his man.

Mrs. Garner had sown the seeds of Caesar's flight in many ways, but one instruction in particular brought him to the attention of the underground railroad. It was a Saturday afternoon and they sat on her front porch. On the main road the weekend spectacle strolled before them. Tradesmen with their carts, families walking to the market. Piteous slaves chained neck to neck, shuffling in step. As Caesar rubbed her feet, the widow encouraged him to cultivate a skill, one that would serve him in good stead as a freeman. He became a woodworker, apprenticing at a nearby shop owned by a broad-minded Unitarian. Eventually he sold his handsomely crafted bowls on the square. As Mrs. Garner remarked, he was good with his hands.

At the Randall plantation he continued his enterprise, joining the Sunday caravan into town with the moss sellers, penny seamstresses, and day laborers. He sold little, but the weekly trip was a small, if bitter, reminder of his life in the north. It tortured him at sundown to tear away from the pageant before him, the mesmerizing dance between commerce and desire.

A stooped, gray-haired white man approached him one Sunday and invited him to his shop. Perhaps he could sell Caesar's crafts during the week, he offered, and they might both profit. Caesar had noticed the man before, strolling among the colored vendors and pausing by his crafts with a curious expression. He hadn't paid him any mind but now the request made him suspicious. Being sold down south had drastically altered his attitude toward whites. He took care.

The man sold provisions, dry goods, and farming tools. The shop was devoid of customers. He lowered his voice and asked, "You can read, can't you?"

"Sir?" Saying it like the Georgia boys said it.

"I've seen you in the square, reading signs. A newspaper. You have to guard over yourself. I'm not the only one can spot such a thing."

Mr. Fletcher was a Pennsylvanian. He relocated to Georgia because, he found out belatedly, his wife refused to live anywhere else. She had a notion about the air down here and its ameliorating effects on the circulation. His wife had a point about the air, he conceded, but in every other way the place was a misery. Mr. Fletcher abhorred slavery as an affront before God. He had never been active in abolitionist circles up north but observing the monstrous system firsthand gave him thoughts he did not recognize. Thoughts that could get him run out of town or worse.

He took Caesar into his confidence, risking that the slave might inform on him for a reward. Caesar trusted him in turn. He had met this sort of white man before, earnest and believing what came out of their mouths. The veracity of their words was another matter, but at least they believed them. The southern white man was spat from the loins of the devil and there was no way to forecast his next evil act.

At the conclusion of that first meeting Fletcher took Caesar's three bowls and told him to return next week. The bowls didn't sell, but the duo's true enterprise thrived as their discussions gave it form. The idea was like a hunk of wood, Caesar thought, requiring human craft and ingenuity to reveal the new shape within.

Sundays were best. Sundays his wife visited her cousins. Fletcher had never warmed to that branch of the family, nor they to him, owing to his peculiar temperament. It was commonly held that the underground railroad did not operate this far south,

Fletcher told him. Caesar already knew this. In Virginia, you could smuggle yourself into Delaware or up the Chesapeake on a barge, evading patrollers and bounty hunters by your wits and the invisible hand of Providence. Or the underground railroad could help you, with its secret trunk lines and mysterious routes.

Antislavery literature was illegal in this part of the nation. Abolitionists and sympathizers who came down to Georgia and Florida were run off, flogged and abused by mobs, tarred and feathered. Methodists and their inanities had no place in the bosom of King Cotton. The planters did not abide contagion.

A station had opened up nonetheless. If Caesar could make it the thirty miles to Fletcher's house, the shopkeeper pledged to convey him to the underground railroad.

"How many slaves he helped?" Cora asked.

"None," Caesar said. His voice did not waver, to fortify Cora as much as himself. He told her that Fletcher had made contact with one slave previous but the man never made it to the rendezvous. Next week the newspaper reported the man's capture and described the nature of his punishment.

"How we know he ain't tricking us?"

"He is not." Caesar had thought it out already. Just talking to Fletcher in his shop provided enough grounds to string him up. No need for elaborate schemes. Caesar and Cora listened to the insects as the enormity of their plan moved over them.

"He'll help us," Cora said. "He has to."

Caesar took her hands in his and then the gesture discomfited him. He let go. "Tomorrow night," he said.

Her final night in the quarters was sleepless, even though she needed her strength. The other Hob women dozed beside her in the loft. She listened to their breathing: That is Nag; that is Rida with her one ragged exhalation every other minute. This time tomorrow she would be loose in the night. Is this what her mother felt when she decided? Cora's image of her was remote. What she remembered most was her sadness. Her mother was a Hob woman before there was a Hob. With the same reluctance to mix, the burden that bent her at all times and set her apart. Cora couldn't put her together in her mind. Who was she? Where was she now? Why had she left her? Without a special kiss to say, When you remember this moment later you will understand that I was saying goodbye even if you did not know it.

Cora's last day in the field she furiously hacked into the earth as if digging a tunnel. Through it and beyond is your salvation.

She said goodbye without saying goodbye. The previous day she sat with Lovey after supper and they talked in a way they hadn't since Jockey's birthday. Cora tried to slide in gentle words about her friend, a gift that she could hold later. *Of course you did that for her, you are a kind person. Of course Major likes you, he can see what I see in you.*

Cora saved her last meal for the Hob women. It was rare for them to spend their free hours together but she rounded them up from their preoccupations. What would become of them? They were exiles, but Hob provided a type of protection once they settled in. By playing up their strangeness, the way a slave simpered and acted childlike to escape a beating, they evaded the entanglements of the quarter. The walls of Hob made a fortress some nights, rescuing them from the feuds and conspiracies. White men eat you up, but sometimes colored folk eat you up, too.

She left a pile of her things by the door: a comb, a square of polished silver that Ajarry had scrounged years ago, the pile of blue stones that Nag called her "Indian rocks." Her farewell.

She took her hatchet. She took flint and tinder. And like her mother she dug up her yams. The next night someone will have claimed the plot, she thought, turned the dirt over. Put a fence around it for chickens. A doghouse. Or maybe she will keep it a garden. An anchor in the vicious waters of the plantation to prevent her from being carried away. Until she chose to be carried away.

They met by the cotton after the village quieted down. Caesar made a quizzical expression at her bulging sack of yams but didn't speak. They moved through the tall plants, so knotted up inside that they forgot to run until they were halfway through. Their speed made them giddy. The impossibility of it. Their fear called after them even if no one else did. They had six hours until their disappearance was discovered and another one or two before the posses reached where they were now. But fear was already in pursuit, as it had been every day on the plantation, and it matched their pace.

They crossed the meadow whose soil was too thin for planting and entered the swamp. It had been years since Cora had played in the black water with the other pickaninnies, scaring each other with tales of bears and hidden gators and fast-swimming water moccasins. Men hunted otter and beaver in the swamp and the moss sellers scavenged from the trees, tracking far but never too far, yanked back to the plantation by invisible chains. Caesar had accompanied some of the trappers on their fishing and hunting expeditions for months now, learning how to step in the peat and silt, where to stick close to the reeds, and how to find the islands of sure ground. He probed the murk before them with his walking stick. The plan was to shoot west until they hit a string of islands a trapper had shown him, and then bow northeast until the swamp dried up. The precious firm footing made it the fastest route north, despite the diversion.

They had made it only a small ways in when they heard the voice and stopped. Cora looked at Caesar for a cue. He held his hands out and listened. It was not an angry voice. Or a man's voice.

Caesar shook his head when he realized the identity of the culprit. "Lovey—shush!"

Lovey had enough sense to be quiet once she got a bead on them. "I knew you were up to something," she whispered when she caught up. "Sneaking around with him but not talking about it. And then you dig up them yams not even ripe yet!" She had cinched some old fabric to make a bag that she slung over her shoulder.

"You get on back before you ruin us," Caesar said.

"I'm going where you going," Lovey said.

Cora frowned. If they sent Lovey back, the girl might be caught sneaking into her cabin. Lovey was not one to keep her tongue still. No more head start. She didn't want to be responsible for the girl, but couldn't figure it.

"He's not going to take three of us," Caesar said.

"He know I'm coming?" Cora asked.

He shook his head.

"Then two surprises as good as one," she said. She lifted her sack. "We got enough food, anyway."

He had all night to get used to the idea. It would be a long time before they slept. Eventually Lovey stopped crying out at every sudden noise from the night creatures, or when she stepped too deep and the water surged to her waist. Cora was acquainted with this squeamish quality of Lovey's, but she did not recognize the other side of her friend, whatever had overtaken the girl and made her run. But every slave thinks about it. In the morning and in the afternoon and in the night. Dreaming of it. Every dream a dream of escape even when it didn't look like it. When it was a dream of new shoes. The opportunity stepped up and Lovey availed herself, heedless of the whip.

The three of them wended west, tromping through the black water. Cora couldn't have led them. She didn't know how Caesar did it. But he was ever surprising her. Of course he had a map in his head and could read stars as well as letters.

Lovey's sighs and curses when she needed a rest saved Cora from asking. When they demanded to look in her tow sack, it contained nothing practical, only odd tokens she had collected, like a small wooden duck and a blue glass bottle. As for his own practicality, Caesar was a capable navigator when it came to finding islands. Whether or not he kept to his route, Cora couldn't tell. They started tracking northeast and by the time it got light they were out of the swamp. "They know," Lovey said when the orange sun broke in the east. The trio took another rest and cut a yam into slices. The mosquitoes and blackflies persecuted them. In the daylight they were a mess, splashed up to their necks in mud, covered in burrs and tendrils. It did not bother Cora. This was the farthest she had ever been from home. Even if she were dragged away at this moment and put in chains, she would still have these miles.

Caesar tossed his walking stick to the ground and they took off again. The next time they stopped, he told them that he had to go find the county road. He promised to return soon, but he needed to take measure of their progress. Lovey had the sense not to ask what happened if he didn't return. To reassure them, he left his sack and waterskin next to a cypress. Or to help them if he did not.

"I knew it," Lovey said, still wanting to pick at it despite her exhaustion. The girls sat against the trees, grateful for solid, dry dirt.

Cora filled her in on what there was left to tell, going back to Jockey's birthday.

"I knew it," Lovey repeated.

"He thinks I'm good luck, because my mother was the only one."

"You want luck, cut off a rabbit foot," Lovey said.

"What your mother gonna do?" Cora asked.

Lovey and her mother arrived on Randall when she was five years old. Her previous master didn't believe in clothing picka-ninnies so it was the first time she had something on her back. Her mother, Jeer, had been born in Africa and loved to tell her daughter and her friends stories of her childhood in a small village by a river and all the animals who lived nearby. Picking broke her body. Her joints were swollen and stiff, making her crooked, and it anguished her to walk. When Jeer could no longer work she looked after babies when their mothers were in the fields. Despite her torments, she was always tender to her girl, even if her big toothless smile fell like an ax the moment Lovey turned away.

"Be proud of me," Lovey answered. She lay down and turned her back.

Caesar appeared sooner than they expected. They were too close to the road, he said, but had made good time. Now their party had to press on, get as far as they could before the riders set out. The horsemen would wipe out their lead in short order.

"When we going to sleep?" Cora asked.

"Let's get away from the road and then we see," Caesar said. From his comportment, he was spent, too.

They set their bags down not long after. When Caesar woke Cora, the sun was getting down. She had not stirred once, even with her body draped awkwardly over the roots of an old oak. Lovey was already awake. They reached the clearing when it was almost dark, a cornfield behind a private farm. The owners were home and busied themselves in their chores, chasing each other in and out of the small cottage. The fugitives withdrew and waited until the family put out their lamps. From here until Fletcher's farm the most direct route was through people's land, but it was too dangerous. They stayed in the forest, looping around.

Ultimately the pigs did them in. They were following the rut of a hog trail when the white men rushed from the trees. There were four of them. Bait laid on the trail, the hog hunters waited for their quarry, which turned nocturnal in the hot weather. The runaways were a different sort of beast but more remunerative.

There was no mistaking the identity of the trio, given the specificity of the bulletins. Two of the hog hunters tackled the smallest of the party, pinning her to the ground. After being so quiet for so long—the slaves to escape the detection of hunters, and the hunters to escape the detection of their prey—all of them cried out and shrieked with their exertions. Caesar grappled with a heavyset man with a long dark beard. The fugitive was younger and stronger, but the man held his ground and seized Caesar by the waist. Caesar fought like he had struck many a white man, an impossible occurrence or else he would have been in the grave long ago. It was the grave the runaways fought against, for that was their destination if these men prevailed and returned them to their master.

Lovey howled as the two men dragged her into the darkness. Cora's assailant was boyish and slender, perhaps the son of one of the other hunters. She was taken unawares but the moment he laid hands on her person, her blood quickened. She was brought back to the night behind the smokehouse when Edward and Pot and the rest brutalized her. She battled. Strength poured into her limbs, she bit and slapped and bashed, fighting now as she had not been able to then. She realized she had dropped her hatchet. She wanted it. Edward was in the dirt and this boy would join him, too, before she was taken.

The boy yanked Cora to the ground. She rolled over and bashed her head against a stump. He scrambled to her, pinning her. Her blood was hot—she reached out and came up with a rock that she slammed into the boy's skull. He reeled and she repeated her assault. His groans ceased.

Time was a figment. Caesar called her name, pulling her up. The bearded man had fled, as much as the darkness allowed her to see. "This way!"

Cora cried after her friend.

There was no sign of her, no way to tell where they had gone. Cora hesitated and he tugged her roughly forward. She followed his instructions.

They stopped running when they realized they had no inkling of where they were headed. Cora saw nothing for the darkness and her tears. Caesar had rescued his waterskin but they had lost the rest of their provisions. They had lost Lovey. He oriented himself with the constellations and the runaways stumbled on, impelled into the night. They didn't speak for hours. From the trunk of their scheme, choices and decisions sprouted like branches and shoots. If they had turned the girl back at the swamp. If they had taken a deeper route around the farms. If Cora had taken the rear and been the one grabbed by the two men. If they had never left at all.

Caesar scouted a promising spot and they climbed trees, sleeping like raccoons.

When she stirred, the sun was up and Caesar paced between two pines, talking to himself. She descended from her roost, numb in her arms and legs from her entanglement in the rough limbs. Caesar's face was serious. By now the word had spread about last night's altercation. The patrollers knew the direction they traveled. "Did you tell her about the railroad?"

"I don't think so."

"I don't think I did. We were foolish not to think on this."

The creek they waded at noon was a landmark. They were close, Caesar said. After a mile, he left her to scout. On his return they adopted a more shallow track in the woods that permitted them to barely see houses through the brush.

"That's it," Caesar said. It was a tidy one-story cottage that looked out on a pasture. The land had been cleared but lay fallow. The red weathervane was Caesar's sign that this was the house, the yellow curtains pulled shut in the back window the signal that Fletcher was home but his wife was not.

"If Lovey told them," Cora said.

They saw no other houses from their vantage, and no people. Cora and Caesar sprinted through the wild grass, exposed for the first time since the swamp. It was unnerving out in the open. She felt like she had been thrown into one of Alice's big black skillets, fires licking below. They waited at the back door for Fletcher to answer their knock. Cora imagined the posses massing in the woods, girding themselves for a dash into the field. Or perhaps they lay wait inside. If Lovey told them. Fletcher finally ushered them into the kitchen.

The kitchen was small but comfortable. Favorite pots showed their dark bottoms from hooks and gaily colored flowers from the pasture leaned out of thin glassware. An old red-eyed hound didn't stir from his corner, indifferent to the visitors. Cora and Caesar drank greedily from the pitcher Fletcher offered them. The host was unhappy to see the extra passenger, but so many things had gone wrong from the very start.

The shopkeeper caught them up. First, Lovey's mother, Jeer, noticed her daughter's absence and left their cabin to make a quiet search. The boys liked Lovey, and Lovey liked the boys. One of the bosses stopped Jeer and got the story out of her.

Cora and Caesar looked at each other. Their six-hour head start had been a fantasy. The patrollers had been deep in the hunt the whole time.

By midmorning, Fletcher said, every spare hand in the county and from all around enlisted in the search. Terrance's reward was unprecedented. Advertisements were posted at every public place. The worst sort of scoundrels took up the chase. Drunkards, incorrigibles, poor whites who didn't even own shoes delighted in this opportunity to scourge the colored population. Patrol bands marauded through the slave villages and ransacked the homes of freemen, stealing and committing assaults.

Providence smiled on the fugitives: The hunters believed they hid in the swamp—with two young females in tow, any other ambitions must have been curtailed. Most slaves made tracks for the black water, as there were no helpful whites this far south, no underground railroad waiting to rescue a wayward nigger. This misstep allowed the trio to get as far northeast as they did.

Until the hog hunters came upon them. Lovey was back on Randall. Posses had called on Fletcher's house twice already to spread the word and sneak a glance at the shadows. But the worst news was that the youngest of the hunters—a boy of twelve—had not awakened from his injuries. Caesar and Cora were as good as murderers in the eyes of the county. The white men wanted blood.

Caesar covered his face and Fletcher placed a reassuring hand on his shoulder. Cora's lack of a response to the information was conspicuous. The men waited. She tore off a piece of bread. Caesar's mortification would have to suffice for the pair.

The story of the escape and their own account of the fight in the woods did much to alleviate Fletcher's dismay. The three of them in his kitchen meant that Lovey didn't know about the railroad, and they hadn't mentioned the shopkeeper's name at any point. They would proceed.

As Caesar and Cora wolfed down the rest of the pumpernickel loaf and slices of ham, the men debated the merits of venturing now or after nightfall. Cora thought better of contributing to the discussion. This was her first time out in the world and there was much she did not know. Her own vote was for lighting out as soon as possible. Every mile between her and the plantation was a victory. She would add to her collection.

The men decided that traveling right under their noses, with the slaves hidden beneath a Hessian blanket in the back of Fletcher's cart, was the most prudent. It removed the difficulty of hiding in the cellar, negotiating Mrs. Fletcher's comings and goings. "If you think so," Cora said. The hound passed gas.

On the silent road Caesar and Cora nestled among Fletcher's crates. The sunlight glowed through the blanket between the shadows of overhanging trees while Fletcher made conversation with his horses. Cora closed her eyes, but a vision of the boy lying in bed, his head bandaged and the big man with the beard standing over him, forestalled her slumber. He was younger than she had reckoned. But he should not have laid his hands on her. The boy should have picked a different pastime than hunting hogs at night. She didn't care if he recovered, she decided. They were going to be killed whether he woke or not.

The noise of the town roused her. She could only imagine what it looked like, the people on their errands, the busy shops, the buggies and carts navigating each other. The voices were close, the mad chatter of a disembodied mob. Caesar squeezed her hand. Their arrangement among the crates prevented her from seeing his face but she knew his expression. Then Fletcher stopped his cart. Cora expected the blanket to be ripped off the next moment and made a portrait of the ensuing mayhem. The roaring sunlight. Fletcher flogged and arrested, more likely lynched for harboring no mere slaves but murderers. Cora and Caesar roundly beaten by the crowd in preparation for their delivery back to Terrance, and whatever their master had devised to surpass Big Anthony's torments. And what he had already meted out to Lovey, if he was not waiting on a reunion of the three runaways. She held her breath.

Fletcher had stopped at the hail of a friend. Cora let out a noise when the man leaned against the cart, rocking it, but he didn't hear. The man greeted Fletcher and gave the shopkeeper an update on the posses and their search—the murderers had been captured! Fletcher thanked God. Another voice joined to rebut this rumor. The slaves were still about, stealing a farmer's chickens in a morning raid, but the hounds had the scent. Fletcher repeated his gratitude toward a God that looked over a white man and his interests. Of the boy there was no news. A pity, Fletcher said.

Directly, the cart was back on the quiet county road. Fletcher said, "You've got them chasing their tails." It wasn't clear if he was talking to the slaves or his horses. Cora dozed again, the rigors of their flight still exacting their toll. Sleeping prevented thoughts of Lovey. When she next opened her eyes, it was dark. Caesar patted her in reassurance. There was a rumbling and a jingling and the sound of a bolt. Fletcher removed the blanket and the fugitives stretched their aching limbs as they took in the barn.

She saw the chains first. Thousands of them dangled off the wall on nails in a morbid inventory of manacles and fetters, of shackles for ankles and wrists and necks in all varieties and combinations. Shackles to prevent a person from absconding, from moving their hands, or to suspend a body in the air for a beating. One row was devoted to children's chains and the tiny manacles and links connecting them. Another row showcased iron cuffs so thick that no saw could bite them, and cuffs so thin that only the thought of punishment prevented their wearer from splitting them. A line of ornate muzzles commanded their own section, and there was a pile of ball and chains in the corner. The balls were arranged in a pyramid, the chains trailing off in S shapes. Some of the shackles were rusted, some were broken, and others seemed as if they had been forged that very morning. Cora moved to one part of the collection and touched a metal loop with spikes radiating toward its center. She decided it was intended for wear around the neck.

"A fearsome display," a man said. "I picked them up here and there."

They hadn't heard him enter; had he been there all along? He wore gray trousers and a shirt of porous cloth that did not hide his skeletal appearance. Cora had seen starving slaves with more meat on their bones. "Some souvenirs from my travels," the white man said. He had an odd manner of speech, a queer lilt that reminded Cora of the way those on the plantation sounded after they lost their wits.

Fletcher introduced him as Lumbly. He shook their hands weakly.

"You the conductor?" Caesar asked.

"No good with steam," Lumbly said. "More of a station agent." When not concerning himself with railroad matters, he said, he led a quiet life on his farm. This was his land. Cora and Caesar needed to arrive under the blanket or else blindfolded, he explained. Best they remain ignorant of their location. "I was expecting three passengers today," he said. "You'll be able to stretch out."

Before they could figure his words, Fletcher informed them it was time for him to return to his wife: "My part is finished, my friends." He embraced the runaways with desperate affection. Cora couldn't help but shrink away. Two white men in two days had their hands around her. Was this a condition of her freedom?

Caesar silently watched the shopkeeper and his cart depart. Fletcher addressed his horses and then his voice trailed away. Concern troubled the features of Cora's companion. Fletcher had undertaken a great risk for them, even when the situation grew more complicated than he had bargained. The only currency to satisfy the debt was their survival and to help others when circumstances permitted. By her accounting, at least. Caesar owed the man much more for taking him into his shop all those months before. That is what she saw in his face—not concern but responsibility. Lumbly shut the barn door, the chains jingling with the vibration.

Lumbly was not as sentimental. He lit a lantern and gave it to Caesar while he kicked some hay and pulled up a trapdoor in the floor. At their trepidation he said, "I'll go first, if you wish." The stairwell was lined with stones and a sour smell emanated from below. It did not open into a cellar but continued down. Cora appreciated the labor that had gone into its construction. The steps were steep, but the stones aligned in even planes and provided an easy descent. Then they reached the tunnel, and appreciation became too mealy a word to contain what lay before her.

The stairs led onto a small platform. The black mouths of the gigantic tunnel opened at either end. It must have been twenty feet tall, walls lined with dark and light colored stones in an alternating pattern. The sheer industry that had made such a project possible. Cora and Caesar noticed the rails. Two steel rails ran the visible length of the tunnel, pinned into the dirt by wooden cross-ties. The steel ran south and north presumably, springing from some inconceivable source and shooting toward a miraculous terminus. Someone had been thoughtful enough to arrange a small bench on the platform. Cora felt dizzy and sat down.

Caesar could scarcely speak. "How far does the tunnel extend?"

Lumbly shrugged. "Far enough for you."

"It must have taken years."

"More than you know. Solving the problem of ventilation, that took a bit of time."

"Who built it?"

"Who builds anything in this country?"

Cora saw that Lumbly relished their astonishment. This was not his first performance.

Caesar said, "But how?"

"With their hands, how else? We need to discuss your departure." Lumbly pulled a yellow paper from his pocket and squinted. "You have two choices. We have a train leaving in one hour and another in six hours. Not the most convenient schedule. Would that our passengers could time their arrivals more appropriately, but we operate under certain constraints."

"The next one," Cora said, standing. There was no question.

"The trick of it is, they're not going to the same place," Lumbly said. "One's going one way and the other . . ."

"To where?" Cora asked.

"Away from here, that's all I can tell you. You understand the difficulties in communicating all the changes in the routes. Locals, expresses, what station's closed down, where they're extending the heading. The problem is that one destination may be more to your liking than another. Stations are discovered, lines discontinued. You won't know what waits above until you pull in."

The runaways didn't understand. From the station agent's words, one route might be more direct but more dangerous. Was he saying one route was longer? Lumbly would not elaborate. He had told them all he knew, he maintained. In the end, the slave's choice lay before them, as ever: anyplace but where they had escaped. After consulting with his partner Caesar said, "We'll take the next one."

"It's up to you," Lumbly said. He motioned toward the bench.

They waited. At Caesar's request the station agent told of how he came to work for the underground railroad. Cora couldn't pay attention. The tunnel pulled at her. How many hands had it required to make this place? And the tunnels beyond, wherever and how far they led? She thought of the picking, how it raced down the furrows at harvest, the African bodies working as one, as fast as their strength permitted. The vast fields burst with hundreds of thousands of white bolls, strung like stars in the sky on the clearest of clear nights. When the slaves finished, they had stripped the fields of their color. It was a magnificent operation, from seed to bale, but not one of them could be prideful of their labor. It had been stolen from them. Bled from them. The tunnel, the tracks, the desperate souls who found salvation in the coordination of its stations and timetables—this was a marvel to be proud of. She wondered if those who had built this thing had received their proper reward.

"Every state is different," Lumbly was saying. "Each one a state of possibility, with its own customs and way of doing things. Moving through them, you'll see the breadth of the country before you reach your final stop."

At that, the bench rumbled. They hushed, and the rumbling became a sound. Lumbly led them to the edge of the platform. The thing arrived in its hulking strangeness. Caesar had seen trains in Virginia; Cora had only heard tell of the machines. It wasn't what she envisioned. The locomotive was black, an ungainly contraption led by the triangular snout of the cowcatcher, though there would be few animals where this engine was headed. The bulb of the smokestack was next, a soot-covered stalk. The main body consisted of a large black box topped by the engineer's cabin. Below that, pistons and large cylinders engaged in a relentless dance with the ten wheels, two sets of small ones in front and three behind. The locomotive pulled one single car, a dilapidated boxcar missing numerous planks in its walls.

The colored engineer waved back at them from his cabin, grinning toothlessly. "All aboard," he said.

To curtail Caesar's annoying interrogations, Lumbly quickly unhooked the boxcar door and slid it wide. "Shall we proceed?"

Cora and Caesar climbed into the car and Lumbly abruptly shut them in. He peered between the gaps in the wood. "If you want to see what this nation is all about, I always say, you have to ride the rails. Look outside as you speed through, and you'll find the true face of America." He slapped the wall of the boxcar as a signal. The train lurched forward.

The runaways lost their balance and stumbled to the nest of hay bales that was to serve as seating. The boxcar creaked and shuddered. It was no new model, and on numerous occasions during their trip Cora feared it was on the verge of collapse. The car was empty apart from hay bales, dead mice, and bent nails. She later discovered a charred patch where someone had started a fire. Caesar was numb from the series of curious events and he curled up on the floor. Following Lumbly's final instructions, Cora looked through the slats. There was only darkness, mile after mile.

When they next stepped into the sunlight, they were in South Carolina. She looked up at the skyscraper and reeled, wondering how far she had traveled.

Ridgeway

ARNOLD Ridgeway's father was a blacksmith. The sunset glow of molten iron bewitched him, the way the color emerged in the stock slow and then fast, overtaking it like an emotion, the sudden pliability and restless writhing of the thing as it waited for purpose. His forge was a window into the primitive energies of the world.

He had a saloon partner named Tom Bird, a half-breed who took a sentimental turn when lubricated by whiskey. On nights when Tom Bird felt separate from his life's design, he shared stories of the Great Spirit. The Great Spirit lived in all things—the earth, the sky, the animals and forests—flowing through and connecting them in a divine thread. Although Ridgeway's father scorned religious talk, Tom Bird's testimony on the Great Spirit reminded him of how he felt about iron. He bent to no god save the glowing iron he tended in his forge. He'd read about the great volcanoes, the lost city of Pompeii destroyed by fire that poured out of mountains from deep below. Liquid fire was the very blood of the earth. It was his mission to upset, mash, and draw out the metal into the useful things that made society operate: nails, horseshoes, plows, knives, guns. Chains. Working the spirit, he called it.

When permitted, young Ridgeway stood in the corner while his father worked Pennsylvania iron. Melting, hammering, dancing around his anvil. Sweat dripping down his face, covered in soot foot to crown, blacker than an African devil. "You got to work that spirit, boy." One day he would find his spirit, his father told him.

It was encouragement. Ridgeway hoisted it as a lonesome burden. There was no model for the type of man he wanted to become. He couldn't turn to the anvil because there was no way to surpass his father's talent. In town he scrutinized the faces of men in the same way that his father searched for impurities in metal. Everywhere men busied themselves in frivolous and worthless occupations. The farmer waited on rain like an imbecile, the shopkeeper arranged row after row of necessary but dull merchandise. Craftsmen and artisans created items that were brittle rumors compared with his father's iron facts. Even the wealthiest men, influencing the far-off London exchanges and local commerce alike, provided no inspiration. He acknowledged their place in the system, erecting their big houses on a foundation of numbers, but he didn't respect them. If you weren't a little dirty at the end of the day, you weren't much of a man.

Every morning, the sounds of his father pounding metal were the footsteps of a destiny that never drew closer.

Ridgeway was fourteen when he took up with the patrollers. He was a hulking fourteen, six and a half feet tall, burly and resolute. His body gave no indication of the confusion within. He beat his fellows when he spied his weaknesses in them. Ridgeway was young for patrol but the business was changing. King Cotton crowded the countryside with slaves. The revolts in the West Indies and disquieting incidents closer to home worried the local planters. What clear-thinking white man wouldn't be worried, slaver or otherwise. The patrols increased in size, as did their mandate. A boy might find a place.

The head patroller in the county was the fiercest specimen Ridgeway had ever laid eyes on. Chandler was a brawler and bully, the local terror decent people crossed the street to avoid even when the rain made it a stew of mud. He spent more days in jail than the runaways he brought in, snoring in a cell next to the miscreant he had stopped hours earlier. An imperfect model, but close to the shape Ridgeway sought. Inside the rules, enforcing them, but also outside. It helped that his father hated Chandler, still smarting from a row years before. Ridgeway loved his father, but the man's constant talk of spirits reminded him of his own lack of purpose.

Patrol was not difficult work. They stopped any niggers they saw and demanded their passes. They stopped niggers they knew to be free, for their amusement but also to remind the Africans of the forces arrayed against them, whether they were owned by a white man or not. Made the rounds of the slave villages in search of anything amiss, a smile or a book. They flogged the wayward niggers before bringing them to the jail, or directly to their owner if they were in the mood and it was not too close to quitting time.

News of a runaway sent them into cheerful activity. They raided the plantations after their quarry, interrogating a host of quivering darkies. Freemen knew what was coming and hid their valuables and moaned when the white men smashed their furniture and glass. Praying that they confined their damage to objects. There were perquisites, apart from the thrill of shaming a man in front of his family or roughing up an unseasoned buck who squinted at you the wrong way. The old Mutter farm had the comeliest colored wenches—Mr. Mutter had a taste—and the excitement of the hunt put a young patroller in a lusty mood. According to some, the backwoods stills of the old men on the Stone plantation produced the best corn whiskey in the county. A roust allowed Chandler to replenish his jars.

Ridgeway commanded his appetites in those days, withdrawing before his confederates' more egregious displays. The other patrollers were boys and men of bad character; the work attracted a type. In another country they would have been criminals, but this was America. He liked the night work best, when they lay in wait for a buck who sneaked through the woods to visit his wife on a plantation up the road, or a squirrel hunter looking to supplement his daily meal of slop. Other patrollers carried guns and eagerly cut down any rascal dumb enough to flee, but Ridgeway copied Chandler. Nature had equipped him with weapons enough. Ridgeway ran them down as if they were rabbits and then his fists subdued them. Beat them for being out, beat them for running, even though the chase was the only remedy for his restlessness. Charging through the dark, branches lashing his face, stumps sending him ass over elbow before he got up again. In the chase his blood sang and glowed.

When his father finished his workday, the fruit of his labor lay before him: a musket, a rake, a wagon spring. Ridgeway faced the man or woman he had captured. One made tools, the other retrieved them. His father teased him about the spirit. What kind of a calling was running down niggers who barely have the wits of a dog?

Ridgeway was eighteen now, a man. "We're both of us working for Mr. Eli Whitney," he said. It was true; his father had just hired two apprentices and contracted work out to smaller smiths. The cotton gin meant bigger cotton yields and the iron tools to harvest it, iron horseshoes for the horses tugging the wagons with iron rims and parts that took it to market. More slaves and the iron to hold them. The crop birthed communities, requiring nails and braces for houses, the tools to build the houses, roads to connect them, and more iron to keep it all running. Let his father keep his disdain and his spirit, too. The two men were parts of the same system, serving a nation rising to its destiny.

An absconded slave might fetch as little as two dollars if the owner was a skinflint or the nigger was busted, and as much as a hundred dollars, double that if captured out of state. Ridgeway became a proper slave catcher after his first trip to New Jersey, when he went up to retrieve the property of a local planter. Betsy made it all the way from the Virginia tobacco fields to Trenton. She hid with cousins until a friend of her owner recognized her at the market. Her master offered the local boys twenty dollars for delivery plus all reasonable expenses.

He'd never traveled so far before. The farther north he got, the more famished his notions. How big the country was! Each town more lunatic and complicated than the last. The hurly-burly of Washington, D.C., made him dizzy. He vomited when he turned a corner and saw the construction site of the Capitol, emptying his guts from either a bad oyster or the hugeness of the thing stirring rebellion in his very being. He sought out the cheapest taverns and turned the stories of the men over in his mind as he scratched at lice. Even the shortest ferry ride delivered him to a new island nation, garish and imposing.

At the Trenton jail the deputy treated him like a man of standing. This was not scourging some colored boy in the twilight or breaking up a slave festival for amusement. This was man's work. In a grove outside Richmond, Betsy made a lewd proposition in exchange for freedom, pulling up her dress with slender fingers. She was slim in the hips, with a wide mouth and gray eyes. He made no promises. It was the first time he lay with a woman. She spat at him when he fastened her chains, and once again when they reached her owner's mansion. The master and his sons laughed as he wiped his face, but the twenty dollars went to new boots and a brocade coat like he'd seen some worthies wear in D.C. He wore the boots for many years. His belly outgrew the coat sooner than that.

New York was the start of a wild time. Ridgeway worked retrieval, heading north when constables sent word they'd captured a runaway from Virginia or North Carolina. New York became a frequent destination, and after exploring new aspects of his character, Ridgeway picked up stakes. The fugitive trade back home was straightforward. Knocking heads. Up north, the gargantuan metropolis, the liberty movement, and the ingenuity of the colored community all converged to portray the true scale of the hunt.

He was a quick study. It was more like remembering than learning. Sympathizers and mercenary captains smuggled fugitives into the city ports. In turn, stevedores and dockhands and clerks furnished him with information and he scooped up the rascals on the threshold of deliverance. Freemen informed on their African brothers and sisters, comparing the descriptions of runaways in the gazettes with the furtive creatures slinking around the colored churches, saloons, and meeting houses. *Barry is a stout well made fellow five feet six or seven, high small eyes and an impudent look. Hasty is far advanced in her pregnancy and is presumed to have been conveyed away by some person, as she could not undergo the fatigue of traveling.* Barry crumpled with a whimper. Hasty and her pup howled all the way to Charlotte.

Soon he owned three fine coats. Ridgeway fell in with a circle of slave catchers, gorillas stuffed into black suits with ridiculous derbies. He had to prove he was not a bumpkin, but just once. Together they shadowed runaways for days, hiding outside places of work until opportunity announced itself, breaking into their negro hovels at night to kidnap them. After years away from the plantation, after taking a wife and starting a family, they had convinced themselves they were free. As if owners forgot about property. Their delusions made them easy prey. He snubbed the blackbirders, the Five Points gangs who hog-tied freemen and dragged them south for auction. That was low behavior, patroller behavior. He was a slave catcher now.

New York City was a factory of antislavery sentiment. The

courts had to sign off before Ridgeway was permitted to take his charges south. Abolitionist lawyers erected barricades of paperwork, every week a new stratagem. New York was a Free State, they argued, and any colored person became magically free once they stepped over the border. They exploited understandable discrepancies between the bulletins and the individual in the courtroom— was there proof that this Benjamin Jones was the Benjamin Jones in question? Most planters couldn't tell one slave from another, even after taking them to bed. No wonder they lost track of their property. It became a game, prying niggers from jail before the lawyers unveiled their latest gambit. High-minded idiocy pitted against the power of coin. For a gratuity, the city recorder tipped him to freshly jailed fugitives and hurriedly signed them over for release. They'd be halfway through New Jersey before the abolitionists had even gotten out of bed.

Ridgeway bypassed the courthouse when needed, but not often. It was a bother to be stopped on the road in a Free State when the lost property turned out to have a silver tongue. Get them off the plantation and they learned to read, it was a disease.

While Ridgeway waited at the docks for smugglers, the magnificent ships from Europe dropped anchor and discharged their passengers. Everything they owned in sacks, half starving. Hapless as niggers, by any measure. But they'd be called to their proper places, as he had been. His whole world growing up in the south was a ripple of this first arrival. This dirty white flood with nowhere to go but out. South. West. The same laws governed garbage and people. The gutters of the city overflowed with offal and refuse—but the mess found its place in time.

Ridgeway watched them stagger down the gangplanks, rheumy and bewildered, overcome by the city. The possibilities lay before these pilgrims like a banquet, and they'd been so hungry their whole lives. They'd never seen the likes of this, but they'd leave their mark on this new land, as surely as those famous souls at Jamestown, making it theirs through unstoppable racial logic. If niggers were supposed to have their freedom, they wouldn't be in chains. If the red man was supposed to keep hold of his land, it'd still be his. If the white man wasn't destined to take this new world, he wouldn't own it now.

Here was the true Great Spirit, the divine thread connecting all human endeavor—if you can keep it, it is yours. Your property, slave or continent. The American imperative.

Ridgeway gathered renown with his facility for ensuring that property remained property. When a runaway took off down an alley, he knew where the man was headed. The direction and aim. His trick: Don't speculate where the slave is headed next. Concentrate instead on the idea that he is running away from you. Not from a cruel master, or the vast agency of bondage, but you specifically. It worked again and again, his own iron fact, in alleys and pine barrens and swamps. He finally left his father behind, and the burden of that man's philosophy. Ridgeway was not working the spirit. He was not the smith, rendering order. Not the hammer. Not the anvil. He was the heat.

His father died and the smith down the road assumed his operation. It was time to return south—back home to Virginia and farther, wherever the work led—and he came with a gang. Too many fugitives to handle by himself. Eli Whitney had run his father into the ground, the old man coughing soot on his death-bed, and kept Ridgeway on the hunt. The plantations were twice as big, twice as numerous, the fugitives more plentiful and nimble, the bounties higher. There was less meddling from the lawmak-ers and abolitionists down south, the planters saw to that. The underground railroad maintained no lines to speak of. The decoys in negro dress, the secret codes in the back pages of newspapers. They openly bragged of their subversion, hustling a slave out the back door as the slave catchers broke down the front. It was a criminal conspiracy devoted to theft of property, and Ridgeway suffered their brazenness as a personal slur.

One Delaware merchant particularly galled him: August Carter. Robust in the Anglo-Saxon tradition, with cool blue eyes that made the lesser sort pay attention to his mealy arguments. That worst sort, an abolitionist with a printing press. "A Mass Meeting of the Friends of Freedom Will Be Held at Miller's Hall at 2 p.m. to Testify Against the Iniquitous Slave Power That Controls the Nation." Everyone knew the Carter home was a station—only a hundred yards separated it from the river—even when raids came up empty. Runaways turned activists saluted his generosity in their Boston speeches. The abolitionist wing of the Methodists circulated his pamphlets on Sunday morning and London periodicals published his arguments without rebuttal. A printing press, and friends among the judges, who forced Ridgeway to relinquish his charges on no less than three occasions. Passing Ridgeway outside the jail, he'd tip his hat.

The slave catcher had little choice but to call upon the man after midnight. He daintily sewed their hoods from white sacks of flour but could barely move his fingers after their visit—his fists swelled for two days from beating the man's face in. He permitted his men to dishonor the man's wife in ways he never let them use a nigger gal. For years after whenever Ridgeway saw a bonfire, the smell reminded him of the sweet smoke of Carter's house going up and a figment of a smile settled on his mouth. He later heard the man moved to Worcester and became a cobbler.

The slave mothers said, Mind yourself or Mister Ridgeway will come for you.

The slave masters said, Send for Ridgeway.

When first summoned to the Randall plantation, he was due for a challenge. Slaves eluded him from time to time. He was extraordinary, not supernatural. He failed, and Mabel's disappearance nagged at him longer than it should have, buzzing in the stronghold of his mind.

On returning, now charged to find that woman's daughter, he knew why the previous assignment had vexed him so. Impossible as it seemed, the underground railroad had a spur in Georgia. He would find it. He would destroy it.

South Carolina

30 **DOLLARS REWARD**

will be given to any person who will deliver to me, or confine in any gaol in the state so that I get her again, a likely yellow NEGRO GIRL 18 years of age who ran away nine months past. She is an artfully lively girl, and will, no doubt, attempt to pass as a free person, has a noticeable scar on her elbow, occasioned by a burn. I have been informed she is lurking in and about Edenton.

BENJ. P. WELLS
MURFREESBORO, JAN. 5, 1812

THE Andersons lived in a lovely clapboard house at the corner of Washington and Main, a few blocks past the hubbub of stores and businesses, where the town settled into private residences for the well-to-do. Beyond the wide front porch, where Mr. and Mrs. Anderson liked to sit in the evenings, the man scooping into his silk tobacco pouch and the woman squinting at her needlework, were the parlor, dining room, and kitchen. Bessie spent most of her time on that first floor, chasing after the children, preparing meals, and tidying up. At the top of the staircase were the bedrooms—Maisie and little Raymond shared theirs—and the second washroom. Raymond took a long nap in the afternoon and Bessie liked to sit in the window seat as he settled into his dreams. She could just make out the top two floors of the Griffin Building, with its white cornices that blazed in the sunlight.

This day she packed a lunch of bread and jam for Maisie, took the boy for a walk, and cleaned the silver and glassware. After Bessie changed the bedding, she and Raymond picked up Maisie from school and they went to the park. A fiddler played the latest melodies by the fountain as the children and their friends diverted themselves with hide-and-seek and hunt the ring. She had to steer Raymond away from a bully, careful not to upset the rascal's mother, whom she could not pick out. It was Friday, which meant that she ended the day with the shopping. The clouds had moved in, anyway. Bessie put the salt beef and milk and the rest of the supper makings on the family's account. She signed with an X.

Mrs. Anderson came home at six o'clock. The family doctor had advised her to spend more time out of the house. Her work raising funds for the new hospital assisted in this regard, in addition to her afternoon lunches with the other ladies of the neighborhood. She was in good spirits, rounding up her children for kisses and hugs and promising a treat after dinner. Maisie hopped and squealed. Mrs. Anderson thanked Bessie for her help and bid her good night.

The walk to the dormitories on the other side of town was not far. There were shortcuts, but Bessie liked to take in the lively activity of Main Street in the evening, mingling with the townsfolk, white and colored. She strolled down the line of establishments, never failing to linger by the big glass windows. The dressmaker with her frilly, colorful creations draped on hooped wire, the overstuffed emporiums and their wonderland of goods, the rival general stores on either side of Main Street. She made a game of picking out the latest additions to the displays. The plenty still astounded her. Most impressive of all was the Griffin Building.

At twelve stories, it was one of the tallest buildings in the nation, certainly it towered over any structure in the south. The pride of the town. The bank dominated the first floor, with its vaulted ceiling and Tennessee marble. Bessie had no business there but was not a stranger to the floors above. The previous week she took the children to see their father on his birthday and got to hear the clopping of her footsteps in the beautiful lobby. The elevator, the only one for hundreds of miles, conveyed them to the eighth floor. Maisie and Raymond were not impressed with the machine, having visited many times, but Bessie never failed to be both delighted and frightened by its magic, bracing herself with the brass rail in case of disaster.

They passed the floors of insurance agents, government offices, and export firms. Vacancies were rare; a Griffin address was a great boon to a business's reputation. Mr. Anderson's floor was a warren of lawyer's offices, with rich carpets, walls of dark brown wood, and doors inlaid with frosted glass. Mr. Anderson himself worked on contracts, primarily in the cotton trade. He was quite surprised to see his family. He received the small cake from the children with good cheer, but made it clear he was anxious to get back to his papers. For a moment Bessie wondered if she was in for a scolding, but none came. Mrs. Anderson had insisted on the trip. Mr. Anderson's secretary held open the door and Bessie hustled the children out to the confectioner.

This evening Bessie passed the shiny brass doors of the bank and continued home. Every day the remarkable edifice served as a monument to her profound change in circumstances. She walked down the sidewalk as a free woman. No one chased her or abused her. Some of Mrs. Anderson's circle, who recognized Bessie as her girl, sometimes even smiled.

Bessie crossed the street to avoid the jumble of saloons and their disreputable clientele. She stopped herself before she searched for Sam's face among the drunkards. Around the corner came the more modest homes of the less prosperous white residents. She picked up her pace. There was a gray house on the corner whose owners were indifferent to their dog's feral displays, and a line of cottages where the wives stared out of the windows with flinty expressions. Many of the white men in this part of town worked as foremen or laborers in the larger factories. They tended not to employ colored help so Bessie had little information about their day to day.

Presently she arrived at the dormitories. The two-story red brick buildings had been completed only a short time before Bessie's arrival. In time the saplings and hedges on the perimeter would provide shade and character; now they spoke of fine intentions. The brick was a pure, unsullied color, without so much as a dot of mud splashed from the rain. Not even a caterpillar crawling in a nook. Inside, the white paint still smelled fresh in the common spaces, dining rooms, and bunk rooms. Bessie wasn't the only girl afraid to touch anything apart from the doorknobs. To even leave a speck or scratch mark.

Bessie greeted the other residents as they crossed each other on the sidewalk. Most were returning from work. Others departed to watch over children so their parents could partake of the pleasant evening. Only half of the colored residents worked on Saturdays, so Friday night was busy.

She reached number 18. She said hello to the girls braiding their hair in the common room and darted upstairs to change before dinner. When Bessie arrived in town, most of the eighty beds in the bunk room had been claimed. A day earlier and she might have been sleeping in a bed beneath one of the windows. It would be some time before someone moved away and she could switch to a better position. Bessie liked the breeze afforded by the windows. If she turned her body the other way she might see stars some nights.

Bessie opened the trunk at the foot of her bed and removed the blue dress she bought her second week in South Carolina. She smoothed it over her legs. The soft cotton on her skin still thrilled her. Bessie bunched her work clothes and put them in the sack under the bed. Lately she did her washing on Saturday afternoons following her school lessons. The chore was her way of making up for sleeping in, an indulgence she allowed herself those mornings.

Supper was roast chicken with carrots and potatoes. Margaret the cook lived over in number 8. The proctors felt it prudent that the people who cleaned and cooked in the dorms did so in buildings other than their own. It was a small but worthy idea. Margaret had a heavy hand with the salt, although her meat and poultry were always exquisitely tender. Bessie mopped up the fat with a crust of bread as she listened to the talk of evening plans. Most of the girls stayed in the night before the social, but some of the younger ones were going out to the colored saloon that had recently opened. Although it wasn't supposed to, the saloon accepted scrip. Another reason to avoid the place, Bessie thought. She brought her dishes to the kitchen and headed back upstairs.

"Bessie?"

"Good evening, Miss Lucy," Bessie said.

It was rare Miss Lucy stayed this late on a Friday. Most proctors disappeared at six o'clock. To hear the girls from the other dormitories tell it, Miss Lucy's diligence put her colleagues to shame. To be sure, Bessie had benefited from her advice many times. She admired the way her clothes were always so crisp and fit just so. Miss Lucy wore her hair in a bun and the thin metal of her eyeglasses lent her a severe aspect, but her quick smile told the story of the woman beneath.

"How are things?" Miss Lucy asked.

"Think I'm gonna spend a quiet night in the quarter, Miss Lucy," Bessie said.

"*Dormitory*, Bessie. Not *quarter.*"

"Yes, Miss Lucy."

"*Going to*, not *gonna.*"

"I am working on it."

"And making splendid progress!" Miss Lucy patted Bessie's arm. "I want to talk to you Monday morning before you head out for work."

"Anything wrong, Miss Lucy?"

"Nothing at all, Bessie. We'll talk then." She gave a little bow and walked to the office.

Bowing to a colored girl.

—

BESSIE Carpenter was the name on the papers Sam gave her at the station. Months later, Cora still didn't know how she had survived the trip from Georgia. The darkness of the tunnel quickly turned the boxcar into a grave. The only light came from the engineer's cabin, through the slats in the front of the rickety car. At one point it shook so much that Cora put her arms around Caesar and they stayed like that for a good while, squeezing each other at the more urgent tremors, pressed against the hay. It felt good to grab him, to anticipate the warm pressure of his rising and falling chest.

Then the locomotive decelerated. Caesar jumped up. They could scarcely believe it, although the runaways' excitement was tempered. Each time they completed one leg of their journey, the next unexpected segment commenced. The barn of shackles, the hole in the earth, this broken-down boxcar—the heading of the underground railroad was laid in the direction of the bizarre. Cora told Caesar that on seeing the chains, she feared Fletcher had conspired with Terrance from the very beginning and that they had been conveyed to a chamber of horrors. Their plot, escape, and arrival were the elements of an elaborate living play.

The station was similar to their point of departure. Instead of a bench, there was a table and chairs. Two lanterns hung on the wall, and a small basket sat next to the stairs.

The engineer set them loose from the boxcar. He was a tall man with a horseshoe of white hair around his pate and the stoop that came from years of field work. He mopped sweat and soot from his face and was about to speak when a ferocious coughing wracked his person. After a few pulls from his flask the engineer regained his composure.

He cut off their thanks. "This is my job," he said. "Feed the boiler, make sure she keeps running. Get the passengers where they got to be." He made for his cabin. "You wait here until they come and fetch you." In moments the train had disappeared, leaving a swirling wake of steam and noise.

The basket contained victuals: bread, half a chicken, water, and a bottle of beer. They were so hungry they shook out the crumbs from the basket to divvy. Cora even took a sip of the beer. At the footsteps on the stairs, they steeled themselves for the latest representative of the underground railroad.

Sam was a white man of twenty-five years and exhibited none of the eccentric mannerisms of his co-workers. Sturdy in frame and jolly, he wore tan trousers with braces and a thick red shirt that had suffered roughly at the washboard. His mustache curled at the ends, bobbing with his enthusiasm. The station agent shook their hands and appraised them, unbelieving. "You made it," Sam said. "You're really here."

He had brought more food. They sat at the wobbly table and Sam described the world above. "You're a long way from Georgia," Sam said. "South Carolina has a much more enlightened attitude toward colored advancement than the rest of the south. You'll be safe here until we can arrange the next leg of your trip. It might take time."

"How long?" Caesar asked.

"No telling. There are so many people being moved around, one station at a time. It's hard to get messages through. The railroad is God's work, but maddening to manage." He watched them devour the food with evident pleasure. "Who knows?" he said. "Perhaps you'll decide to stay. As I said, South Carolina is like nothing you've ever seen."

Sam went upstairs and returned with clothes and a small barrel of water. "You need to wash up," he said. "I intend that in the kindest way." He sat on the stairs to give them privacy. Caesar bid Cora to wash up first, and joined Sam. Her nakedness was no novelty, but she appreciated the gesture. Cora started with her face. She was dirty, she smelled, and when she wrung the cloth, dark water spilled out. The new clothes were not stiff negro cloth but a cotton so supple it made her body feel clean, as if she had actually scrubbed with soap. The dress was simple, light blue with plain lines, like nothing she had worn before. Cotton went in one way, came out another.

When Caesar finished washing up, Sam gave them their papers.

"The names are wrong," Caesar said.

"You're runaways," Sam said. "This is who you are now. You need to commit the names and the story to memory."

More than runaways—murderers, maybe. Cora hadn't thought of the boy since they stepped underground. Caesar's eyes narrowed as he made the same calculation. She decided to tell Sam about the fight in the woods.

The station agent made no judgments and looked genuinely aggrieved by Lovey's fate. He told them he was sorry about their friend. "Hadn't heard about that. News like that doesn't travel here like it does some places. The boy may have recovered for all we know, but that does not change your position. All the better that you have new names."

"It says here we're the property of the United States Government," Caesar pointed out.

"That's a technicality," Sam said. White families packed up and flocked to South Carolina for opportunities, from as far as New York according to the gazettes. So did free men and women, in a migration the country had never witnessed before. A portion of the colored were runaways, although there was no telling how many, for obvious reasons. Most of the colored folk in the state had been bought up by the government. Saved from the block in some cases or purchased at estate sales. Agents scouted the big auctions. The majority were acquired from whites who had turned their back on farming. Country life was not for them, even if planting was how they had been raised and their family heritage. This was a new era. The government offered very generous terms and incentives to relocate to the big towns, mortgages and tax relief.

"And the slaves?" Cora asked. She did not understand the money talk, but she knew people being sold as property when she heard it.

"They get food, jobs, and housing. Come and go as they please, marry who they wish, raise children who will never be taken away. Good jobs, too, not slave work. But you'll see soon enough." There was a bill of sale in a file in a box somewhere, from what he understood, but that was it. Nothing that would be held over them. A confidante in the Griffin Building had forged these papers for them.

"Are you ready?" Sam asked.

Caesar and Cora looked at each other. Then he extended his hand like a gentleman. "My lady?"

She could not prevent herself from smiling, and they stepped into the daylight together.

The government had purchased Bessie Carpenter and Christian Markson from a bankruptcy hearing in North Carolina. Sam helped them rehearse as they walked to town. He lived two miles outside, in a cottage his grandfather had built. His parents had operated the copper shop on Main Street, but Sam chose a different path after they died. He sold the business to one of the many transplants who'd come to South Carolina for a fresh start and Sam now worked at one of the saloons, the Drift. His friend owned the place, and the atmosphere suited his personality. Sam liked the spectacle of the human animal up close, as well as his access to the workings of the town, once the drink loosened tongues. He made his own hours, which was an asset in his other enterprise. The station was buried beneath his barn, as with Lumbly.

At the outskirts Sam gave them detailed directions to the Placement Office. "And if you get lost, just head for that"—he pointed at the skyscraping wonder—"and make a right when you hit Main Street." He would contact them when he had more information.

Caesar and Cora made their way up the dusty road into town, unbelieving. A buggy rounded the turn and the pair nearly dove into the woods. The driver was a colored boy who tipped his cap in a jaunty fashion. Nonchalant, as if it were nothing. To have such bearing at his young age! When he was out of sight they laughed at their ridiculous behavior. Cora straightened her back and held her head level. They would have to learn how to walk like freemen.

In the following months, Cora mastered posture. Her letters and speech required more attention. After her talk with Miss Lucy, she removed her primer from her trunk. While the other girls gossiped and said good night one by one, Cora practiced her letters. The next time she signed for the Andersons' groceries, she would write *Bessie* in careful print. She blew out the candle when her hand cramped.

It was the softest bed she had ever lain in. But then, it was the only bed she had ever lain in.

Miss Handler must have been raised in the bosom of saints. Even though the old man was utterly incompetent with regards to the rudiments of writing and speaking, the teacher was never less than polite and indulgent. The entire class—the schoolhouse was full on Saturday mornings—shifted at their desks while the old man sputtered and choked on the day's lessons. The two girls in front of Cora made cross-eyes at each other and giggled at his botched sounds.

Cora joined the class in exasperation. It was nigh impossible to understand Howard's speech under normal circumstances. He favored a pidgin of his lost African tongue and slave talk. In the old days, her mother had told her, that half language was the voice of the plantation. They had been stolen from villages all over Africa and spoke a multitude of tongues. The words from across the ocean were beaten out of them over time. For simplicity, to erase their identities, to smother uprisings. All the words except for the ones locked away by those who still remembered who they had been before. "They keep 'em hid like precious gold," Mabel said.

These were not her mother's and grandmother's times. Howard's attempts at "I am" consumed precious lesson time, already too short after the work week. She had come here to learn.

A gust sent the shutters wheezing on their hinges. Miss Handler put down her chalk. "In North Carolina," she said, "what we are doing is a crime. I would be fined a hundred dollars and you would receive thirty-nine lashes. That's from the law. Your master would likely have a more severe punishment." The woman met Cora's eyes. The teacher was only a few years older than her but she made Cora feel like an ignorant pickaninny. "It's hard to start from nothing. A few weeks ago, some of you were where Howard is now. It takes time. And patience."

She dismissed them. Chastened, Cora snatched up her things, wishing to be the first one out the door. Howard wiped his tears with his sleeve.

The schoolhouse lay south of the rows of girls' dormitories. The building was also used for meetings in need of a more serious atmosphere than that of the common rooms, Cora noticed, such as the assemblies on hygiene and feminine matters. It looked out on the green, the colored population's park. Tonight one of the bands from the men's dormitory was playing in the gazebo for the social.

They deserved Miss Handler's scolding. South Carolina maintained a different attitude toward colored progress, as Sam had told Cora on the platform. Cora had savored this fact in a multitude of ways over the months, but the provision for colored education was among the most nourishing. Connelly once put out a slave's eyes for looking at words. He lost Jacob's labor, though if the man had been talented the overseer would have subjected him to a less drastic punishment. In return he gained the eternal fear of any slave with a notion to learn his letters.

Don't need eyes to shuck corn, Connelly told them. Or to starve yourself to death, as Jacob did presently.

She put the plantation behind her. She did not live there anymore.

A page slipped out of her primer and she chased it onto the grass. The book was falling apart, from her use and that of the previous owners. Cora had seen little children, ones younger than Maisie, use the same primer for their lessons. New copies with fresh spines. The ones from the colored schoolhouse were well-thumbed and she had to squeeze her letters above and in between other people's scribblings, but there was no whipping attached just for looking at it.

Her mother would be proud of her. As Lovey's mother was likely proud of her daughter for running away, for a day and a half. Cora replaced the page in her book. She pushed the plantation from her again. She was getting better at it. Her mind was wily though, twisty. Thoughts she did not like wormed in from the sides, from beneath, through the cracks, from places she had battened down.

Of her mother, for example. Her third week in the dormitory, she knocked on the door of Miss Lucy's office. If the government kept records of all the colored arrivals, perhaps among the many names was that of her mother. Mabel's life after her escape was an enigma. It was possible she was one of the freemen who came to South Carolina for the opportunities.

Miss Lucy worked in a room down the hallway from number 18's common room. Cora did not trust her, yet there she stood. Miss Lucy admitted her. The office was cramped, with filing cabinets the proctor had to squeeze through to get to her desk, but she kept it pleasant with samplers on the walls detailing farming scenes. There was no room for a second chair. Visitors stood for their audience, which kept the visits short.

Miss Lucy regarded Cora over her glasses. "What's her name?"

"Mabel Randall."

"Your name is Carpenter," Miss Lucy said.

"That my daddy's name. My mother, she a Randall."

"*That is*," Miss Lucy said. "*She is.*"

She stooped before one of the cabinets and ran her fingers over the blue-tinted papers, glancing in Cora's direction every so often. Miss Lucy had mentioned that she lived with a group of proctors in a boardinghouse near the square. Cora tried to picture what the woman did when she was not managing the dormitory, how she spent her Sundays. Did she have a young gentleman who took her places? How did an unattached white woman occupy herself in South Carolina? Cora was getting braver but still stuck close to the dormitories when not attending to the Andersons. It seemed prudent, those early days out of the tunnel.

Miss Lucy moved to another cabinet, tugging open a series of drawers, but came up empty. "These records are only of who's here at our dormitories," she said. "But we have locations all over the state." The proctor wrote down her mother's name and promised to check the master records in the Griffin Building. For the second time she reminded Cora of the lessons in reading and writing, which were optional but recommended, in keeping with their mission of colored uplift, especially for those with aptitude. Then Miss Lucy returned to her work.

It had been a whim. Once Mabel ran, Cora thought of her as little as possible. After landing in South Carolina, she realized that she had banished her mother not from sadness but from rage. She hated her. Having tasted freedom's bounty, it was incomprehensible to Cora that Mabel had abandoned her to that hell. A child. Her company would have made the escape more difficult, but Cora hadn't been a baby. If she could pick cotton, she could run. She would have died in that place, after untold brutalities, if Caesar had not come along. In the train, in the deathless tunnel, she had finally asked him why he brought her with him. Caesar said, "Because I knew you could do it."

How she hated her. The nights without number she spent up in the miserable loft, tossing about, kicking the woman next to her, devising ways off the plantation. Sneaking into a cartload of cotton and leaping to the road outside New Orleans. Bribing an overseer with her favors. Taking her hatchet and running through the swamp as her wretched mother had done. All the sleepless nights. In the light of morning she convinced herself that her scheming had been a dream. Those were not her thoughts, not at all. Because to walk around with that in your mind and do nothing was to die.

She didn't know where her mother had fled. Mabel hadn't spent her freedom saving money to buy her daughter out of bondage, that was certain. Randall would not have allowed it, but nonetheless. Miss Lucy never did find her mother's name in her files. If she had, Cora would have walked up to Mabel and knocked her flat.

"Bessie—you all right with yourself?"

It was Abigail from number 6, who came by for supper occasionally. She was friendly with the girls who worked on Montgomery Street. Cora had been standing in the middle of the grass, staring. She told Abigail everything was fine and returned to the dormitory to do her chores. Yes, Cora needed to keep better guard over her thoughts.

If Cora's own mask was occasionally askew, she proved adept at maintaining the disguise of Bessie Carpenter, late of North Carolina. She had prepared herself for Miss Lucy's question about her mother's surname and for other tracks the conversation might have taken. The interview at the Placement Office that first day had concluded after a few brief questions. The newcomers had toiled either in the house or in the field. In either case, the majority of the openings were domestic work. The families were told to exercise forbearance with inexperienced help.

The doctor's examination gave her a scare, but not on account of the questions. The gleaming steel instruments in the examination room looked like tools Terrance Randall might have ordered from the blacksmith for sinister purposes.

The doctor's offices were on the tenth floor of the Griffin. She survived the shock of her first elevator ride and stepped into a long corridor lined with chairs, all of which were full of colored men and women awaiting examinations. After a nurse in a stark white uniform checked her name off a list, Cora joined the group of women. The nervous talk was understandable; for most, this was their first visit with a doctor. On the Randall plantation, the doctor was only called when the slave remedies, the roots and salves, had failed and a valued hand was near death. In most cases there was nothing for the doctor to do at that point but complain about the muddy roads and receive his payment.

They called her name. The window in the examination room granted her a view of the configuration of the town and the verdant countryside for miles and miles. That men had built such a thing as this, a stepping-stone to heaven. She might have stayed there all day, gazing at the landscape, but the examination cut short her reverie. Dr. Campbell was an efficient sort, a portly gentleman who buzzed around the room with his white coat flapping behind him like a cape. He probed about her general health as his young nurse recorded it all on blue paper. From which tribe did her ancestors originate and what did she know of their constitutions? Had she ever been sick? How was the condition of her heart, her lungs? She realized the headaches she had suffered since Terrance's blows had disappeared since she came to South Carolina.

The intelligence test was brief, consisting of playing with wooden shapes and a series of illustrated quizzes. She undressed for the physical examination. Dr. Campbell looked at her hands. They had softened but were still those of one who had worked the fields. His fingers traced the scars from her whippings. Hazarding a guess as to the number of lashes, he was off by two. He examined her privates with his tools. The exam was painful and made her ashamed, the doctor's cold attitude doing nothing to ease her discomfort. Cora answered his questions about the assault. Dr.

Campbell turned to the nurse and she wrote down his speculations over her ability to mother a child.

A collection of imposing metal instruments lay on a nearby tray. He picked up one of the most terrifying, a thin spike attached to a glass cylinder. "We're going to take some blood," he said.

"What for?"

"Blood tells us a lot," the doctor said. "About diseases. How they spread. Blood research is the frontier." The nurse grabbed Cora's arm and Dr. Campbell stabbed the needle in. This explained the howls she had heard in the hall outside. She made her own contribution. Then she was done. In the hall, only the men remained. The chairs were full.

That was her last visit to the tenth floor of the building. Once the new hospital opened, Mrs. Anderson told her one day, the offices of the government doctors were relocating. The floor was already fully leased, Mr. Anderson added. Mrs. Anderson's own doctor ran his practice on Main Street, above the optician. He sounded like a capable man. In the months that Cora had worked for the family, the mother's bad days had markedly reduced in number. The tantrums, the afternoons she spent locked in her room with the drapes shut, her severe manner with the children occurred less frequently. Spending more time outside the house, and the pills, had worked wonders.

When Cora finished her Saturday washing and had supper, it was almost time for the social. She put on her new blue dress. It was the prettiest one at the colored emporium. She shopped there as little as possible on account of the markup. From shopping for Mrs. Anderson, she was horrified that things in their local establishment cost two or three times as much as those in the white stores. As for the dress, it had cost a week's wages and she was forced to use scrip. She had been careful about her spending for the most part. Money was new and unpredictable and liked to go where it pleased. Some of the girls owed months of wages and resorted to scrip for everything now. Cora understood why—after the town deducted for food, housing, and miscellany like upkeep on the dormitories and schoolbooks, there was little left. Best to rely on scrip's credit sparingly. The dress was a one-time affair, Cora assured herself.

The girls in the bunk room were in a state of great excitement over the evening's gathering. Cora was no exception. She finished primping. Perhaps Caesar was already on the green.

He waited on one of the benches affording a view of the gazebo and the musicians. He knew she was not going to dance. From across the green, Caesar seemed older than he had in his Georgia days. She recognized his evening clothes from the stacks in the colored emporium, but he wore them with more confidence than other men his age who hailed from plantations. The factory work agreed with him. As well as the other elements of their improved circumstances, of course. In the week since they last saw each other, he had cultivated a mustache.

Then she saw the flowers. She complimented him on the bouquet and thanked him. He complimented her on her dress. He had tried to kiss her a month after they emerged from the tunnel. She pretended it didn't happen and since then he had joined this performance. One day they would address it. Maybe at that time she would kiss him, she didn't know.

"I know them," Caesar said. He pointed at the band as they took their places. "I think they might even be better than George and Wesley."

Cora and Caesar grew more casual about referring to Randall in public as the months passed. Much of what they said could apply to any former slave who overheard them. A plantation was a plantation; one might think one's misfortunes distinct, but the true horror lay in their universality. In any event, the music would soon cover their talk of the underground railroad. Cora hoped the musicians wouldn't think them rude for their inattention. It was unlikely. Playing their music as freemen and not chattel was probably still a cherished novelty. To attack the melody without the burden of providing one of the sole comforts of their slave village. To practice their art with liberty and joy.

The proctors arranged the socials to foster healthy relations between colored men and women, and to undo some of the damage to their personalities wrought by slavery. By their reckoning, the music and dancing, the food and punch, all unfolding on the green in the flickering lantern light, were a tonic for the battered soul. For Caesar and Cora it was one of their few opportunities to catch each other up.

Caesar worked in the machine factory outside town and his changing schedule rarely overlapped with hers. He liked the work. Every week the factory assembled a different machine, determined by the volume of orders. The men arranged themselves before the conveyor belt and each was responsible for attaching his assigned component to the shape moving down the line. At the start of the belt there was nothing, a pile of waiting parts, and when the last man was finished, the result lay before them, whole. It was unexpectedly fulfilling, Caesar said, to witness the complete product, in contrast to the disembodied toil on Randall.

The work was monotonous but not taxing; the changing products helped with the tedium. The lengthy rest breaks were well distributed throughout the shift, arranged according to a labor theorist often quoted by the foremen and managers. The other men were fine fellows. Some still bore the marks of plantation behavior, eager to redress perceived slights and acting as if they still lived under the yoke of reduced resources, but these men improved every week, fortified by the possibilities of their new lives.

The former fugitives traded news. Maisie lost a tooth. This

week the factory manufactured locomotive engines—Caesar wondered whether they would one day be used by the underground
railroad. The prices at the emporium had gone up again, he
observed. This was not news to Cora.

"How is Sam?" Cora asked. It was easier for Caesar to meet
with the station agent.

"In his usual temper—cheerful for no reason you can tell. One
of the louts at the tavern gave him a black eye. He's proud of it.
Says he'd always wanted one."

"And the other?"

He crossed his hands on his thighs. "There's a train in a few
days. If we want to take it." He said that last part as if he knew
her attitude.

"Perhaps the next one."

"Yes, maybe the next one."

Three trains had passed through since the pair arrived. The
first time they talked for hours over whether it was wiser to depart
the dark south immediately or see what else South Carolina had
to offer. By then they had gained a few pounds, earned wages,
and begun to forget the daily sting of the plantation. But there
had been real debate, with Cora agitating for the train and Caesar
arguing for the local potential. Sam was no help—he was fond of
his birthplace and an advocate of South Carolina's evolution on
matters of race. He didn't know how the experiment would turn
out, and he came from a long line of rabble-rousers distrustful of
the government, but Sam was hopeful. They stayed. Maybe the
next one.

The next one came and went with a shorter discussion. Cora
had just finished a splendid meal in her dormitory. Caesar had
bought a new shirt. The thought of starving again on the run was
not attractive, nor was the prospect of leaving behind the things

they had purchased with their toil. The third train came and went, and now this fourth one would, too.

"Maybe we should stay for good," Cora said.

Caesar was silent. It was a beautiful night. As he promised, the musicians were very talented and played the rags that had made everyone happy at previous socials. The fiddler came from this or that plantation, the banjo man from another state: Every day the musicians in the dormitories shared the melodies from their regions and the body of music grew. The audience contributed dances from their own plantations and copied each other in the circles. The breeze cooled them when they broke away to rest and flirt. Then they started in again, laughing and clapping hands.

"Maybe we should stay," Caesar repeated. It was decided.

The social ended at midnight. The musicians put out a hat for donations, but most people were deep in scrip by Saturday night so it remained empty. Cora said good night to Caesar and was on her way home when she witnessed an incident.

The woman ran through the green near the schoolhouse. She was in her twenties, of slender build, and her hair stuck up wildly. Her blouse was open to her navel, revealing her breasts. For an instant, Cora was back on Randall and about to be educated in another atrocity.

Two men grabbed the woman and, as gently as they could, stopped her flailing. A crowd gathered. One girl went to fetch the proctors from over by the schoolhouse. Cora shouldered her way in. The woman blubbered incoherently and then said suddenly, "My babies, they're taking away my babies!"

The onlookers sighed at the familiar refrain. They had heard it so many times in plantation life, the lament of the mother over her tormented offspring. Cora remembered Caesar's words about the men at the factory who were haunted by the plantation, carrying it here despite the miles. It lived in them. It still lived in all of them, waiting to abuse and taunt when chance presented itself.

The woman calmed down somewhat and was led back to the dormitory at the very rear of the line. Despite the comfort brought by their decision to stay, it was a long night for Cora as her thoughts returned to the woman's screams, and the ghosts she called her own.

"Will I be able to say goodbye? To the Andersons and the children?" Cora asked.

Miss Lucy was sure that could be arranged. The family was fond of her, she said.

"Did I do a bad job?" Cora thought she had made a fine adjustment to the more delicate rhythms of domestic work. She ran her thumb across the pads of her fingers. They were so soft now.

"You did a splendid job, Bessie," Miss Lucy said. "That's why when this new placement came up, we thought of you. It was my idea and Miss Handler seconded it. The museum needs a special kind of girl," she said, "and not many of the residents have adapted as well as you have. You should take it as a compliment."

Cora was reassured but lingered in the doorway.

"Anything else, Bessie?" Miss Lucy asked, squaring her papers.

Two days after the incident at the social, Cora was still troubled. She asked after the screaming woman.

Miss Lucy nodded in sympathy. "You're referring to Gertrude," she said. "I know it was upsetting. She's fine. They're keeping her in bed for a few days until she's herself again." Miss Lucy explained that there was a nurse on hand checking on her. "That's why we reserved that dormitory for residents with nervous disorders. It doesn't make sense for them to mix with the larger population. In number 40, they can get the care they require."

"I didn't know 40 was special," Cora said. "It's your Hob."

"I'm sorry?" Miss Lucy asked, but Cora didn't elaborate.

"They're only there for a short time," the white woman added. "We're optimistic."

Cora didn't know what *optimistic* meant. She asked the other girls that night if they were familiar with the word. None of them had heard it before. She decided that it meant *trying*.

The walk to the museum was the same route she took to the Andersons', until she turned right at the courthouse. The prospect of leaving the family made her sorrowful. She had little contact with the father, as he left the house early and his office window was one of those in the Griffin that stayed lit the latest. Cotton had made him a slave, too. But Mrs. Anderson had been a patient employer, especially after her doctor's prescriptions, and the children were pleasant. Maisie was ten. By that age on the Randall plantation all the joy was ground out. One day a pickaninny was happy and the next the light was gone from them; in between they had been introduced to a new reality of bondage. Maisie was spoiled, doubtless, but there were worse things than being spoiled if you were colored. The little girl made Cora wonder what her own children might be like one day.

She'd seen the Museum of Natural Wonders many times on her strolls but never knew what the squat limestone building was for. It occupied an entire block. Statues of lions guarded the long flat steps, seeming to gaze thirstily at the large fountain. Once Cora walked into its influence, the sound of the splashing water dampened the street noise, lifting her into the auspices of the museum.

Inside, she was taken through a door that was off-limits to the public and led into a maze of hallways. Through half-opened doors, Cora glimpsed curious activities. A man put a needle and thread to a dead badger. Another held up yellow stones to a bright light. In a room full of long wooden tables and apparatus she saw her first microscopes. They squatted on the tables like black frogs.

Then she was introduced to Mr. Fields, the curator of Living History.

"You'll do perfectly," he said, scrutinizing her as the men in the rooms had scrutinized the projects on their worktables. His speech at all times was quick and energetic, without a trace of the south. She later discovered that Mr. Fields had been hired from a museum in Boston to update the local practices. "Been eating better since you came, I see," he said. "To be expected, but you'll do fine."

"I start cleaning in here first, Mr. Fields?" Cora had decided on the way over that in her new position she would avoid the cadences of plantation speech the best she could.

"Cleaning? Oh, no. You know what we do here—" He stopped. "Have you been here before?" He explained the business of museums. In this one, the focus was on American history—for a young nation, there was so much to educate the public about. The untamed flora and fauna of the North American continent, the minerals and other splendors of the world beneath their feet. Some people never left the counties where they were born, he said. Like a railroad, the museum permitted them to see the rest of the country beyond their small experience, from Florida to Maine to the western frontier. And to see its people. "People like you," Mr. Fields said.

Cora worked in three rooms. That first day, gray drapes covered the large glass windows that separated them from the public. The next morning the drapes were gone and the crowds arrived.

The first room was Scenes from Darkest Africa. A hut dominated the exhibit, its walls wooden poles lashed together under a peaked thatch roof. Cora retreated into its shadows when she needed a break from the faces. There was a cooking fire, the flames represented by shards of red glass; a small, roughly made bench;

and assorted tools, gourds, and shells. Three large black birds hung from the ceiling on a wire. The intended effect was that of a flock circling over the activity of the natives. They reminded Cora of the buzzards that chewed the flesh of the plantation dead when they were put on display.

The soothing blue walls of Life on the Slave Ship evoked the Atlantic sky. Here Cora stalked a section of a frigate's deck, around the mast, various small barrels, and coils of rope. Her African costume was a colorful wrap; her sailor outfit made her look like a street rascal, with a tunic, trousers, and leather boots. The story of the African boy went that after he came aboard, he helped out on deck with various small tasks, a kind of apprentice. Cora tucked her hair under the red cap. A statue of a sailor leaned against the gunwale, spyglass pointed. The eyes, mouth, and skin color were painted on its wax head in disturbing hues.

Typical Day on the Plantation allowed her to sit at a spinning wheel and rest her feet, the seat as sure as her old block of sugar maple. Chickens stuffed with sawdust pecked at the ground; from time to time Cora tossed imaginary seed at them. She had numerous suspicions about the accuracy of the African and ship scenes but was an authority in this room. She shared her critique. Mr. Fields did concede that spinning wheels were not often used outdoors, at the foot of a slave's cabin, but countered that while authenticity was their watchword, the dimensions of the room forced certain concessions. Would that he could fit an entire field of cotton in the display and had the budget for a dozen actors to work it. One day perhaps.

Cora's criticism did not extend to Typical Day's wardrobe, which was made of coarse, authentic negro cloth. She burned with shame twice a day when she stripped and got into her costume.

Mr. Fields had the budget for three actors, or types as he referred to them. Also recruited from Miss Handler's schoolhouse,

Isis and Betty were similar in age and build to Cora. They shared costumes. On their breaks, the three discussed the merits and disadvantages of their new positions. Mr. Fields let them be, after a day or two of adjustments. Betty liked that he never showed his temper, as opposed to the family she had just worked for, who were generally nice but there was always the possibility of a misunderstanding or a bad mood that was none of her doing. Isis enjoyed not having to speak. She hailed from a small farm where she was often left to her own devices, save on those nights when the master needed company and she was forced to drink the cup of vice. Cora missed the white stores and their abundant shelves, but she still had her evening walks home, and her game with the changing window displays.

On the other hand, ignoring the museum visitors was a prodigious undertaking. The children banged on the glass and pointed at the types in a disrespectful fashion, startling them as they pretended to fuss with sailor's knots. The patrons sometimes yelled things at their pantomimes, comments that the girls couldn't make out but that gave every indication of rude suggestions. The types rotated through the exhibits every hour to ease the monotony of pretending to swab the deck, carve hunting tools, and fondle the wooden yams. If Mr. Fields had one constant instruction, it was that they not sit so much, but he didn't press it. They teased Skipper John, as they nicknamed the dummy sailor, from their stools as they fiddled with the hemp rope.

THE exhibits opened the same day as the hospital, part of a celebration trumpeting the town's recent accomplishments. The new mayor had been elected on the progress ticket and wanted to ensure that the residents associated him with his predecessor's forward-looking initiatives, which had been implemented while he was still a property lawyer in the Griffin Building. Cora did not attend the festivities, although she saw the glorious fireworks that night from the dormitory window and got to see the hospital up close when her checkup came around. As the colored residents settled into South Carolina life, the doctors monitored their physical well-being with as much dedication as the proctors who took measure of their emotional adjustments. Some day, Miss Lucy told Cora one afternoon while they walked the green, all the numbers and figures and notes would make a great contribution to their understanding of colored life.

From the front, the hospital was a smart, sprawling single-floor complex that seemed as long as the Griffin Building was tall. It was stark and unadorned in its construction in a way Cora had never seen before, as if to announce its efficiency in its very walls. The colored entrance was around the side but apart from that was identical to the white entrance, in the original design and not an afterthought, as was so often the case.

The colored wing was having a busy morning when Cora gave her name to the receptionist. A group of men, some of whom she recognized from socials and afternoons on the green, filled the adjacent room while they waited for their blood treatments. She hadn't heard of blood trouble before arriving in South Carolina, but it afflicted a great number of the men in the dormitories and was the source of tremendous effort on the part of the town doctors. The specialists had their own section it seemed, the patients disappearing down a long hall when their name was called.

She saw a different physician this time, one more pleasant than Dr. Campbell. His name was Stevens. He was a northerner, with black curls that verged on womanish, an effect he tempered with his carefully tended beard. Dr. Stevens seemed young for a doctor. Cora took his precociousness as a tribute to his talents. As she moved through the examination, Cora got the impression she was being conveyed on a belt, like one of Caesar's products, tended down the line with care and diligence.

The physical examination was not as extensive as the first. He consulted the records from her previous visit and added his own notes on blue paper. In between he asked her about dormitory life. "Sounds efficient," Dr. Stevens said. He declared the museum work "an intriguing public service."

After she dressed, Dr. Stevens pulled over a wooden stool. His manner remained light as he said, "You've had intimate relations. Have you considered birth control?"

He smiled. South Carolina was in the midst of a large public health program, Dr. Stevens explained, to educate folks about a new surgical technique wherein the tubes inside a woman were severed to prevent the growth of a baby. The procedure was simple, permanent, and without risk. The new hospital was specially equipped, and Dr. Stevens himself had studied under the man who pioneered the technique, which had been perfected on the colored inmates of a Boston asylum. Teaching the surgery to local doctors and offering its gift to the colored population was part of the reason he was hired.

"What if I don't want to?"

"The choice is yours, of course," the doctor said. "As of this week, it is mandatory for some in the state. Colored women who have already birthed more than two children, in the name of population control. Imbeciles and the otherwise mentally unfit, for obvious reasons. Habitual criminals. But that doesn't apply to you, Bessie. Those are women who already have enough burdens. This is just a chance for you to take control over your own destiny."

She wasn't his first recalcitrant patient. Dr. Stevens put the matter aside without losing his warm demeanor. Her proctor had more information about the program, he told Cora, and was available to talk about any concern.

She walked down the hospital corridor briskly, hungry for air. Cora had become too accustomed to escaping unscathed from encounters with white authority. The directness of his questions and his subsequent elaborations threw her. To compare what had happened the night of the smokehouse with what passed between a man and his wife who were in love. Dr. Stevens's speech made them the same. Her stomach twisted at the idea. Then there was the matter of *mandatory*, which sounded as if the women, these Hob women with different faces, had no say. Like they were property that the doctors could do with as they pleased. Mrs. Anderson suffered black moods. Did that make her unfit? Was her doctor offering her the same proposal? No.

As she turned these thoughts over, she found herself in front of the Andersons' house. Her feet took over when her mind was elsewhere. Perhaps underneath, Cora was thinking about children. Maisie would be at school, but Raymond might be home. She had been too busy the last two weeks to make a proper goodbye.

The girl who opened the door looked at Cora with suspicion, even after she explained who she was.

"I thought her name was Bessie," the girl said. She was skinny and small, but she held on to the door as if more than happy to throw her weight against it to keep out intruders. "You said you was Cora."

Cora cursed the doctor's distraction. She explained that her master named her Bessie, but in the quarter everyone called her Cora because she looked so much like her mother.

"Mrs. Anderson is not at home," the girl said. "And the children are playing with they friends. You best come back when she's home." She shut the door.

For once, Cora took the shortcut home. Talking to Caesar would have helped, but he was at the factory. She lay in her bed until supper. From that day on, she took a route to the museum that avoided the Anderson home.

Two weeks later Mr. Fields decided to give his types a proper tour of the museum. Isis and Betty's time behind the glass had improved their acting skills. The duo affected a plausible interest as Mr. Fields held forth on the cross-sections of pumpkins and the life rings of venerable white oaks, the cracked-open geodes with their purple crystals like glass teeth, the tiny beetles and ants the scientists had preserved with a special compound. The girls chuckled at the stuffed wolverine's frozen smile, the red-tailed hawk caught mid-dive, and the lumbering black bear that charged the window. Predators captured in the moment they went in for the kill.

Cora stared at the wax faces of the white people. Mr. Fields's types were the only living exhibits. The whites were made of plaster, wire, and paint. In one window, two pilgrims in thick wool breeches and doublets pointed at Plymouth rock while their fellow voyagers looked on from ships in the mural. Delivered to safety after the hazardous passage to a new beginning. In another window, the museum arranged a harbor scene, where white colonists dressed like Mohawk Indians hurled crates of tea over the side of the ship with exaggerated glee. People wore different kinds of chains across their lifetimes, but it wasn't hard to interpret rebellion, even when the rebels wore costumes to deny blame.

The types walked before the displays like paying customers. Two determined explorers posed on a ridge and gazed at the mountains of the west, the mysterious country with its perils and discoveries before them. Who knew what lay out there? They were masters of their lives, lighting out fearlessly into their futures.

In the final window, a red Indian received a piece of parchment from three white men who stood in noble postures, their hands open in gestures of negotiation.

"What's that?" Isis asked.

"That's a real tepee," Mr. Fields said. "We like to tell a story in each one, to illuminate the American experience. Everyone knows the truth of the historic encounter, but to see it before you—"

"They sleep in there?" Isis said.

He explained. And with that, the girls returned to their own windows.

"What do you say, Skipper John," Cora asked her fellow sailor. "Is this the truth of our historic encounter?" She had lately taken to making conversation with the dummy to add some theater for the audience. Paint had flaked from his cheek, exposing the gray wax beneath.

The stuffed coyotes on their stands did not lie, Cora supposed. And the anthills and the rocks told the truth of themselves. But the white exhibits contained as many inaccuracies and contradictions as Cora's three habitats. There had been no kidnapped boys swabbing the decks and earning pats on the head from white kidnappers. The enterprising African boy whose fine leather boots she wore would have been chained belowdecks, swabbing his body in his own filth. Slave work was sometimes spinning thread, yes; most times it was not. No slave had ever keeled over dead at a spinning wheel or been butchered for a tangle. But nobody wanted to speak on the true disposition of the world. And no one wanted to hear it. Certainly not the white monsters on the other side of the exhibit at that very moment, pushing their greasy snouts against the window, sneering and hooting. Truth was a changing display in a shop window, manipulated by hands when you weren't looking, alluring and ever out of reach.

The whites came to this land for a fresh start and to escape the tyranny of their masters, just as the freemen had fled theirs. But the ideals they held up for themselves, they denied others. Cora had heard Michael recite the Declaration of Independence back on the Randall plantation many times, his voice drifting through the village like an angry phantom. She didn't understand the words, most of them at any rate, but *created equal* was not lost on her. The white men who wrote it didn't understand it either, if *all men* did not truly mean all men. Not if they snatched away what belonged to other people, whether it was something you could hold in your hand, like dirt, or something you could not, like freedom. The land she tilled and worked had been Indian land. She knew the white men bragged about the efficiency of the massacres, where they killed women and babies, and strangled their futures in the crib.

Stolen bodies working stolen land. It was an engine that did not stop, its hungry boiler fed with blood. With the surgeries that Dr. Stevens described, Cora thought, the whites had begun stealing futures in earnest. Cut you open and rip them out, dripping. Because that's what you do when you take away someone's babies—steal their future. Torture them as much as you can when they are on this earth, then take away the hope that one day their people will have it better.

"Ain't that right, Skipper John?" Cora asked. Sometimes, if Cora turned her head fast, it looked as if the thing were winking at her.

A few nights later, she noticed the lights in number 40 were out, even though it was early in the evening. She asked the other girls. "They were moved to the hospital," one said. "So they can get better."

The night before Ridgeway put an end to South Carolina, Cora lingered on the roof of the Griffin Building, trying to see where she had come from. There was an hour until her meeting with Caesar and Sam and she didn't relish the idea of fretting on her bed, listening to the chirping of the other girls. Last Saturday after school, one of the men who worked in the Griffin, a former tobacco hand named Martin, told her that the door to the roof was unlocked. Access was easy. If Cora worried about one of the white people who worked on the twelfth floor questioning her when she got off the elevator, Martin told her, she could take the stairs for the final flights.

This was her second twilight visit. The height made her giddy. She wanted to jump up and snatch the gray clouds roiling overhead. Miss Handler had taught the class about the Great Pyramids in Egypt and the marvels the slaves made with their hands and sweat. Were the pyramids as tall as this building, did the pharaohs sit on top and take the measure of their kingdoms, to see how diminished the world became when you gained the proper distance? On Main Street below workmen erected three- and four-story buildings, taller than the old line of two-floor establishments. Cora walked by the construction every day. Nothing as big as the Griffin yet, but one day the building would have brothers and sisters, striding over the land. Whenever she let her dreams take her down hopeful avenues, this notion stirred her, that of the town coming into its own.

To the east side of the Griffin were the white people's houses and their new projects—the expanded town square, the hospital, and the museum. Cora crossed to the west, where the colored dormitories lay. From this height, the red boxes crept up on the uncleared woods in impressive rows. Is that where she would live one day? A small cottage on a street they hadn't laid yet? Putting the boy and the girl to sleep upstairs. Cora tried to see the face of the man, conjure the names of the children. Her imagination failed her. She squinted south toward Randall. What did she expect to see? The night took the south into darkness.

And north? Perhaps she would visit one day.

The breeze made her shiver and she headed for the street. It was safe to go to Sam's now.

Caesar didn't know why the station agent wanted to see them. Sam had signaled as he passed the saloon and told him, "Tonight." Cora had not returned to the railroad station since her arrival, but the day of her deliverance was so vivid she had no trouble finding the road. The animal noises in the dark forest, the branches snapping and singing, reminded her of their flight, and then of Lovey disappearing into the night.

She walked faster when the light from Sam's windows fluttered through the branches. Sam embraced her with his usual enthusiasm, his shirt damp and reeking with spirits. She had been too distracted to notice the house's disarray on her previous visit, the grimed plates, sawdust, and piles of clothes. To get to the kitchen she had to step over an upturned toolbox, its contents jumbled on the floor, nails fanned like pick-up-sticks. Before she left, she would recommend he contact the Placement Office for a girl.

Caesar had already arrived and sipped a bottle of ale at the kitchen table. He'd brought one of his bowls for Sam and ran his fingers over its bottom as if testing an imperceptible fissure. Cora had almost forgotten he liked to work with wood. She had not seen much of him lately. He had bought more fancy clothes from the colored emporium, she noted with pleasure, a dark suit that fit him well. Someone had taught him how to tie a tie, or perhaps that was a token of his time in Virginia, when he had believed the old white woman would free him and he had worked on his appearance.

"Is there a train coming in?" Cora asked.

"In a few days," Sam said.

Caesar and Cora shifted in their seats.

"I know you don't want to take it," Sam said. "It's no matter."

"We decided to stay," Caesar said.

"We wanted to make sure before we told you," Cora added.

Sam huffed and leaned back in the creaky chair. "It made me happy to see you skipping the trains and making a go of things here," the station agent said. "But you may reconsider after my story."

Sam offered them some sweetmeats—he was a faithful customer of Ideal Bakery off Main Street—and revealed his purpose. "I want to warn you away from Red's," Sam said.

"You scared of the competition?" Caesar joked. There was no question on that front. Sam's saloon did not serve colored patrons. No, Red's had exclusive claim to the residents of the dormitories with a hankering for drink and dance. It didn't hurt that they took scrip.

"More sinister," Sam said. "I'm not sure what to make of it, to be honest." It was a strange story. Caleb, the owner of the Drift, possessed a notoriously sour disposition; Sam had a reputation as the barkeep who enjoyed conversation. "You get to know the real life of a place, working there," Sam liked to say. One of Sam's regulars was a doctor by the name of Bertram, a recent hospital hire. He didn't mix socially with the other northerners, preferring the atmosphere and salty company at the Drift. He had a thirst for whiskey. "To drown out his sins," Sam said.

On a typical night, Bertram kept his thoughts close until his third drink, when the whiskey unstoppered him and he rambled animatedly about Massachusetts blizzards, medical-school hazing rituals, or the relative intelligence of Virginia opossum. His discourse the previous evening had turned to female companionship, Sam said. The doctor was a frequent visitor at Miss Trumball's establishment, preferring it to the Lanchester House, whose girls had a saturnine disposition in his opinion, as if imported from Maine or other gloom-loving provinces.

"Sam?" Cora said.

"I'm sorry, Cora." He abridged. Dr. Bertram enumerated some of the virtues of Miss Trumball's, and then added, "Whatever you do, man, keep out of Red's Café, if you have a taste for nigger gals." Several of his male patients frequented the saloon, carrying on with the female patrons. His patients believed they were being treated for blood ailments. The tonics the hospital administered, however, were merely sugar water. In fact, the niggers were participants in a study of the latent and tertiary stages of syphilis.

"They think you're helping them?" Sam asked the doctor. He kept his voice neutral, even as his face got hot.

"It's important research," Bertram informed him. "Discover how a disease spreads, the trajectory of infection, and we approach a cure." Red's was the only colored saloon in the town proper; the proprietor got a break on the rent for a watchful eye. The syphilis program was one of many studies and experiments under way at the colored wing of the hospital. Did Sam know that the Igbo tribe of the African continent is predisposed to nervous disorders? Suicide and black moods? The doctor recounted the story of forty slaves, shackled together on a ship, who jumped overboard en masse rather than live in bondage. The kind of mind that could conceive of and execute such a fantastic course! What if we performed adjustments to the niggers' breeding patterns and removed those of melancholic tendency? Managed other attitudes, such as sexual aggression and violent natures? We could protect our women and daughters from their jungle urges, which Dr. Bertram understood to be a particular fear of southern white men.

The doctor leaned in. Had Sam read the newspaper today?

Sam shook his head and topped off the man's drink.

Still, the barkeep must have seen the editorials over the years, the doctor insisted, expressing anxiety over this very topic. America has imported and bred so many Africans that in many states the whites are outnumbered. For that reason alone, emancipation is impossible. With strategic sterilization—first the women but both sexes in time—we could free them from bondage without fear that they'd butcher us in our sleep. The architects of the Jamaica uprisings had been of Beninese and Congolese extraction, willful and cunning. What if we tempered those bloodlines carefully over time? The data collected on the colored pilgrims and their descendants over years and decades, the doctor said, will prove one of the boldest scientific enterprises in history. Controlled sterilization, research into communicable diseases, the perfection of new surgical techniques on the socially unfit—was it any wonder the best medical talents in the country were flocking to South Carolina?

A group of rowdies stumbled in and crowded Bertram to the end of the bar. Sam was occupied. The doctor drank quietly for a time and then slipped out. "You two are not the sort that goes to Red's," Sam said, "but I wanted you to know."

"Red's," Cora said. "This is more than the saloon, Sam. We have to tell them they're being lied to. They're sick."

Caesar was in agreement.

"Will they believe you over their white doctors?" Sam asked. "With what proof? There is no authority to turn to for redress—the town is paying for it all. And then there are all the other towns where colored pilgrims have been installed in the same system. This is not the only place with a new hospital."

They worked it out over the kitchen table. Was it possible that not only the doctors but everyone who ministered to the colored population was involved in this incredible scheme? Steering the colored pilgrims down this or that path, buying them from estates and the block in order to conduct this experiment? All those white hands working in concert, committing their facts and figures down on blue paper. After Cora's discussion with Dr. Stevens, Miss Lucy had stopped her one morning on her way to the museum. Had Cora given any thought to the hospital's birth control program? Perhaps Cora could talk to some of the other girls about it, in words they could understand. It would be very appreciated, the white woman said. There were all sorts of new positions opening up in town, opportunities for people who had proven their worth.

Cora thought back to the night she and Caesar decided to stay, the screaming woman who wandered into the green when the social came to an end. "They're taking away my babies." The woman wasn't lamenting an old plantation injustice but a crime perpetrated here in South Carolina. The doctors were stealing her babies from her, not her former masters.

"They wanted to know what part of Africa my parents hailed from," Caesar said. "How was I to know? He said I had the nose of a Beninese."

"Nothing like flattery before they geld a fellow," Sam said.

"I have to tell Meg," Caesar said. "Some of her friends spend evenings at Red's. I know they have a few men they see there."

"Who's Meg?" Cora said.

"She's a friend I've been spending time with."

"I saw you walk down Main Street the other day," Sam said. "She's very striking."

"It was a nice afternoon," Caesar said. He took a sip of his beer, focusing on the black bottle and avoiding Cora's eyes.

They made little progress on a course of action, struggling with the problem of whom to turn to and the possible reaction from the other colored residents. Perhaps they would prefer not to know, Caesar said. What were these rumors compared to what they had been freed from? What sort of calculation would their neighbors make, weighing all the promises of their new circumstances against the allegations and the truth of their own pasts? According to the law, most of them were still property, their names on pieces of paper in cabinets kept by the United States Government. For the moment, warning people was all they could do.

Cora and Caesar were almost to town when he said, "Meg works for one of those Washington Street families. One of those big houses you see?"

Cora said, "I'm glad you have friends."

"You sure?"

"Were we wrong to stay?" Cora asked.

"Maybe this is where we were supposed to get off," Caesar said. "Maybe not. What would Lovey say?"

Cora had no answer. They didn't speak again.

SHE slept poorly. In the eighty bunks the women snored and shifted under their sheets. They had gone to bed believing themselves free from white people's control and commands about what they should do and be. That they managed their own affairs. But the women were still being herded and domesticated. Not pure merchandise as formerly but livestock: bred, neutered. Penned in dormitories that were like coops or hutches.

In the morning, Cora went to her assigned work with the rest of the girls. As she and the other types were about to get dressed, Isis asked if she could switch rooms with Cora. She was feeling poorly and wanted to rest at the spinning wheel. "If I could just get off my feet for a bit."

After six weeks at the museum, Cora hit upon a rotation that suited her personality. If she started in Typical Day on the Plantation, she could get her two plantation shifts finished just after the midday meal. Cora hated the ludicrous slave display and preferred to get it over as soon as possible. The progression from Plantation to Slave Ship to Darkest Africa generated a soothing logic. It was like going back in time, an unwinding of America. Ending her day in Scenes from Darkest Africa never failed to cast her into a river of calm, the simple theater becoming more than theater, a genuine refuge. But Cora agreed to Isis's request. She would end the day a slave.

In the fields, she was ever under the merciless eye of the overseer or boss. "Bend your backs!" "Work that row!" At the Andersons', when Maisie was at school or with her playmates and little Raymond was asleep, Cora worked unmolested and unwatched. It was a small treasure in the middle of the day. Her recent installation in the exhibition returned her to the furrows of Georgia, the dumb, open-jawed stares of the patrons stealing her back to a state of display.

One day she decided to retaliate against a red-haired white woman who scowled at the sight of Cora's duties "at sea." Perhaps the woman had wed a seaman of incorrigible appetites and hated the reminder—Cora didn't know the source of her animus, or care. The woman irked her. Cora stared into her eyes, unwavering and fierce, until the woman broke, fairly running from the glass toward the agricultural section.

From then on Cora selected one patron per hour to evil-eye.

A young clerk ducking out from his desk in the Griffin, a man of enterprise; a harried matron corralling an unruly clutch of children; one of the sour youths who liked to batter the glass and startle the types. Sometimes this one, sometimes that one. She picked the weak links out from the crowd, the ones who broke under her gaze. The weak link—she liked the ring of it. To seek the imperfection in the chain that keeps you in bondage. Taken individually, the link was not much. But in concert with its fellows, a mighty iron that subjugated millions despite its weakness. The people she chose, young and old, from the rich part of town or the more modest streets, did not individually persecute Cora. As a community, they were shackles. If she kept at it, chipping away at weak links wherever she found them, it might add up to something.

She got good at her evil eye. Looking up from the slave wheel or the hut's glass fire to pin a person in place like one of the beetles or mites in the insect exhibits. They always broke, the people, not expecting this weird attack, staggering back or looking at the floor or forcing their companions to pull them away. It was a fine lesson, Cora thought, to learn that the slave, the African in your midst, is looking at you, too.

The day Isis felt under the weather, during Cora's second rotation on the ship, she looked past the glass and saw pigtailed Maisie, wearing one of the dresses Cora used to wash and hang on the line. It was a school trip. Cora recognized the boys and girls who accompanied her, even if the children did not remember her as the Andersons' old girl. Maisie didn't place her at first. Then Cora fixed her with the evil eye and the girl knew. The teacher elaborated on the meaning of the display, the other children pointed and jeered at Skipper John's garish smile—and Maisie's face twitched in fear. From the outside, no one could tell what passed between them, just like when she and Blake faced each other the day of the doghouse. Cora thought, I'll break you, too, Maisie, and she did, the little girl scampering out of the frame. She didn't know why she did it, and was abashed until she took off her costume and returned to the dormitory.

SHE called upon Miss Lucy that evening. Cora had been figuring on Sam's news all day, holding it up to the light like a hideous bauble, tilting it so. The proctor had aided Cora many times. Now her suggestions and advice resembled maneuvers, the way a farmer tricks a donkey into moving in line with his intentions.

The white woman was gathering a stack of her blue papers when Cora poked her head into the office. Was her name written down there, and what were the notes beside it? No, she corrected: Bessie's name, not hers.

"I only have a moment," the proctor said.

"I saw people moving back into number 40," Cora said. "But no one who used to live there. Are they still in the hospital for their treatment?"

Miss Lucy looked at her papers and stiffened. "They were moved to another town," she said. "We need room for all the new arrivals, so women like Gertrude, the ones who need help, are being sent to where they can get more suitable attention."

"They're not coming back?"

"They are not." Miss Lucy appraised her visitor. "It troubles you, I know. You're a smart girl, Bessie. I still hope you'll take on the mantle of leadership with the other girls, even if you don't think the operation is what you need right now. You could be a true credit to your race if you put your mind to it."

"I can decide for myself," Cora said. "Why can't they? On the plantation, master decided everything for us. I thought we were done with that here."

Miss Lucy recoiled from the comparison. "If you can't see the difference between good, upstanding people and the mentally disturbed, with criminals and imbeciles, you're not the person I thought you were."

I'm not the person you thought I was.

One of the proctors interrupted them, an older woman named Roberta who often coordinated with the Placement Office. She had placed Cora with the Andersons, those months ago. "Lucy? They're waiting on you."

Miss Lucy grumbled. "I have them all right here," Miss Lucy told her colleague. "But the records in the Griffin are the same. The Fugitive Slave Law says we have to hand over runaways and not impede their capture—not drop everything we're doing just because some slave catcher thinks he's onto his bounty. We don't harbor murderers." She rose, holding the stack of papers to her chest. "Bessie, we'll take this up tomorrow. Please think about our discussion."

Cora retreated to the bunkhouse stairs. She sat on the third step. They could be looking for anyone. The dormitories were full of runaways who'd taken refuge here, in the wake of a recent escape from their chains or after years of making a life for themselves elsewhere. They could be looking for anyone.

They hunted murderers.

Cora went to Caesar's dormitory first. She knew his schedule but in her fright could not remember his shifts. Outside, she didn't see any white men, the rough sort she imagined slave catchers to look like. She sprinted across the green. The older man at the dormitory leered at her—there was always a licentious implication when a girl visited the men's housing—and informed her that Caesar was still at the factory. "You want to wait with me?" he asked.

It was getting dark. She debated whether or not to risk Main Street. The town records had her name as Bessie. The sketches on the fliers Terrance had printed after their escape were crudely drawn but resembled them enough that any savvy hunter would look at her twice. There was no way she would rest until she conferred with Caesar and Sam. She took Elm Street, parallel to Main, until she reached the Drift's block. Each time she turned a corner, she expected a posse on horses, with torches and muskets and mean smiles. The Drift was full with early-evening carousers, men she recognized and those she did not. She had to pass by the saloon's window twice before the station agent saw her and motioned for her to come around back.

The men in the saloon laughed. She slipped through the light cast in the alley from inside. The outhouse door was ajar: empty. Sam stood in the shadows, his foot on a crate as he laced his boots. "I was trying to figure out how to get word," he said. "The slave catcher's name is Ridgeway. He's talking to the constable now, about you and Caesar. I've been serving two of his men whiskey."

He handed her a flier. It was one of the bulletins Fletcher had described in his cottage, with one change. Now that she knew her letters, the word *murder* hooked her heart.

There was a ruckus from inside the bar and Cora stepped farther into the shadows. Sam couldn't leave for another hour, he said. He'd gather as much information as he could and try to intercept Caesar at the factory. It was best if Cora went ahead to his house and waited.

She ran as she had not in a long time, sticking to the side of the road and darting into the woods at the sound of a traveler. She entered Sam's cottage through the back door and lit a candle in the kitchen. After pacing, unable to sit, Cora did the only thing that calmed her. She had cleaned all the dishware when Sam returned home.

"It's bad," the station agent said. "One of the bounty hunters came in right after we spoke. Had a ring of ears around his neck like a red Indian, a real tough character. He told the others that they knew where you were. They left to meet their man in front,

Ridgeway." He panted from the run over. "I don't know how, but they know who you are."

Cora had grabbed Caesar's bowl. She turned it over in her hands.

"They got a posse together," Sam said. "I couldn't get to Caesar. He knows to come here or the saloon—we had a plan. He may already be on his way." Sam intended to return to the Drift to wait for him.

"Do you think anyone saw us talking?"

"Maybe you should go down to the platform."

They dragged the kitchen table and the thick gray rug. Together they lifted the door in the floor—it was a tight fit—and the musty air flickered the candles. She took some food and a lantern and descended into the darkness. The door closed above her and the table rumbled back into place.

She had avoided the services at the colored churches in town. Randall forbade religion on his plantation to eliminate the distraction of deliverance, and churching never interested her once she came to South Carolina. It made her seem strange to the other colored residents, she knew, but seeming strange had not bothered her for a long time. Was she supposed to pray now? She sat at the table in the thin lamplight. It was too dark on the platform to make out where the tunnel began. How long would it take them to root out Caesar? How fast could he run? She was aware of the bargains people made in desperate situations. To reduce the fever in a sick baby, to halt the brutalities of an overseer, to deliver one from a host of slave hells. From what she saw, the bargains never bore fruit. Sometimes the fever subsided, but the plantation was always still there. Cora did not pray.

She fell asleep waiting. Later, Cora crawled back up the steps, perching just beneath the door, and listened. It might be day or night in the world. She was hungry and thirsty. She ate some of the bread and sausage. Moving up and down the steps, putting her ear to the door and then retreating after a time, she passed the hours. When she finished the food, her despair was complete. She listened by the door. There was not a sound.

The thundering above woke her, terminating the void. It was not one person, or two, but many men. They ransacked the house and shouted, knocking over cabinets and upending furniture. The noise was loud and violent and so near, she shrank down the steps. She could not make out their words. Then they were done.

The seams in the door permitted no light and no draft. She could not smell the smoke, but she heard the glass shatter and the pop and crackle of the wood.

The house was on fire.

Stevens

THE Anatomy House of the Proctor Medical School was three blocks away from the main building, second from last on the dead-end street. The school wasn't as discriminating as the better-known medical colleges in Boston; the press of acceptances necessitated an expansion. Aloysius Stevens worked nights to satisfy the terms of his fellowship. In exchange for tuition relief and a place to work—the late-night shift was quiet and conducive to study—the school got someone to admit the body snatcher.

Carpenter usually delivered just before dawn, before the neighborhood roused, but tonight he called at midnight. Stevens blew out the lamp in the dissection room and ran up the stairs. He almost forgot his muffler, then remembered how cold it had been last time, when autumn crept in to remind them of the bitter season to come. It rained that morning and he hoped it wouldn't be too muddy. He had one pair of brogues and the soles were in a miserable state.

Carpenter and his man Cobb waited in the driver's seat. Stevens settled in the cart with the tools. He slid down until they got a healthy distance away, in case any of the faculty or students were about. It was late, but a bone expert from Chicago had presented that night and they might still be carousing in the local saloons. Stevens was disappointed about missing the man's talk—his fellowship often prevented his attendance at guest lectures—but the money would remove some of the sting. Most of the other students came from well-off Massachusetts families, spared worries over rent or food. When the cart passed McGinty's and he heard the laughter inside, Stevens pulled his hat down.

Cobb leaned around. "Concord tonight," he said, and offered his flask. As a matter of policy Stevens declined when Cobb shared his liquor. Though still in his studies he was certain of various diagnoses he'd made about the state of the man's health. But the wind was brisk and mean and they had hours in the dark and mud before the return to the Anatomy House. Stevens took a long pull and choked on fire. "What is this?"

"One of my cousin's concoctions. Too strong for your taste?" He and Carpenter chortled.

More likely he had collected last night's dregs at the saloon. Stevens took the prank in good cheer. Cobb had warmed to Stevens over the months. He could imagine the man's complaints when Carpenter suggested that he stand in whenever one of their gang was too besotted, or incarcerated, or otherwise unavailable for their nocturnal missions. Who's to say this fancy rich boy could keep his tongue? (Stevens was not rich and was fancy only in his aspirations.) The city had started hanging grave robbers lately— which was ironic or fitting depending on one's perspective, as the bodies of the hanged were given to medical schools for dissection.

"Don't mind the gallows," Cobb had told Stevens. "It's quick enough. The people are the thing—it should be a private viewing, if you ask me. Watching a man shit his guts, it's indecent."

Digging up graves had fastened the bonds of friendship. Now when Cobb called him Doctor, it was with respect and not derision. "You're not like that other sort," Cobb told him one night when they carried a cadaver through the back door. "You're a wee shady."

That he was. It helped to be a wee disreputable when you were a young surgeon, especially when it came to materials for postmortem dissection. There had been a body shortage ever since the study of anatomy came into its own. The law, the jail, and the judge provided only so many dead murderers and prostitutes. Yes, persons afflicted with rare diseases and curious deformities sold their bodies for study after their demise, and some doctors donated their cadavers in the spirit of scientific inquiry, but their numbers scarcely met the demand. The body game was fierce, for buyers and sellers alike. Rich medical schools outbid the less fortunate ones. Body snatchers charged for the body, then added a retainer, then a delivery fee. They raised prices at the start of the teaching period when demand was high, only to offer bargains at the end of the term when there was no longer a need for a specimen.

Morbid paradoxes confronted Stevens daily. His profession worked to extend life while secretly hoping for an increase in the deceased. A malpractice suit called you before the judge for want of a skill, but get caught with an ill-gotten cadaver and the judge punished you for trying to obtain that skill. Proctor made its students pay for their own pathological specimens. Stevens's first anatomy course required two complete dissections—how was he supposed to pay for that? Back home in Maine, he'd been spoiled by his mother's cooking; the women on her side were gifted. Here in the city, tuition, books, lectures, and rent had him subsisting on crusts for days on end.

When Carpenter invited Stevens to work for him, he did not hesitate. His appearance scared Stevens, that first delivery months before. The grave robber was an Irish giant, imposing in frame, uncouth in manner and speech, and carried with him the reek of damp earth. Carpenter and his wife had six children; when two of them passed from yellow fever, he sold them for anatomical study. Or so it was said. Stevens was too scared to ask for refutation. When trafficking in cadavers, it helped to be immune to sentimentality.

He wouldn't be the first body snatcher to open a grave to find the face of a long-lost cousin or a dear friend.

Carpenter recruited his gang at the saloon, rowdies all. They slept the day, drank well into the evening, and then set off for their pastime. "The hours are not great, but suit a certain character." Criminal character, incorrigible by any measure. It was a low enterprise. Raiding cemeteries was the least of it. The competition was a pack of rabid animals. Leave a prospect to too late in the evening and you were liable to discover someone else had pilfered the body first. Carpenter reported his competition's clients to the police, broke into dissection rooms to mutilate their deliveries. Brawls erupted when rival gangs converged on the same pauper's field. They smashed one another's faces among the tombstones. "It was raucous," Carpenter always said when he finished one of his stories, grinning through his mossy teeth.

In his glory days, Carpenter elevated the ploys and chicanery of his trade to a devilish art. He brought rocks in wheelbarrows for undertakers to bury and carried away the deceased. An actor taught his nieces and nephews to cry on demand, the craft of bereavement. Then they made the rounds of the morgue, claiming bodies as long-lost relatives—although Carpenter was not above simply stealing bodies from the coroner when he had to. On more than one occasion, Carpenter sold a cadaver to an anatomical school, reported the body to the police, and then had his wife, dressed in mourning clothes, claim it as her son. Whereupon Carpenter sold the body again to another school. It saved the county the expense of burial; no one looked too closely.

Eventually the body trade grew so reckless that relatives took to holding graveside vigils, lest their loved ones disappear in the night. Suddenly every missing child was perceived to have been a victim of foul play—snatched, dispatched, and then sold for dissection. The newspapers took up the cause in outraged editorials; the law stepped in. In this new climate, most body snatchers extended their territory, riffling the graves of distant cemeteries to space out their raids. Carpenter turned to niggers exclusively.

The niggers did not post sentries over their dead. Niggers did not pound on the door of the sheriff, they did not haunt the offices of the newspapermen. No sheriff paid them any mind, no journalist listened to their stories. The bodies of their loved ones disappeared into sacks and reappeared in the cool cellars of medical schools to relinquish their secrets. Every one of them a miracle, in Stevens's view, providing instruction into the intricacies of God's design.

Carpenter snarled when he said the word, a mangy dog hoarding his bone: *nigger*. Stevens never used the word. He disapproved of racial prejudice. Indeed, an uneducated Irishman like Carpenter, steered by society to a life of rummaging graves, had more in common with a negro than a white doctor. If you considered the matter at length. He wouldn't say that aloud, of course. Sometimes Stevens wondered if his views weren't quaint, given the temper of the modern world. The other students uttered the most horrible things about the colored population of Boston, about their smell, their intellectual deficiencies, their primitive drives. Yet when his classmates put their blades to a colored cadaver, they did more for the cause of colored advancement than the most high-minded abolitionist. In death the negro became a human being. Only then was he the white man's equal.

On the outskirts of Concord, they stopped at the small wooden gate and waited for the custodian's signal. The man waved his lantern back and forth and Carpenter drove the cart inside the cemetery. Cobb paid the man's fee and he directed them to this night's bounty: two large, two medium, and three infants. The rain had softened the earth. They'd be done in three hours. After they refilled the graves, it would be as if they were never there.

"Your surgeon's knife." Carpenter handed Stevens a spade.

He'd be a medical student again in the morning. Tonight he was a resurrection man. Body snatcher was an accurate name. Resurrection man was a bit florid, but it held a truth. He gave these people a second chance to contribute, one denied them in their previous life.

And if you could make a study of the dead, Stevens thought from time to time, you could make a study of the living, and make them testify as no cadaver could.

He rubbed his hands to stir the blood and started to dig.

North Carolina

Runaway or conveyed off, From the subscriber's residence, near Henderson, on the 16th inst. a negro girl named MARTHA, belonging to the Subscriber. Said girl is of a dark brown complexion, slightly made, and very free spoken, about 21 years of age; she wore a black silk bonnet with feathers; and had in her possession two calico bed quiltings. I understand she will try to pass as a free girl.

RIGDON BANKS
GRANVILLE COUNTY, AUGUST 28, 1839

SHE lost the candles. One of the rats woke Cora with its teeth and when she settled herself, she crawled across the dirt of the platform in her search. She came up with nothing. It was the day after Sam's house collapsed, though she couldn't be sure. Best to measure time now with one of the Randall plantation's cotton scales, her hunger and fear piling on one side while her hopes were removed from the other in increments. The only way to know how long you are lost in the darkness is to be saved from it.

By then Cora only needed the candlelight for company, having collected the particulars of her prison. The platform was twenty-eight paces long, and five and a half from wall to tracks' edge. It was twenty-six steps up to the world above. The trapdoor was warm when she placed her palm against it. She knew which step snagged her dress when she crawled up (the eighth) and which liked to scrape her skin if she scrabbled down too fast (the fifteenth). Cora remembered seeing a broom in a corner of the platform. She used it to tap the ground like the blind lady in town, the way Caesar had probed the black water during their flight. Then she got clumsy or cocky and fell onto the tracks, losing both the broom and any desire beyond huddling on the ground.

She had to get out. In those long hours, she could not keep from devising cruel scenes, arranging her own Museum of Terrible Wonders. Caesar strung up by the grinning mob; Caesar a brutalized mess on the floor of the slave catcher's wagon, halfway back to Randall and the waiting punishments. Kind Sam in jail; Sam tarred and feathered, interrogated about the underground railroad, broken-boned and senseless. A faceless white posse sifted through the smoldering remains of the cabin, pulled up the trapdoor and delivered her into wretchedness.

Those were the scenes she decorated in blood when awake. In nightmares the exhibits were more grotesque. She strolled back and forth before the glass, a customer of pain. She was locked in Life on the Slave Ship after the museum had closed, ever between ports and waiting for the wind while hundreds of kidnapped souls screamed belowdecks. Behind the next window, Miss Lucy cut open Cora's stomach with a letter opener and a thousand black spiders spilled from her guts. Over and over, she was transported back to the night of the smokehouse, held down by nurses from the hospital as Terrance Randall grunted and thrusted above her. Usually the rats or bugs woke her when their curiosity became too much, interrupting her dreams and returning her to the darkness of the platform.

Her stomach quivered under her fingers. She had starved before, when Connelly got it in his mind to punish the quarter for mischief and cut off rations. But they needed food to work and the cotton demanded the punishment be brief. Here, there was no way to know when she would eat next. The train was late. The night Sam told them about the bad blood—when the house still stood—the next train was due in two days. It should have arrived. She didn't know how late it was, but the delay signified nothing good. Maybe this branch was shut down. The entire line exposed and canceled. No one was coming. She was too weak to walk the unknowable miles to the next station, in the dark, let alone face whatever waited at the following stop.

Caesar. If they had been sensible and kept running, she and Caesar would be in the Free States. Why had they believed that two lowly slaves deserved the bounty of South Carolina? That a new life existed so close, just over the state line? It was still the south, and the devil had long nimble fingers. And then, after all the world had taught them, not to recognize chains when they were snapped to their wrists and ankles. The South Carolina chains were of new manufacture—the keys and tumblers marked by regional design—but accomplished the purpose of chains. They had not traveled very far at all.

She could not see her own hand in front of her but saw Caesar's capture many times. Seized at his factory station, snatched en route to meet Sam at the Drift. Walking down Main Street, arm in arm with his girl Meg. Meg cries out when they seize him, and they knock her to the sidewalk. That was one thing that would be different if she had made Caesar her lover: They might have been captured together. They would not be alone in their separate prisons. Cora drew her knees to her chest and wrapped her arms around them. In the end she would have disappointed him. She was a stray after all. A stray not only in its plantation meaning—orphaned, with no one to look after her—but in every other sphere as well. Somewhere, years ago, she had stepped off the path of life and could no longer find her way back to the family of people.

The earth trembled faintly. In days to come, when she remembered the late train's approach, she would not associate the vibration with the locomotive but with the furious arrival of a truth she had always known: She was a stray in every sense. The last of her tribe.

The light of the train shuddered around the bend. Cora reached for her hair before realizing that after her interment there was no improving her appearance. The engineer would not judge her; their secret enterprise was a fraternity of odd souls. She waved her hands animatedly, savoring the orange light as it expanded on the platform like a warm bubble.

The train sped past the station and out of sight.

She almost keeled over into the tracks as she howled after the train, her throat raspy and raw after days of privation. Cora stood and shook, incredulous, until she heard the train stop and back up on the tracks.

The engineer was apologetic. "Will you take my sandwich, as well?" he asked as Cora guzzled from his waterskin. She ate the sandwich, oblivious to his jest, even though she had never been partial to hog tongue.

"You're not supposed to be here," the boy said, adjusting his spectacles. He was no older than fifteen, raw-boned and eager.

"Well, you see me, don't you?" She licked her fingers and tasted dirt.

The boy cried "Gosh!" and "Sweet mother!" at every complication in her story, tucking his thumbs into the pockets of his overalls and rocking on his heels. He spoke like one of the white children Cora had observed in the town square playing kick-the-ball, with a carefree authority that did not jibe with the color of his skin, let alone the nature of his job. How he came to command the locomotive was a story, but now was not the time for the unlikely histories of colored boys.

"Georgia station is closed," he said finally, scratching his scalp beneath his blue cap. "We're supposed to stay away. Patrollers must have smoked it out, I figure." He clambered into his cabin after his pisspot, then went to the edge of the tunnel and emptied it. "The bosses hadn't heard from the station agent, so I was running express. This stop wasn't on my schedule." He wanted to leave immediately.

Cora hesitated, unable to stop herself from looking at the stairs for a last-minute addition. The impossible passenger. Then she started for the cabin.

"You can't go up here!" the boy said. "It's regulations."

"You can't expect me to ride on that," Cora said.

"All passengers ride coach on this train, miss. They're pretty strict about that."

To call the flatcar a coach was an abuse of the word. It was a boxcar like the one she rode to South Carolina, but only in foundation. The plane of wooden planks was riveted to the undercarriage, without walls or ceiling. She stepped aboard and the train jolted with the boy's preparations. He turned his head and waved at his passenger with disproportionate enthusiasm.

Straps and ropes for oversize freight lay on the floor, loose and serpentine. Cora sat in the center of the flatcar, wrapped one around her waist three times, grabbed another two and fashioned reins. She pulled tight.

The train lurched into the tunnel. Northward. The engineer yelled, "All aboard!" The boy was simple, Cora decided, responsibilities of his office notwithstanding. She looked back. Her underground prison waned as the darkness reclaimed it. She wondered if she was its final passenger. May the next traveler not tarry and keep moving up the line, all the way to liberty.

In the journey to South Carolina, Cora had slept in the turbulent car, nestled against Caesar's warm body. She did not sleep on her next train ride. Her so-called coach was sturdier than the boxcar, but the rushing air made the ride into a blustery ordeal. From time to time, Cora had to turn her body to catch her breath. The engineer was more reckless than his predecessor, going faster, goading the machine into velocity. The flatcar jumped whenever they took a turn. The closest she had ever been to the sea was her term in the Museum of Natural Wonders; these planks taught her about ships and squalls. The engineer's crooning drifted back, songs she did not recognize, debris from the north kicked up by the gale. Eventually she gave up and lay on her stomach, fingers dug into the seams.

"How goes it back there?" the engineer asked when they stopped. They were in the middle of the tunnel, no station in sight.

Cora flapped her reins.

"Good," the boy said. He wiped the soot and sweat from his forehead. "We're about halfway there. Needed to stretch my legs." He slapped the side of the boiler. "This old girl, she bucks."

It wasn't until they were moving again that Cora realized she forgot to ask where they were headed.

A careful pattern of colored stones decorated the station beneath Lumbly's farm, and wooden slabs covered the walls of Sam's station. The builders of this stop had hacked and blasted it from the unforgiving earth and made no attempt at adornment, to showcase the difficulty of their feat. Stripes of white, orange, and rust-colored veins swam through the jags, pits, and knobs. Cora stood in the guts of a mountain.

The engineer lit one of the torches on the wall. The laborers hadn't cleaned up when they finished. Crates of gear and mining equipment crowded the platform, making it a workshop. Passengers chose their seating from empty cases of explosive powder. Cora tested the water in one of the barrels. It tasted fresh. Her mouth was an old dustpan after the rain of flying grit in the tunnel. She drank from the dipper for a long time as the engineer watched her, fidgeting. "Where is this place?" she asked.

"North Carolina," the boy replied. "This used to be a popular stop, from what I'm told. Not anymore."

"The station agent?" Cora asked.

"I've never met him, but I'm sure he's a fine fellow."

He required fine character and a tolerance for gloom to operate in this pit. After her days beneath Sam's cottage, Cora declined the challenge. "I'm going with you," Cora said. "What's the next station?"

"That's what I was trying to say before, miss. I'm in maintenance." Because of his age, he told her, he was entrusted with the engine but not its human freight. After the Georgia station shut down—he didn't know the details, but gossip held it had been discovered—they were testing all the lines in order to reroute traffic. The train she had been waiting for was canceled, and he didn't know when another one would be through. His instructions were to make a report on conditions and then head back to the junction.

"Can't you take me to the next stop?"

He motioned her to the edge of the platform and extended his lantern. The tunnel terminated fifty feet ahead in a ragged point.

"We passed a branch back there, heads south," he said. "I've got just enough coal to check it out and make it back to the depot."

"I can't go south," Cora said.

"The station agent will be along. I'm sure of it."

She missed him when he was gone, in all of his foolishness.

Cora had light, and another thing she did not have in South Carolina—sound. Dark water pooled between the rails, fed in steady drips from the station ceiling. The stone vault above was white with splashes of red, like blood from a whipping that soaked a shirt. The noise cheered her, though. As did the plentiful drinking water, the torches, and the distance she had traveled from the slave catchers. North Carolina was an improvement, beneath the surface.

She explored. The station abutted a rough-hewn tunnel. Support struts shored up the wooden ceiling and stones embedded in the dirt floor made her stumble. She chose to go left first, stepping over spill that had come loose from the walls. Rusting tools littered the path. Chisels, sledges, and picks—weaponry for battling mountains. The air was damp. When she ran her hand along the wall it came back coated in cool white dust. At the end of the corridor, the ladder bolted into the stone led up into a snug passage. She lifted the torch. There was no telling how far the rungs extended. She braved the climb only after discovering that the other end of the corridor narrowed into a glum dead end.

A few feet into the level above, she saw why the equipment had been abandoned by the work gangs. A sloping mound of rocks and dirt, floor to ceiling, cut off the tunnel. Opposite the cave-in, the tunnel terminated after a hundred feet, confirming her fear. She was trapped once more.

Cora collapsed on the rocks and wept until sleep overtook her. The station agent woke her. "Oh!" the man said. His round red face poked through the space he'd made at the top of the rubble. "Oh, dear," he said. "What are you doing here?"

"I'm a passenger, sir."

"Don't you know this station is closed?"

She coughed and rose, straightening her filthy dress.

"Oh dear, oh dear," he said.

His name was Martin Wells. Together they widened the hole in the wall of stone and she squeezed through to the other side. The man helped her clamber down to level ground as if helping a lady from the finest carriage. After several turns, the mouth of the tunnel extended a dim invitation. A breeze tickled her skin. She gulped the air like water, the night sky the best meal she had ever had, the stars made succulent and ripe after her time below.

The station agent was a barrel-shaped man deep in his middle age, pasty-complected and soft. For an agent of the underground railroad, presumably no stranger to peril and risk, he evinced a nervous personality. "You're not supposed to be here," he said, repeating the engineer's assessment. "This is a very regrettable turn."

Martin huffed through his explanation, washing his sweaty gray hair from his face as he spoke. The night riders were on patrol, he explained, casting agent and passenger into dangerous waters. The old mica mine was remote, to be sure, exhausted long ago by Indians and forgotten by most, but the regulators routinely checked the caves and mines, anyplace a fugitive might seek refuge from their justice.

The cave-in that had so distressed Cora was a ruse to camouflage the operation below. Despite its success, the new laws in North Carolina had rendered the station inoperable—he was visiting the mine merely to leave a message for the underground railroad that he could accept no more passengers. When it came to harboring Cora, or any other runaway, Martin was unprepared in every way. "Especially given the present circumstances," he whispered, as if the patrollers waited at the top of the gully.

Martin told her he needed to fetch a wagon and Cora wasn't convinced he was coming back. He insisted he wouldn't be long—dawn was approaching and after that it would be impossible to move her. She was so grateful to be outside in the living world that she decided to believe him, and almost threw her arms around him when he reappeared, driving a weather-beaten wagon pulled by two bony draft horses. They repositioned the sacks of grain and seed to make a slim pocket. The last time Cora needed to hide in this manner, they required room for two. Martin draped a tarpaulin over his cargo and they rumbled out of the cut, the station agent grumbling profane commentary until they gained the road.

They had not traveled long when Martin stopped the horses. He removed the tarpaulin. "It will be sunrise soon, but I wanted you to see this," the station agent said.

Cora did not immediately know what he meant. The country road was quiet, crowded on both sides by the forest canopy. She saw one shape, then another. Cora got out of the wagon.

The corpses hung from trees as rotting ornaments. Some of them were naked, others partially clothed, the trousers black where their bowels emptied when their necks snapped. Gross wounds and injuries marked the flesh of those closest to her, the two caught by the station agent's lantern. One had been castrated, an ugly mouth gaping where his manhood had been. The other was a woman. Her belly curved. Cora had never been good at knowing if a body was with a child. Their bulging eyes seemed to rebuke her stares, but what were the attentions of one girl, disturbing their rest, compared to how the world had scourged them since the day they were brought into it?

"They call this road the Freedom Trail now," Martin said as he covered the wagon again. "The bodies go all the way to town."

In what sort of hell had the train let her off?

When she next emerged from the wagon, Cora sneaked around the side of Martin's yellow house. The sky was growing light. Martin had brought the wagon as far back into his property as he dared. The homes on either side of his were quite close— anyone awakened by the horses' noise could see her. Toward the front of the house, Cora saw the street, and beyond that, a grass field. Martin urged her on and she crept onto the back porch and then inside. A tall white woman in her nightclothes leaned against the wainscoting in the kitchen. She sipped a glass of lemonade and did not look at Cora as she said, "You're going to get us murdered."

This was Ethel. She and Martin had been married for thirty-five years. The couple did not speak as he washed his trembling hands in the basin. They had quarreled over her while she waited at the mine, Cora knew, and would resume that argument once they dealt with the matter before them.

Ethel led Cora upstairs while Martin returned the wagon to his store. Cora got a brief look at the parlor, which was modestly furnished; after Martin's warnings, the morning light through the window quickened her step. Ethel's long gray hair extended half-way down her back. The woman's manner of walking unnerved Cora—she seemed to float, aloft on her fury. At the top of the stairs, Ethel stopped and pointed to the washroom. "You smell," she said. "Be quick about it."

When Cora stepped into the hallway again, the woman summoned her up the stairs to the attic. Cora's head almost brushed the ceiling of the small, hot room. Between the sloping walls of the peaked roof, the attic was crammed with years of castoffs. Two broken washboards, piles of moth-eaten quilts, chairs with split seats. A rocking horse, covered in matted hide, sat in the corner under a curl of peeling yellow wallpaper.

"We're going to have to cover that now," Ethel said, referring to the window. She moved a crate from the wall, stood on it, and nudged the hatch in the ceiling. "Come, come," she said. Her face set in a grimace. She still had not looked at the fugitive.

Cora pulled herself up above the false ceiling, into the cramped nook. It came to a point three feet from the floor and ran fifteen feet in length. She moved the stacks of musty gazettes and books to make more room. Cora heard Ethel descend the stairs, and when her host returned she handed Cora food, a jug of water, and a chamber pot.

Ethel looked at Cora for the first time, her drawn face framed by the hatch. "The girl is coming by and by," she said. "If she hears you, she'll turn us in and they will kill us all. Our daughter and her family arrive this afternoon. They cannot know you are here. Do you understand?"

"How long will it be?"

"You stupid thing. Not a sound. Not a single sound. If anyone hears you, we are lost." She pulled the hatch shut.

The only source of light and air was a hole in the wall that faced the street. Cora crawled to it, stooping beneath the rafters. The jagged hole had been carved from the inside, the work of a previous occupant who'd taken issue with the state of the lodgings. She wondered where the person was now.

That first day, Cora acquainted herself with the life of the park, the patch of green she'd seen across the street from the house. She pressed her eye to the spy hole, shifting around to capture the entire view. Two- and three-story wood-frame houses bordered the park on all sides, identical in construction, distinguished by paint color and the type of furniture on their long porches. Neat brick walkways crisscrossed the grass, snaking in and out of the shadows of the tall trees and their luxurious branches. A fountain warbled near the main entrance, surrounded by low stone benches that were occupied soon after sunup and remained popular well into the night.

Elderly men with handkerchiefs full of crusts for the birds, children with their kites and balls, and young couples under the spell of romance took their shifts. A brown mutt owned the place, known to all, yipping and scampering. Across the afternoon, children chased it through the grass and onto the sturdy white bandstand at the edge of the park. The mutt dozed in the shade of the benches and the gigantic oak that dominated the green with majestic ease. It was well-fed, Cora observed, gobbling down the treats and bones offered by the citizens. Her stomach never failed to rumble at the sight. She named him Mayor.

As the sun approached its zenith, and the park bustled with midday traffic, the heat transformed the hidey-hole into a wretched furnace. Crawling to different sections of the attic nook, searching for imaginary oases of cool, became her principal activity after her vigil over the park. She learned that her hosts would not visit her during the day, when their girl Fiona was working. Martin tended to his store, Ethel came and went on her social rounds, but Fiona was always downstairs. She was young, with a prominent Irish accent. Cora heard her going about her duties, sighing to herself and muttering invectives toward her absent employers. Fiona did not enter the attic that first day, but the sound of her steps turned Cora as stiff as her old sailing mate Skipper John. Ethel's warnings the first morning made their intended impression.

On her arrival day there were additional visitors—Martin and Ethel's daughter, Jane, and her family. From the daughter's bright and pleasant manner, Cora decided she took after her father, and filled in her broad face using Martin as a template. The son-in-law and the two granddaughters were an unceasing commotion, thundering through the house. At one point the girls started for the attic but reconsidered after a discussion about the habits and customs of ghosts. There was indeed a ghost in the house, but she was done with chains, rattling or no.

In the evening the park remained busy. The main street must be nearby, Cora thought, funneling the town. Some older women in blue gingham dresses nailed white-and-blue bunting to the bandstand. Garlands of orange leaves added a flourish. Families staked out spots before the stage, unrolling blankets and removing supper from baskets. Those who lived next to the park gathered on their porches with jugs and glasses.

Preoccupied by her uncomfortable refuge and the parade of misfortunes since the slave catchers found them out, Cora did not immediately notice an important feature of the park: Everyone was white. She had never left the plantation before she and Caesar ran away, so South Carolina gave Cora her first glimpse of the mingling of races in towns and cities. On Main Street, in stores, in factories and offices, in every sector, black and white mixed all day as a matter of course. Human commerce withered without it. In liberty or bondage, the African could not be separated from the American.

In North Carolina the negro race did not exist except at the ends of ropes.

Two able young men helped the matrons hang a banner over the bandstand: Friday Festival. A band took its place onstage, the sounds of their warming up gathering the scattered parkgoers. Cora hunkered and pressed her face to the wall. The banjo man displayed some talent, the horn player and fiddler less so. Their melodies were bland in comparison to those of the colored musicians she'd heard, on Randall and off, but the townspeople enjoyed the denatured rhythms. The band closed with spirited renditions of two colored songs Cora recognized, which proved the most popular of the night. On the porch below, Martin and Ethel's grandchildren squealed and clapped.

A man in a rumpled linen suit took the stage to deliver a brief welcome. Martin told Cora later that this was Judge Tennyson, a respected figure in town when abstemious. This night he tottered. She couldn't make out the judge's introduction of the next act, a coon show. She'd heard of them but had never witnessed their travesties; the colored evening at the theater in South Carolina offered different fare. Two white men, their faces blackened by burned cork, capered through a series of skits that brought the park to exuberant laughter. Dressed in mismatched, gaudy clothes and chimney-pot hats, they molded their voices to exaggerate colored speech; this seemed to be the source of the humor. A sketch where the skinnier performer took off his dilapidated boot and counted his toes over and over again, constantly losing his place, generated the loudest reaction.

The final performance, following a notice from the judge regarding the chronic drainage issues at the lake, was a short play. From what Cora put together from the actors' movements and the bits of dialogue that traveled to her suffocating nook, the play concerned a slave—again, a white man in burned cork, pink showing on his neck and wrists—who ran north after a light rebuke from his master. He suffered on his journey, delivering a pouty soliloquy on hunger, cold, and wild beasts. In the north, a saloon keeper took him on. The saloon keeper was a ruthless boss, beating and insulting the wayward slave at every turn, stealing wages and dignity, the hard image of northern white attitudes.

The last scene depicted the slave on his master's doorstep, having once again run away, this time from the false promises of the Free States. He begged after his former position, lamenting his folly and asking for forgiveness. With kind and patient words, the master explained that it was impossible. In the slave's absence, North Carolina had changed. The master whistled and two patrollers ushered the prostrate slave from the premises.

The town appreciated the moral of the performance, their applause resounding through the park. Toddlers clapped from the shoulders of their fathers, and Cora caught Mayor nipping at the air. She had no idea of the size of the town but felt that every citizen was in the park now, waiting. The true purpose of the evening revealed itself. A sturdy-built man in white trousers and a bright red coat took command of the stage. Despite his size, he moved with force and authority—Cora recalled the mounted bear in the museum, posed at the dramatic moment of his charge. He twisted one end of his handlebar mustache with patient amusement as the crowd quieted. His voice was firm and clear and for the first time that evening Cora did not miss a single word.

He introduced himself as Jamison, though every soul in the park was aware of his identity. "Each Friday I awake full of vigor," he said, "knowing that in a few hours we'll gather here again and celebrate our good fortune. Sleep used to come so hard to me, in the days before our regulators secured the darkness." He gestured to the formidable band, fifty-strong, who had assembled at the side of the bandstand. The town cheered when the men waved and nodded at Jamison's acknowledgment.

Jamison caught the crowd up. God had given one regulator the gift of a newborn son, and two others had observed their birthdays. "We have a new recruit with us tonight," Jamison continued, "a young man from a fine family who joined the ranks of the night riders this week. Come on up, Richard, and let them have a look at you."

The slender red-haired boy advanced tentatively. Like his fellows, he wore his uniform of black trousers and white shirt of thick cloth, his neck swimming in the collar. The boy mumbled. From Jamison's side of the conversation, Cora gathered that the recruit had been making the rounds of the county, learning the protocols of his squad.

"And you had an auspicious start, didn't you, son?"

The lanky boy bobbed his head. His youth and slight frame reminded Cora of the engineer of her last train trip, inducted by circumstance into the work of men. His freckled skin was lighter-hued, but they shared the same fragile eagerness. Born the same day, perhaps, then steered by codes and circumstances to serve disparate agencies.

"It's not every rider who makes a catch his first week out," Jamison said. "Let's see what young Richard has for us."

Two night riders dragged a colored girl onstage. She had a house girl's tender physique and shrank further in her simpering. Her gray tunic was torn and smeared with blood and filth, and her head had been crudely shaved. "Richard was searching the hold of a steamship bound for Tennessee when he found this rascal hiding below," Jamison said. "Louisa is her name. She absconded from her plantation in the confusion of the reorganization and hid in the woods these many months. Believing she had escaped the logic of our system."

Louisa rolled over to survey the crowd, lifted her head briefly, and was still. It would have been difficult to make out her tormentors with all the blood in her eyes.

Jamison raised his fists in the air, as if daring something in the sky. The night was his opponent, Cora decided, the night and the phantoms he filled it with. In the dark, he said, colored miscreants lurked to violate the citizens' wives and daughters. In the deathless dark, their southern heritage lay defenseless and imperiled.

The riders kept them safe. "We have each of us made sacrifices for this new North Carolina and its rights," Jamison said. "For this separate nation we have forged, free from northern interference and the contamination of a lesser race. The black horde has been beaten back, correcting the mistake made years ago at this nation's nativity. Some, like our brothers just over the state line, have embraced the absurd notion of nigger uplift. Easier to teach a donkey arithmetic." He bent down to rub Louisa's head. "When we find the odd rascal, our duty is clear."

The crowd separated, tutored by routine. With Jamison leading the procession, the night riders dragged the girl to the great oak in the middle of the park. Cora had seen the wheeled platform in the corner of the park that day; children climbed and jumped on it all afternoon. At some point in the evening it had been pushed beneath the oak tree. Jamison called for volunteers, and people of all ages rushed to their places on either side of the platform. The noose lowered around Louisa's neck and she was led up the stairs. With the precision born of practice, a night rider threw the rope over the thick, sturdy branch with a single toss.

One of those who had gathered to push the ramp away was ejected—he'd already taken his turn at a previous festival. A young brunette in a pink polka-dot dress rushed to take his place.

Cora turned away before the girl swung. She crawled to the opposite side of the nook, in the corner of her latest cage. Over the next several months, on nights when it was not too suffocating, she preferred that corner for sleeping. It was as far from the park, the miserable thumping heart of the town, as she could get.

The town hushed. Jamison gave the word.

‒‒◆‒‒

To explain why he and his wife kept Cora imprisoned in their attic, Martin had to go back a ways. As with everything in the south, it started with cotton. The ruthless engine of cotton required its fuel of African bodies. Crisscrossing the ocean, ships brought bodies to work the land and to breed more bodies.

The pistons of this engine moved without relent. More slaves led to more cotton, which led to more money to buy more land to farm more cotton. Even with the termination of the slave trade, in less than a generation the numbers were untenable: all those niggers. Whites outnumbered slaves two to one in North Carolina, but in Louisiana and Georgia the populations neared parity. Just over the border in South Carolina, the number of blacks surpassed that of whites by more than a hundred thousand. It was not difficult to imagine the sequence when the slave cast off his chains in pursuit of freedom—and retribution.

In Georgia and Kentucky, South America and the Caribbean Isles, the Africans turned on their masters in short but disturbing encounters. Before the Southampton rebellion was smothered, Turner and his band murdered sixty-five men, women, and children. Civilian militias and patrollers lynched three times that in response—conspirators, sympathizers, and innocents—to set an example. To clarify the terms. But the numbers remained, declaring a truth unclouded by prejudice.

"Around here, the closest thing to a constable was the patroller," Martin said.

"Most places," Cora said. "Patroller will harass you anytime they feel like." It was after midnight, her first Monday. Martin's daughter and her family had returned home, as had Fiona, who lived down the road in Irishtown. Martin perched on a crate in the attic, fanning himself. Cora paced and stretched her sore limbs. She had not stood in days. Ethel declined to appear. Dark blue drapes hid the windows and the small candle licked at the gloom.

Despite the hour, Martin spoke in a whisper. His next-door neighbor's son was a night rider.

As the slave owners' enforcers, the patrollers were the law: white, crooked, and merciless. Drawn from the lowest and most vicious segment, too witless to even become overseers. (Cora nodded in agreement.) The patroller required no reason to stop a person apart from color. Slaves caught off the plantation need passes, unless they wanted a licking and a visit to the county jail. Free blacks carried proof of manumission or risked being conveyed into the clutches of slavery; sometimes they were smuggled to the auction block anyway. Rogue blacks who did not surrender could be shot. They searched slave villages at will and took liberties as they ransacked the homes of freemen, stealing hard-earned linens or making licentious advances.

In war—and to put down a slave rebellion was the most glorious call to arms—the patrollers transcended their origins to become a true army. Cora pictured the insurrections as great, bloody battles, unfurling beneath a night sky lit by vast fires. From Martin's accounts, the actual uprisings were small and chaotic. The slaves walked the roads between towns with their scavenged weapons: hatchets and scythes, knives and bricks. Tipped by colored turncoats, the white enforcers organized elaborate ambushes, decimating the insurgents with gunfire and running them down on horseback, reinforced by the might of the United States Army. At the first alarms, civilian volunteers joined the patrollers to quell the disturbance, invading the quarters and putting freemen's homes to the torch. Suspects and bystanders crammed the jails. They strung up the guilty and, in the interest of prevention, a robust percentage of the innocent. Once the slain had been avenged—and more important, the insult to white order repaid with interest—the civilians returned to their farms and factories and stores, and the patrollers resumed their rounds.

The revolts were quashed, but the immensity of the colored population remained. The verdict of the census lay in glum columns and rows.

"We know it, but don't say it," Cora told Martin.

The crate creaked as Martin shifted.

"And if we say, we don't say it for anyone to hear," Cora said. "How big we are."

On a chilly evening last autumn, the powerful men of North Carolina convened to solve the colored question. Politicians attuned to the shifting complexities of the slavery debate; wealthy farmers who drove the beast of cotton and felt the reins slipping; and the requisite lawyers to fire the soft clay of their schemes into permanence. Jamison was present, Martin told Cora, in his capacities as a senator and local planter. It was a long night.

They assembled in Oney Garrison's dining room. Oney lived atop Justice Hill, so named because it allowed one to see everything below for miles and miles, placing the world in proportion. After this night their meeting would be known as the Justice Convention. Their host's father had been a member of the cotton vanguard and a savvy proselytizer of the miracle crop. Oney grew up surrounded by the profits of cotton, and its necessary evil, niggers. The more he thought about it—as he sat there in his dining room, taking in the long, pallid faces of the men who drank his liquor and overstayed their welcome—what he really wanted was simply more of the former and less of the latter. Why were they spending so much time worrying about slave uprisings and northern influence in Congress when the real issue was who was going to pick all this goddamned cotton?

In the coming days the newspapers printed the numbers for all to see, Martin said. There were almost three hundred thousand slaves in North Carolina. Every year that same number of Europeans—Irish and Germans mostly, fleeing famine and political unpleasantness—streamed into the harbors of Boston, New York, Philadelphia. On the floor of the state house, in the editorial pages, the question was put forth: Why cede this supply to the Yankees? Why not alter the course of that human tributary so that it fed southward? Advertisements in overseas papers promoted the benefits of term labor, advance agents expounded in taverns and town meetings and poorhouses, and in due course the charter ships teemed with their willing human cargo, bringing dreamers to the shores of a new country. Then they disembarked to work the fields.

"Never seen a white person pick cotton," Cora said.

"Before I came back to North Carolina, I'd never seen a mob rip a man limb from limb," Martin said. "See that, you stop saying what folks will do and what they won't."

True, you couldn't treat an Irishman like an African, white nigger or no. There was the cost of buying slaves and their upkeep on one hand and paying white workers meager but livable wages on the other. The reality of slave violence versus stability in the long term. The Europeans had been farmers before; they would be farmers again. Once the immigrants finished their contracts (having paid back travel, tools, and lodging) and took their place in American society, they would be allies of the southern system that had nurtured them. On Election Day when they took their turn at the ballot box, theirs would be a full vote, not three-fifths. A financial reckoning was inevitable, but come the approaching conflict over the race question, North Carolina would emerge in the most advantageous position of all the slave states.

In effect, they abolished slavery. On the contrary, Oney Garrison said in response. We abolished niggers.

"All the women and children, the men—where did they go?" Cora asked. Someone shouted in the park, and the two in the attic were still for a while.

"You saw," Martin said.

The North Carolina government—half of which crowded into Garrison's dining room that night—purchased existing slaves from farmers at favorable rates, just as Great Britain had done when it abolished slavery decades ago. The other states of the cotton empire absorbed the stock; Florida and Louisiana, in their explosive growth, were particularly famished for colored hands, especially the seasoned variety. A short tour of Bourbon Street forecast the result to any observer: a repulsive mongrel state in which the white race is, through amalgamation with negro blood, made stained, obscured, confused. Let them pollute their European bloodlines with Egyptian darkness, produce a river of half-breeds, quadroons, and miscellaneous dingy yellow bastards—they forge the very blades that will be used to cut their throats.

The new race laws forbid colored men and women from setting foot on North Carolina soil. Freemen who refused to leave their land were run off or massacred. Veterans of the Indian campaigns earned generous mercenary coin for their expertise. Once the soldiers finished their work, the former patrollers took on the mantle of night riders, rounding up strays—slaves who tried to outrun the new order, dispossessed freemen without the means to make it north, luckless colored men and women lost in the land for any number of reasons.

When Cora woke up that first Saturday morning, she put off looking through the spy hole. When she finally steeled herself, they had already cut down Louisa's body. Children skipped underneath the spot where she had dangled. "The road," Cora said, "the Freedom Trail, you called it. How far does it go?"

It extended as far as there were bodies to feed it, Martin said. Putrefying bodies, bodies consumed by carrion eaters were constantly replaced, but the heading always advanced. Every town of any real size held their Friday Festival, closing with the same grim finale. Some places reserved extra captives in the jail for a fallow week when the night riders returned empty-handed.

Whites punished under the new legislation were merely hung, not put on display. Although, Martin qualified, there was the case of a white farmer who had sheltered a gang of colored refugees. When they combed through the ashes of the house it was impossible to pick his body from those he had harbored, as the fire had eliminated the differences in their skin, leveling them. All five bodies were hung on the trail and nobody made much of a fuss over the breach in protocol.

With the topic of white persecution, they had arrived at the reason for her term in the nook. "You understand our predicament," Martin said.

Abolitionists had always been run off here, he said. Virginia or Delaware might tolerate their agitating, but no cotton state. Owning the literature was enough for a spell in jail, and when you were released you did not stay in town long. In the amendments to the state's constitution, the punishment for possessing seditious writings, or for aiding and abetting a colored person, was left to the discretion of local authorities. In practice, the verdict was death. The accused were dragged from their homes by their hair. Slave owners who refused to comply—from sentiment or a quaint notion about property rights—were strung up, as well as kindhearted citizens who hid niggers in their attics and cellars and coal bins.

After a lull in white arrests, some towns increased the rewards for turning in collaborators. Folks informed on business rivals, ancient nemeses, and neighbors, recounting old conversations where the traitors had uttered forbidden sympathies. Children tattled on their parents, taught by schoolmistresses the hallmarks of sedition. Martin related the story of a man in town who had been trying to rid himself of his wife for years, to no avail. The details of her crime did not hold up under scrutiny, but she paid the ultimate price. The gentleman remarried three months later.

"Is he happy?" Cora asked.

"What?"

Cora waved her hand. The severity of Martin's account had sent her down an avenue of odd humor.

Before, slave patrollers searched the premises of colored individuals at will, be they free or enslaved. Their expanded powers permitted them to knock on anyone's door to pursue an accusation and for random inspections as well, in the name of public safety. The regulators called at all hours, visiting the poorest trapper and wealthiest magistrate alike. Wagons and carriages were stopped at checkpoints. The mica mine was only a few miles away—even if Martin had the grit to run with Cora, they would not make it to the next county without an examination.

Cora thought that the whites would be loath to give up their freedoms, even in the name of security. Far from instilling resentment, Martin told her, the patrollers' diligence was a point of pride from county to county. Patriots boasted of how often they'd been searched and given a clean bill. A night rider's call on the home of a comely young woman had led to more than one happy engagement.

They twice searched Martin and Ethel's house before Cora appeared. The riders were perfectly pleasant, complimenting Ethel on her ginger cake. They did not look askance at the attic hatch, but that was no guarantee that next time things would proceed along the same lines. The second visit caused Martin to resign from his duties with the railroad. There were no plans for the next leg of Cora's journey, no word from associates. They would have to wait for a sign.

Once again, Martin apologized for his wife's behavior. "You understand she's scared to death. We're at the mercy of fate."

"You feel like a slave?" Cora asked.

Ethel hadn't chosen this life, Martin said.

"You were born to it? Like a slave?"

That put an end to their conversation that night. Cora climbed up into the nook with fresh rations and a clean chamber pot.

Her routine established itself quickly. It could not have been otherwise, given the constraints. After she knocked her head into the roof a dozen times, her body remembered the limits on her movement. Cora slept, nestled between the rafters as if in the cramped hold of a ship. She watched the park. She worked on her reading, making the best of the education that had been cut short in South Carolina, squinting in the spy hole's dim light. She wondered why there were only two kinds of weather: hardship in the morning, and tribulation at night.

Every Friday the town held its festival and Cora retreated to the opposite side of the nook.

The heat was impossible most days. On the worst she gulped at the hole like a fish in a bucket. Sometimes she neglected to ration her water, imbibing too much in the morning and staring with bitterness at the fountain the rest of the day. That damned dog cavorting in the spray. When the heat made her faint, she awoke with her head smeared into a rafter, her neck feeling like a chicken's after Alice the cook tried to wring it for supper. The meat she put on her bones in South Carolina melted away. Her host replaced her soiled dress with one his daughter had left behind. Jane was scarce-hipped and Cora now fit into her clothes with room.

Near midnight, after all the lights in the houses facing the park were extinguished and Fiona had long gone home, Martin brought food. Cora descended into the attic proper, to stretch and breathe different air. They talked some, then at a certain point Martin would stand with a solemn expression and Cora clambered back into the nook. Every few days Ethel permitted Martin to give her a brief visit to the washroom. Cora always fell asleep following Martin's visit, sometimes after an interval of sobbing and sometimes so quickly she was like a candle being blown out. She returned to her violent dreams.

She tracked the regulars on their daily transits through the park, assembling notes and speculations like the compilers of her almanacs. Martin kept abolitionist newspapers and pamphlets in the nook. They were a danger; Ethel wanted them gone, but they had been his father's and predated their residence in the house so Martin figured they could deny ownership. Once Cora had gleaned what she could from the yellowed pamphlets, she started on the old almanacs, with their projections and ruminations about the tides and stars, and bits of obscure commentary. Martin brought her a Bible. On one of her short interludes down in the attic, she saw a copy of *The Last of the Mohicans* that had been warped and swollen by water. She huddled by the spy hole for reading light, and in the evening curled around a candle.

Cora opened Martin's visits with the same question. "Any word?"

After a few months, she stopped.

The silence from the railroad was complete. The gazettes printed reports of raided depots and station agents brought to raw justice, but those were common slave-state fables. Previously, strangers knocked on Martin's door with messages concerning routes, and once, news of a confirmed passenger. Never the same person twice. No one had come in a long time, Martin said. By his lights, there was nothing for him to do.

"You won't let me leave," Cora said.

His reply was a whimper: "The situation is plain." It was a perfect trap, he said, for everyone. "You won't make it. They'll catch you. Then you'll tell them who we are."

"On Randall, when they want you in irons, they put you in irons."

"You'll bring us to ruin," Martin said. "Yourself, me, and Ethel, and all who helped you up and down the line."

She wasn't being fair but didn't much care, feeling mulish. Martin gave her a copy of that day's newspaper and pulled the hatch into place.

Any noise from Fiona sent her stock-still. She could only imagine what the Irish girl looked like. Occasionally Fiona dragged junk up to the attic. The stairs complained loudly at the slightest pressure, an efficient alarm. Once the maid moved on, Cora returned to her tiny range of activities. The girl's vulgarities reminded Cora of the plantation and the stream of oaths delivered by the hands when master's eye was not on them. The small rebellion of servants everywhere. She assumed Fiona spat in the soup.

The maid's route home did not include a cut across the park. Cora never saw her face even as she became a student of the girl's sighs. Cora pictured her, scrappy and determined, a survivor of famine and the hard relocation. Martin told her she'd come to America on a Carolina charter with her mother and brother. The mother got lung sickness and died a day out from land. The boy was too young to work and had a puny constitution overall; older Irish ladies passed him around most days. Was Irishtown similar to the colored streets in South Carolina? Crossing a single street transformed the way people talked, determined the size and condition of the homes, the dimension and character of the dreams.

In a few months it would be the harvest. Outside the town, in the fields, the cotton would pop into bolls and travel into sacks, picked this time by white hands. Did it bother the Irish and Germans to do nigger work, or did the surety of wages erase dishonor? Penniless whites took over the rows from penniless blacks, except at the end of the week the whites were no longer penniless. Unlike their darker brethren, they could pay off their contracts with their salaries and start a new chapter.

Jockey used to talk on Randall about how the slavers needed to roam deeper and deeper into Africa to find the next bunch of slaves, kidnapping tribe after tribe to feed the cotton, making the plantations into a mix of tongues and clans. Cora figured that a new wave of immigrants would replace the Irish, fleeing a different but no less abject country, the process starting anew. The engine huffed and groaned and kept running. They had merely switched the fuel that moved the pistons.

The sloping walls of her prison were a canvas for her morbid inquiries, particularly between sundown and Martin's late-night visit. When Caesar had approached her, she envisioned two outcomes: a contented, hard-won life in a northern city, or death. Terrance would not be content to merely discipline her for running away; he would make her life an ornate hell until he got bored, then have her dispatched in a gory exhibition.

Her northern fantasy, those first weeks in the attic, was a mere sketch. Glimpses of children in a bright kitchen—always a boy and a girl—and a husband in the next room, unseen but loving. As the days stretched, other rooms sprouted off the kitchen. A parlor with simple but tasteful furniture, things she had seen in the white shops of South Carolina. A bedroom. Then a bed covered in white sheets that shone in the sun, her children rolling on it with her, the husband's body half visible at the edges. In another scene, years hence, Cora walked down a busy street in her city and came across her mother. Begging in the gutter, a broken old woman bent into the sum of her mistakes. Mabel looked up but did not recognize her daughter. Cora kicked her beggar's cup, the few coins flew into the hubbub, and she continued on her afternoon errand to fetch flour for her son's birthday cake.

In this place to come, Caesar occasionally came for supper and they laughed ruefully about Randall and the travails of their escape, their eventual freedom. Caesar told the children how he got the small scar over his eyebrow, dragging a finger across it: He was caught by a slave catcher in North Carolina but got free.

Cora rarely thought of the boy she had killed. She did not need to defend her actions in the woods that night; no one had the right to call her to account. Terrance Randall provided a model for a mind that could conceive of North Carolina's new system, but the scale of the violence was hard to settle in her head. Fear drove these people, even more than cotton money. The shadow of the black hand that will return what has been given. It occurred to her one night that she was one of the vengeful monsters they were scared of: She had killed a white boy. She might kill one of them next. And because of that fear, they erected a new scaffolding of oppression on the cruel foundation laid hundreds of years before. That was Sea Island cotton the slaver had ordered for his rows, but scattered among the seeds were those of violence and death, and that crop grew fast. The whites were right to be afraid. One day the system would collapse in blood.

An insurrection of one. She smiled for a moment, before the facts of her latest cell reasserted themselves. Scrabbling in the walls like a rat. Whether in the fields or underground or in an attic room, America remained her warden.

⸺ ❖ ⸺

It was a week before the summer solstice. Martin stuffed one of the old quilts into a chair without a seat and sank into it by degrees over the course of his visit. As was her habit, Cora asked for help with words. This time they came from the Bible, through which she made desultory progress: *gainsay, ravening, hoar.* Martin admitted he didn't know the meanings of gainsay and ravening. Then, as if to prepare for the new season, Martin reviewed the series of bad omens.

The first had occurred the previous week, when Cora knocked over the chamber pot. She'd been in the nook for four months and made noise before, knocking her head against the roof or her knee against a rafter. Fiona had never reacted. This time the girl was puttering around in the kitchen when Cora kicked the pot against the wall. Once Fiona came upstairs she wouldn't be able to overlook the dripping sound of the mess leaking between the boards into the attic, or the smell.

The noon whistle had just sounded. Ethel was out. Fortunately, another girl from Irishtown visited after lunch and the two gossiped in the parlor for so long that afterward Fiona had to speed through her chores. She either didn't notice the odor or pretended not to, shirking the responsibility for cleaning after whatever rodent's nest was up there. When Martin came that night and they cleaned, he told Cora it was best if he didn't mention the close call to Ethel. Her nerves were especially brittle with the rise in the humidity.

Informing Ethel was up to Martin. Cora hadn't seen the woman since the night of her arrival. As far as she could tell, her host didn't speak of her—even when Fiona was off the premises—beyond infrequent mentions of *that creature*. The slam of the bedroom door often preceded Martin's upstairs visit. The only thing that kept Ethel from turning her in, Cora decided, was complicity.

"Ethel is a simple woman," Martin said, sinking in the chair. "She couldn't foresee these troubles when I asked for her hand."

Cora knew that Martin was about to recount his accidental recruitment, which meant extra time outside the nook. She stretched her arms and encouraged him. "How could you, Martin."

"Lord, how could I," Martin said.

He was a most unlikely instrument of abolition. In Martin's recollection, his father, Donald, had never expressed an opinion about the peculiar institution, although their family was rare in their circle in not owning slaves. When Martin was little, the stock boy at the feed store was a wizened, stooped man named Jericho, freed many years previously. To his mother's dismay, Jericho came over every Thanksgiving bearing a tin of turnip mash. Donald grunted in disapproval or shook his head at newspaper items about the latest slave incident, but it wasn't clear if he judged the brutality of the master or the intransigence of the slave.

At eighteen, Martin left North Carolina and after a period of lonesome meandering took a position as a clerk in a Norfolk shipping office. The quiet work and sea air suited him. He developed a fondness for oysters and his constitution improved generally. Ethel's face appeared one day in a crowd, luminous. The Delanys had old ties to the region, pruning the family tree into a lopsided sight: abundant and many-cousined in the north, sparse and faceless in the south. Martin rarely visited his father. When Donald fell while fixing the roof, Martin hadn't been home in five years.

The men had never communicated easily. Before Martin's

mother passed, it was her lot to translate the ellipses and muttered asides that constituted conversation between father and son. At Donald's deathbed, there was no interpreter. He made Martin promise to finish his work, and the son assumed the old man meant him to take over the feed store. That was the first misunderstanding. The second was taking the map he discovered in his father's papers for directions to a cache of gold. In his life, Donald wrapped himself in a kind of quiet that, depending on the observer, signaled imbecility or a reservoir of mystery. It would be just like his father, Martin thought, to comport himself like a pauper while hiding a fortune.

The treasure, of course, was the underground railroad. Some might call freedom the dearest currency of all, but it was not what Martin expected. Donald's diary—set on a barrel on the station platform and surrounded by colored stones in a kind of shrine—described how his father had always been disgusted by his country's treatment of the Ethiopian tribe. Chattel slavery was an affront to God, and slavers an aspect of Satan. Donald had provided aid to slaves his whole life, whenever possible and with whatever means at hand, ever since he was a small boy and misdirected some bounty men who badgered him over a runaway.

His many work trips during Martin's childhood were in fact abolitionist missions. Midnight meetings, riverbank chicanery, intrigue at the crossroads. It was ironic that given his communication difficulties, Donald functioned as a human telegraph, relaying messages up and down the coast. The U.G.R.R. (as he referred to it in his notes) operated no spurs or stops in North Carolina until Donald made it his mission. Working this far south was suicide, everyone said. He added the nook to the attic nonetheless, and if the false ceiling was not without seams, it kept his charges aloft. By the time a loose shingle undid him, Donald had conveyed a dozen souls to the Free States.

Martin helped a considerably smaller number. Both he and Cora decided his skittish personality had not helped them during the close call the previous night, when in another bad omen the regulators knocked on the front door.

IT had been just after dark and the park was full of those afraid to go home. Cora wondered what waited for them that they lingered so purposefully, the same people week after week. The fast-walking man who sat on the fountain's rim, dragging his fingers through his wispy hair. The slovenly, wide-hipped lady who always wore a black bonnet and muttered to herself. They weren't here to drink the night air or sneak a kiss. These people slumped on their distracted circuits, looking this way and that, never in front. As if to avoid the eyes of all the ghosts, the dead ones who had built their town. Colored labor had erected every house on the park, laid the stones in the fountain and the paving of the walkways. Hammered the stage where the night riders performed their grotesque pageants and the wheeled platform that delivered the doomed men and women to the air. The only thing colored folks hadn't built was the tree. God had made that, for the town to bend to evil ends.

No wonder the whites wandered the park in the growing darkness, Cora thought, her forehead pressed into the wood. They were ghosts themselves, caught between two worlds: the reality of their crimes, and the hereafter denied them for those crimes.

Cora was informed of the night riders' rounds by the ripple passing through the park. The evening crowd turned to gawk at a house on the opposite side. A young girl in pigtails let a trio of regulators inside her home. Cora remembered the girl's father had trouble with their porch steps. She hadn't seen him for weeks. The girl clutched her robe to her neck and closed the door behind them. Two night riders, tall and densely proportioned, idled on the porch smoking their pipes with complacent sloth.

The door opened half an hour later and the team huddled on the sidewalk in a lantern's circle, consulting a ledger. They crossed the park, eventually stepping beyond the spy hole's domain. Cora had closed her eyes when their loud rapping on the front door shocked her. They stood directly beneath.

The next minutes moved with appalling slowness. Cora huddled in a corner, making herself small behind the final rafter. Sounds furnished details of the action below. Ethel greeted the night riders warmly; anyone who knew her would be certain she was hiding something. Martin made a quick tour of the attic to make sure nothing was amiss, and then joined everyone downstairs.

Martin and Ethel answered their questions quickly as they showed the group around. It was just the two of them. Their daughter lived elsewhere. (The night riders searched the kitchen and parlor.) The maid Fiona had a key but no one else had access to the house. (Up the stairs.) They had been visited by no strangers, heard no strange noises, noted nothing out of the ordinary. (They searched the two bedrooms.) Nothing was missing. There was no cellar—surely they knew by now that the park houses did not have cellars. Martin had been in the attic that very afternoon and noticed nothing amiss.

"Do you mind if we go up?" The voice was gruff and low. Cora assigned it to the shorter night rider, the one with the beard.

Their footfalls were loud on the attic stairs. They navigated around the junk. One of them spoke, startling Cora—his head was inches below her. She kept her breath close. The men were sharks moving their snouts beneath a ship, looking for the food they sensed was close. Only thin planks separated hunter and prey.

"We don't go up here that much since the raccoons made a nest," Martin said.

"You can smell their mess," the other night rider said.

The regulators departed. Martin skipped his midnight rounds in the attic, scared that they were in the teeth of an elaborate trap. Cora in her comfortable darkness patted the sturdy wall: It had kept her safe.

They had survived the chamber pot and the night riders. Martin's final bad omen happened that morning: A mob strung up a husband and wife who hid two colored boys in their barn. Their daughter turned them in, jealous of the attention. Despite their youth, the colored boys joined the grisly gallery on the Freedom Trail. One of Ethel's neighbors told her about it in the market and Ethel fainted dead away, pitching into a row of preserves.

Home searches were on the rise. "They've been so successful rounding up people that now they have to work hard to meet their quotas," Martin said.

Cora offered that perhaps it was good the house had been searched—it would be some time before they returned. More time for the railroad to reach out, or for another opportunity to present itself.

Martin always fidgeted when Cora raised the idea of initiative. He cradled one of his childhood toys in his hands, a wooden duck. He'd worried the paint from it these last months. "Or it means the roads will be twice as hard to pass," he said. "The boys'll be hungry for a souvenir." His face lit up. "Ravening—I think it means very hungry."

Cora had been feeling poorly all day. She said good night and climbed into her nook. For all the close calls, she was in the same place she had been in for months: becalmed. Between departure and arrival, in transit like the passenger she'd been ever since she ran. Once the wind picked up she would be moving again, but for now there was only the blank and endless sea.

What a world it is, Cora thought, that makes a living prison into your only haven. Was she out of bondage or in its web: how to describe the status of a runaway? Freedom was a thing that shifted as you looked at it, the way a forest is dense with trees up close but from outside, from the empty meadow, you see its true limits. Being free had nothing to do with chains or how much space you had. On the plantation, she was not free, but she moved unrestricted on its acres, tasting the air and tracing the summer stars. The place was big in its smallness. Here, she was free of her master but slunk around a warren so tiny she couldn't stand.

Cora hadn't left the top floors of the house in months but her perspective roved widely. North Carolina had its Justice Hill, and she had hers. Looking down over the universe of the park, she saw the town drift where it wanted, washed by sunlight on a stone bench, cooled in the shadows of the hanging tree. But they were prisoners like she was, shackled to fear. Martin and Ethel were terrified of the watchful eyes behind every darkened window. The town huddled together on Friday nights in the hope their numbers warded off the things in the dark: the rising black tribe; the enemy who concocts accusations; the child who undertakes a magnificent revenge for a scolding and brings the house down around them. Better to hide in attics than to confront what lurked behind the faces of neighbors, friends, and family.

The park sustained them, the green harbor they preserved as the town extended itself outward, block by block and house by house. Cora thought of her garden back on Randall, the plot she cherished. Now she saw it for the joke it was—a tiny square of dirt that had convinced her she owned something. It was hers like the cotton she seeded, weeded, and picked was hers. Her plot was a shadow of something that lived elsewhere, out of sight. The way poor Michael reciting the Declaration of Independence was an echo of something that existed elsewhere. Now that she had run away and seen a bit of the country, Cora wasn't sure the document described anything real at all. America was a ghost in the darkness, like her.

THAT night she took ill. Spasms in her belly woke her. In her dizziness, the nook lurched and rocked. She lost the contents of her stomach in the small space, and control of her bowels. Heat besieged the tiny room, firing the air and inside her skin. Somehow she made it to morning's light and the lifting of the veil. The park was still there; in the night she had dreamed she was at sea and chained belowdecks. Next to her was another captive, and another, hundreds of them crying in terror. The ship bucked on swells, dove and slammed into anvils of water. She heard footsteps on the stairs, the sound of the hatch scraping, and she closed her eyes.

Cora woke in a white room, a soft mattress cupping her body. The window delivered more than a stingy puncture of sunlight. Park noise was her clock: It was late afternoon.

Ethel sat in the corner of her husband's childhood bedroom. Her knitting piled in her lap, she stared at Cora. She felt her patient's forehead. "Better," Ethel said. She poured a glass of water, then brought a bowl of beef broth.

Ethel's attitude had softened during Cora's delirium. The runaway made so much noise moaning in the night and was so ill when they lowered her from the attic nook that they were obliged to let Fiona go for a few days. Martin had the Venezuelan pox, they told the Irish girl, caught from a tainted bag of feed, and the doctor forbid anyone to enter the house until it had run its course. He'd read about one such quarantine in a magazine, the first excuse that came into his head. They paid the girl her wages for the week. Fiona tucked the money into her purse and asked no more questions.

It was Martin's turn to absent himself while Ethel assumed responsibility for their guest, nursing Cora through two days of fever and convulsions. The couple had made few friends during their time in the state, making it easier to abstain from the life of town. While Cora twisted in her delirium, Ethel read from the Bible to speed her recuperation. The woman's voice entered her dreams. So stern the night Cora emerged from the mine, it now contained a quality of tenderness. She dreamed the woman kissed her forehead, motherly. Cora listened to her stories, drifting. The ark delivered the worthy, bringing them to the other side of the catastrophe. The wilderness stretched for forty years before others found their promised land.

The afternoon stretched the shadows like taffy and the park entered its period of diminished popularity as supper approached. Ethel sat in the rocking chair, smiled, and looked through the Scripture, trying to find an appropriate section.

Now that she was awake and could speak for herself, Cora told her host that the verses were unnecessary.

Ethel's mouth formed a line. She closed the book, one thin finger holding her place. "We are all in need of our Savior's grace," Ethel said. "It wouldn't be very Christian of me to let a heathen into my house, and not share His word."

"It has been shared," Cora said.

It had been Ethel's childhood Bible that Martin gave to Cora, smudged and stained by her fingers. Ethel quizzed Cora, dubious as to how much their guest could read and understand. To be sure, Cora was not a natural believer, and her education had been terminated sooner than she wished. In the attic she had struggled with the words, pressed on, doubled back to difficult verses. The contradictions vexed her, even half-understood ones.

"I don't get where it says, He that stealeth a man and sells him, shall be put to death," Cora said. "But then later it says, Slaves should be submissive to their masters in everything—and be well-pleasing." Either it was a sin to keep another as property, or it had God's own blessing. But to be well-pleasing in addition? A slaver must have snuck into the printing office and put that in there.

"It means what it says," Ethel said. "It means that a Hebrew may not enslave a Hebrew. But the sons of Ham are not of that tribe. They were cursed, with black skin and tails. Where the Scripture condemns slavery, it is not speaking of negro slavery at all."

"I have black skin, but I don't have a tail. As far as I know—I never thought to look," Cora said. "Slavery is a curse, though, that much is true." Slavery is a sin when whites were put to the yoke, but not the African. All men are created equal, unless we decide you are not a man.

Under the Georgia sun, Connelly had recited verses while scourging field hands for infractions. "Niggers, obey your earthly masters in everything and do it not only when their eye is on you and to win their favor but with sincerity of heart and reverence for the Lord." The slash of the cat-o'-nine-tails punctuating every syllable, and a wail from the victim. Cora remembered other passages on slavery in the Good Book and shared them with her host. Ethel said she didn't wake up that morning to get into a theological argument.

Cora enjoyed the woman's company and frowned when she left. For her part, Cora blamed the people who wrote it down. People always got things wrong, on purpose as much as by accident. The next morning Cora asked for the almanacs.

They were obsolete, last year's weather, but Cora adored the old almanacs for containing the entire world. They didn't need people to say what they meant. The tables and facts couldn't be shaped into what they were not. The vignettes and parodies between the lunar tables and weather reports—about cranky old widows and simple darkies—confused her as much as the moral lessons in the holy book. Both described human behavior beyond her ken. What did she know, or need to know, of fancy wedding manners, or moving a herd of lambs through the desert? One day she might use the almanac's instructions, at least. Odes to the Atmosphere, Odes to the Cocoa-Tree of the South Sea Islands. She hadn't heard of odes or atmospheres before, but as she worked through the pages, these creatures took up residence in her mind. Should she ever own boots, she now knew the trick of tallow and wax that extended their use. If one of her chickens got the snuffles one day, rubbing asafetida in butter on their nostrils would set them straight.

Martin's father had needed the almanacs to plan for the full moon—the books held prayers for runaways. The moon grew fat and thin, there were solstices, first frosts, and spring rains. All these things proceeded without the interference of men. She tried to imagine what the tide looked like, coming in and going out, nipping at the sand like a little dog, heedless of people and their machinations. Her strength returned.

On her own, she couldn't understand all the words. Cora asked Ethel, "Can you read some to me?"

Ethel growled. But she opened an almanac where the spine broke and in compromise with herself used the same cadences she used for the Bible. "'Transplanting the Evergreens. It seems not very material whether evergreen trees are transplanted in April, May, or June . . .'"

When Friday arrived, Cora was much improved. Fiona was set to come back on Monday. They agreed that in the morning

Cora should return to the nook. Martin and Ethel would invite a neighbor or two for cake to dispel any gossip or speculation. Martin practiced a wan demeanor. Perhaps even host someone for the Friday Festival. Their porch had a perfect view.

That evening Ethel let Cora stay in the extra bedroom, provided she kept the room dark and stayed away from the window. Cora had no intention of watching the weekly spectacle but looked forward to one last stretch in the bed. In the end, Martin and Ethel thought better of inviting people over, so the only guests were the uninvited ones that stepped out of the crowd at the start of the coon show.

The regulators wanted to search the house.

The performance stopped, the town buzzing at the commotion at the side of the park. Ethel tried to stall the night riders. They pushed past her and Martin. Cora started for the stairs but they complained reliably, warning her so often these last few months, that she knew she wouldn't be able to make it. She crawled under Martin's old bed and that's where they found her, snatching her ankles like irons and dragging her out. They tossed her down the stairs. She jammed her shoulder into the banister at the bottom. Her ears rang.

She laid eyes on Martin and Ethel's porch for the first time. It was the stage for her capture, a second bandstand for the town's amusement as she lay on the planks at the feet of four regulators in their white and black uniforms. Another four restrained Martin and Ethel. One more man stood on the porch, dressed in a worsted plaid vest and gray trousers. He was one of the tallest men Cora had ever seen, solidly built with an arresting gaze. He surveyed the scene and smiled at a private joke.

The town filled the sidewalk and the street, jostling each other for a view of this new entertainment. A young redheaded girl pushed through. "Venezuelan pox! I told you they had someone up there!"

So here was Fiona, finally. Cora propped herself up for a look at the girl she knew so well but had never seen.

"You'll get your reward," the night rider with the beard said. He'd been to the house on the previous search.

"You say, you lummox," Fiona said. "You said you checked the attic last time, but you didn't, did you?" She turned to the town to establish witnesses for her claim. "You all see—it's my reward. All that food missing?" Fiona kicked Cora lightly with her foot. "She'd make a big roast and then the next day it was gone. Who was eating all that food? Always looking up at the ceiling. What were they looking at?"

She was so young, Cora thought. Her face was a round and freckled apple, but there was hardness in her eyes. It was difficult to believe the grunts and cusses she'd heard over the months had come out of that little mouth, but the eyes were proof enough.

"We treated you nice," Martin said.

"You have an awful queer way, both of you," Fiona said. "And you deserve whatever you get."

The town had seen justice served too many times to count, but the rendering of the verdict was a new experience. It made them uneasy. Were they a jury now, in addition to the gallery? They looked at each other for cues. An old-timer made his hand into a cone and hollered nonsense through it. A half-eaten apple hit Cora's stomach. On the bandstand, the coon-show players stood with their disheveled hats in their hands, deflated.

Jamison appeared, rubbing his forehead with a red handkerchief. Cora had not seen him since the first night, but she had heard every speech of the Friday-night finales. Every joke and grandiose claim, the appeals to race and statehood, and then the order to kill the sacrifice. The interruption in the proceedings confounding him. Absent its usual bluster, Jamison's voice squeaked. "This is something," he said. "Aren't you Donald's son?"

Martin nodded, his soft body quivering with quiet sobs.

"I know your daddy would be ashamed," Jamison said.

"I had no idea what he was up to," Ethel said. She tugged against the night riders who gripped her tight. "He did it himself! I didn't know anything!"

Martin looked away. From the people on the porch, from the town. He turned his face north toward Virginia, where he had been free of his hometown for a time.

Jamison gestured and the night riders pulled Martin and Ethel to the park. The planter looked Cora over. "A nice treat," Jamison said. Their scheduled victim was in the wings somewhere. "Should we do both?"

The tall man said, "This one is mine. I've made it clear."

Jamison's expression curdled. He was not accustomed to ignorance of his status. He asked for the stranger's name.

"Ridgeway," the man said. "Slave catcher. I go here, I go there. I've been after this one for a long time. Your judge knows all about me."

"You can't just come in here, muscling about." Jamison was aware that his usual audience, milling outside the property, observed him with undefined expectations. At the new tremor in his words two night riders, young bucks both, stepped forward to crowd Ridgeway.

Ridgeway exhibited no bother over the display. "You all have your local customs going on here—I get that. Having your fun." He pronounced *fun* like a temperance preacher. "But it doesn't belong to you. The Fugitive Slave Law says I have a right to return this property to its owner. That's what I aim to do."

Cora whimpered and felt her head. She was dizzy, like she'd

been after Terrance struck her. This man was going to return her to him.

The night rider who threw Cora down the stairs cleared his throat. He explained to Jamison that the slave catcher had led them to the house. The man had visited Judge Tennyson that afternoon and made an official request, although the judge had been enjoying his customary Friday whiskey and might not remember. No one was keen on executing the raid during the festival, but Ridgeway had insisted.

Ridgeway spat tobacco juice on the sidewalk, at the feet of some onlookers. "You can keep the reward," he told Fiona. He bent slightly and lifted Cora by her arm. "You don't have to be afraid, Cora. You're going home."

A little colored boy, about ten years old, drove a wagon up the street through the crowd, shouting at the two horses. On any other occasion the sight of him in his tailored black suit and stovepipe hat would have been a cause of bewilderment. After the dramatic capture of the sympathizers and the runaway, his appearance nudged the night into the realm of the fantastical. More than one person thought what had just transpired was a new wrinkle in the Friday entertainment, a performance arranged to counter the monotony of the weekly skits and lynchings, which, to be honest, had grown predictable.

At the foot of the porch, Fiona held forth to a group of girls from Irishtown. "A girl's got to look after her interests if she's going to get ahead in this country," she explained.

Ridgeway rode with another man in addition to the boy, a tall white man with long brown hair and a necklace of human ears around his neck. His associate shackled Cora's ankles, and then ran the chains through a ring in the floor of the wagon. She arranged herself on the bench, her head pulsing in agony with every heartbeat. As they pulled away, she saw Martin and Ethel.

They had been tied to the hanging tree. They sobbed and heaved at their bonds. Mayor ran in mad circles at their feet. A blond girl picked up a rock and threw it at Ethel, hitting her in the face. A segment of the town laughed at Ethel's piteous shrieks. Two more children picked up rocks and threw them at the couple. Mayor yipped and jumped as more people bent to the ground. They raised their arms. The town moved in and then Cora couldn't see them anymore.

Ethel

EVER since she saw a woodcut of a missionary surrounded by jungle natives, Ethel thought it would be spiritually fulfilling to serve the Lord in dark Africa, delivering savages to the light. She dreamed of the ship that would take her, a magnificent schooner with sails like angel wings, cutting across the violent sea. The perilous journey into the interior, up rivers, wending mountain passes, and the dangers escaped: lions, serpents, man-killing plants, duplicitous guides. And then the village, where the natives receive her as an emissary of the Lord, an instrument of civilization. In gratitude the niggers lift her to the sky, praising her name: Ethel, Ethel.

She was eight years old. Her father's newspapers contained tales of explorers, unknown lands, pygmy peoples. The nearest she could get to the image in the newspaper was playing mission-ary and native with Jasmine. Jasmine was like a sister to her. The game never lasted long before they switched to husband and wife, practicing kisses and arguments in the cellar of Ethel's house. Given the color of their skins, there was never any doubt over their roles in either game, Ethel's habit of rubbing soot onto her face notwithstanding. Her face blackened, she practiced expres-sions of amazement and wonder in front of the mirror so she'd know what to expect when she met her heathens.

Jasmine lived in the upstairs room with her mother, Felice. The Delany family owned Felice's mother, and when little Edgar Delany turned ten, he received Felice as a present. Now that he was a man, Edgar recognized that Felice was a miracle, tending to the affairs of his house as if she were born to it. He recounted her darky wisdom as a matter of routine, sharing her parables about human nature with guests whenever she disappeared into the kitchen so that when she returned their faces glowed with affection and jealousy. He gave her passes to visit the Parker plantation every New Year's Day feast; Felice's sister was a washwoman there. Jasmine was born nine months after one such visit, and now the Delanys owned two slaves.

Ethel thought that a slave was someone who lived in your house like family but was not family. Her father explained the origin of the negro to disabuse her of this colorful idea. Some maintained that the negro was the remnant of a race of giants who had ruled the earth in an ancient time, but Edgar Delany knew they were descendants of cursed, black Ham, who had survived the Flood by clinging to the peaks of a mountain in Africa. Ethel thought that if they were cursed, they required Christian guidance all the more.

On her eighth birthday, Ethel's father forbid her to play with Jasmine so as not to pervert the natural state of relations between the races. Ethel did not make friends easily, even then. She sobbed and stomped for days; Jasmine was more adaptable. Jasmine assumed simple duties around the household and took over her mother's position when Felice's heart seized and she fell mute and paralyzed. Felice lingered for months, her mouth open and pink, eyes foggy, until Ethel's father had her removed. Ethel observed no disturbance in her old playmate's face when they loaded her mother into the cart. By then the two did not speak outside of household matters.

The house had been built fifty years before and the stairs creaked. A whisper in one room carried into the next two. Most nights after supper and prayers, Ethel heard her father going up the crooked stairs, guided by the bobbing light of the candle. Sometimes she sneaked to her bedroom door and caught a glimpse of his white bedclothes disappearing around the corner.

"Where are you going, Father?" she asked one night. Felice had been gone two years. Jasmine was fourteen.

"Going upstairs," he said, and both experienced a strange relief now that they had a term for his nocturnal visits. He was going upstairs—where else did the stairs lead? Her father had given one explanation for the separation of the races in fratricidal punishment. His nighttime trips elaborated on the arrangement. Whites lived downstairs and blacks lived upstairs, and to bridge that separation was to heal a biblical wound.

Her mother held a low opinion about her husband going upstairs but was not without resources. When their family sold Jasmine to the coppersmith on the other side of town, Ethel knew it was her mother's doing. There was no more going upstairs when the new slave took residence. Nancy was a grandmother, slow in her steps and half blind. Now it was her wheezing that penetrated the walls, not footsteps and squeals. The house had not been so clean and orderly since Felice; Jasmine had been efficient but distracted. Jasmine's new home was across the way in colored town. Everyone whispered that the child had his father's eyes.

One day over lunch Ethel announced that when she was old enough, she intended to spread the Christian word to African primitives. Her parents scoffed. It was not something that good young women from Virginia did. If you want to help savages, her father said, teach school. The brain of a five-year-old is more savage and unruly than the oldest jungle darky, he said. Her course was set. Ethel filled in for the regular teacher when she was under the weather. Little white children were primitive in their own way, chirping and undeveloped, but it wasn't the same. Her thoughts of the jungle and a ring of dark admirers remained in her private preserve.

Resentment was the hinge of her personality. The young women in her circle comported themselves in a foreign ritual, undecipherable. She had little use for boys and, later, men. When Martin appeared, introduced by one of her cousins who worked at the shipping company, she had tired of the gossip and long relinquished an interest in happiness. A panting badger, Martin wore her down. The game of husband and wife was even less fun than she supposed. Jane, at least, turned out to be an unexpected mercy, a tidy bouquet in her arms, even if conception proved yet another humiliation. Over the years life on Orchard Street passed with a tedium that eventually congealed into comfort. She pretended not to see Jasmine when they passed on the street, especially when her former playmate was in the company of her son. His face was a dark mirror.

Then Martin was summoned to North Carolina. He arranged Donald's funeral on the hottest day of the year; they thought she fainted from sadness when it was just the barbaric humidity. Once they got a taker for the feed shop, they were done, he assured her. The place was backward. If it wasn't the heat, it was the flies; if not the mice, then the people. At least in Virginia, lynch mobs maintained a pretext of spontaneity. They didn't string up people practically on your front lawn, the same time every week, like church. North Carolina was to be a brief interlude, or so she thought until she came across the nigger in her kitchen.

George had dropped out of the attic for some food, the lone slave Martin helped before the girl arrived. It was a week before the race laws went into effect and violence against the colored population was on the rise in rehearsal. A note on their doorstep had directed Martin to the mica mine, he told her. George waited for him, hungry and irritated. The tobacco picker thumped around the attic for a week before a railroad agent took him on the next leg, boxing him up in a crate and shoving the thing through the front door. Ethel was livid, then despairing—George acted as Donald's executor, illuminating Martin's secret inheritance. He'd lost three fingers on his hand cutting cane.

Slavery as a moral issue never interested Ethel. If God had not meant for Africans to be enslaved, they wouldn't be in chains. She did, however, have firm ideas about not getting killed for other people's high-minded ideas. She and Martin argued over the underground railroad as they hadn't argued in a long time, and that was before the murderous fine print of the race laws manifested itself. Through Cora—that termite in the attic—Donald reached from beyond the grave to punish her for her joke those many years before. When their families met for the first time, Ethel made a remark about Donald's simple country suit. She was trying to call attention to the two families' different ideas of proper attire, to get it out of the way so they could all enjoy the meal Ethel had spent so much time planning. But Donald had never forgiven her, she told Martin, she was sure of it, and now they were going to swing from the branches of the tree right outside their front door.

When Martin went upstairs to help the girl it was not in the same way her father had gone upstairs, but both men came down transformed. They reached across the biblical rift for a selfish purpose.

If they could, why not her?

Everything had been denied Ethel her whole life. To mission, to help. To give love in the way she wanted. When the girl got sick, the moment Ethel awaited for so long had finally arrived. In the end she had not gone to Africa, Africa had come to her. Ethel went upstairs, as her father had done, to confront the stranger who lived in her house as family. The girl lay on the sheets, curved like a primeval river. She cleaned the girl, washing her filth from her. She kissed the girl on her forehead and neck in her restless slumber with two kinds of feeling mixed up in those kisses. She gave her the Holy Word.

A savage to call her own, at last.

Tennessee

25 DOLLARS REWARD

RAN AWAY from the subscriber on the 6th of February last, his Negro Girl PEGGY. She is about 16 years of age, and is a bright mulatto, about the ordinary height, with straight hair and tolerable good features—she has a ragged scar on her neck occasioned by a burn. She will no doubt attempt to pass for a free girl, and it is likely she has obtained a free pass. She has a down look when spoken to, and not remarkably intelligent. She speaks quick, with a shrill voice.

JOHN DARK.
CHATHAM COUNTY, MAY 17.

"JESUS, carry me home, home to that land . . ."

Jasper wouldn't stop singing. Ridgeway shouted from the head of their little caravan for him to shut his mouth, and sometimes they halted so Boseman could climb into the wagon and clout the runaway on the head. Jasper sucked the scars on his fingers for a short interval, then resumed his crooning. Quietly at first so that only Cora could hear. But soon he'd be singing again, to his lost family, to his god, to everyone they passed on the trail. He'd have to be disciplined again.

Cora recognized some of the hymns. She suspected he made up many of them; the rhymes were crooked. She wouldn't have minded it so much if Jasper had a better voice, but Jesus had not blessed him in that department. Or with looks—he had a lopsided frog face and oddly thin arms for a field hand—or with luck. Luck least of all.

He and Cora had that in common.

They picked up Jasper three days out of North Carolina. Jasper was a delivery. He absconded from the Florida cane fields and made it to Tennessee before a tinker caught him stealing food from his pantry. After a few weeks the deputy located his owner, but the tinker had no means of transport. Ridgeway and Boseman were drinking in a tavern around the corner from the jail while little Homer waited with Cora and the wagon. The town clerk approached the famous slave catcher, brokered an arrangement, and Ridgeway now had the nigger chained in the wagon. He hadn't reckoned the man for a songbird.

The rain tapped on the canopy. Cora enjoyed the breeze and then felt ashamed for enjoying something. They stopped to eat when the rain let up. Boseman slapped Jasper, chuckled, and unchained the two fugitives from the wagon floor. He offered his customary vulgar promise as he knelt before Cora, sniffing. Jasper's and Cora's wrists and ankles remained manacled. It was the longest she had ever been in chains.

Crows glided over. The world was scorched and harrowed as far as they could see, a sea of ash and char from the flat planes of the fields up to the hills and mountains. Black trees tilted, stunted black arms pointing as if to a distant place untouched by flame. They rode past the blackened bones of houses and barns without number, chimneys sticking up like grave markers, the husked stone walls of ravaged mills and granaries. Scorched fences marked where cattle had grazed; it was not possible the animals survived.

After two days of riding through it, they were covered in black grime. Ridgeway said it made him feel at home, the blacksmith's son.

This is what Cora saw: Nowhere to hide. No refuge between those black stalks, even if she weren't fettered. Even if she had an opportunity.

An old white man in a gray coat trotted by on a dun horse. Like the other travelers they passed on the black road, he slowed in curiosity. Two adult slaves were common enough. But the colored boy in the black suit driving the wagon and his queer smile discomfited strangers. The younger white man with the red derby wore a necklace adorned with pieces of shriveled leather. When they figured out these were human ears, he bared a line of intermittent teeth browned by tobacco. The older white man in command discouraged all conversation with his glowering. The traveler moved on, around the bend where the road limped between the denuded hills.

Homer unfolded a moth-eaten quilt for them to sit on and distributed their portions on tin plates. The slave catcher allowed his prisoners an equal share of the food, a custom dating to his earliest days in the job. It reduced complaints and he billed the client. At the edge of the blackened field they ate the salt pork and the beans Boseman had prepared, the dry flies screeching in waves.

Rain agitated the smell of the fire, making the air bitter. Smoke flavored every bite of food, each sip of water. Jasper sang, "Jump up, the redeemer said! Jump up, jump up if you want to see His face!"

"Hallelujah!" Boseman shouted. "Fat little Jesus baby!" His words echoed and he did a dance, splashing dark water.

"He's not eating," Cora said. Jasper had foregone the last few meals, screwing his mouth shut and crossing his arms.

"Then it doesn't eat," Ridgeway said. He waited for her to say something, having grown used to her chirping at his remarks. They were on to each other. She kept silent to interrupt their pattern.

Homer scampered over and gobbled down Jasper's portion. He sensed Cora staring at him and grinned without looking up.

The driver of the wagon was an odd little imp. Ten years old, Chester's age, but imbued with the melancholy grace of an elderly house slave, the sum of practiced gestures. He was fastidious about his fine black suit and stovepipe hat, extracting lint from the fabric and glaring at it as if it were a poison spider before flicking it. Homer rarely spoke apart from his hectoring of the horses. Of racial affinity or sympathy, he gave no indication. Cora and Jasper might as well have been invisible most of the time, smaller than lint.

Homer's duties encompassed driving the team, sundry maintenance, and what Ridgeway termed "bookkeeping." Homer maintained the business accounts and recorded Ridgeway's stories in a small notebook he kept in his coat pocket. What made this or that utterance from the slave catcher worthy of inclusion, Cora could not discern. The boy preserved worldly truism and matter-of-fact observations about the weather with equal zeal.

Prompted by Cora one night, Ridgeway maintained that he'd never owned a slave in his life, save for the fourteen hours Homer was his property. Why not? she asked. "What for?" he said. Ridgeway was riding through the outskirts of Atlanta—he'd just delivered a husband and wife to their owner, all the way from New York—when he came upon a butcher trying to square a gambling debt. His wife's family had given them the boy's mother as a wedding gift. The butcher had sold her during his previous stretch of bad luck. Now it was the boy's turn. He painted a crude sign to hang around the boy's neck advertising the offer.

The boy's strange sensibility moved Ridgeway. Homer's shining eyes, set in his round pudgy face, were at once feral and serene. A kindred spirit. Ridgeway bought him for five dollars and drew up emancipation papers the next day. Homer remained at his side despite Ridgeway's halfhearted attempts to shoo him away. The butcher had held no strong opinions on the subject of colored education and had permitted the boy to study with the children of some freemen. Out of boredom, Ridgeway helped him with his letters. Homer pretended he was of Italian extraction when it suited him and let his questioners sit with their bewilderment. His unconventional attire evolved over time; his disposition remained unchanged.

"If he's free, why don't he go?"

"Where?" Ridgeway asked. "He's seen enough to know a black boy has no future, free papers or no. Not in this country. Some disreputable character would snatch him and put him on the block lickety-split. With me, he can learn about the world. Find purpose."

Each night, with meticulous care, Homer opened his satchel and removed a set of manacles. He locked himself to the driver's seat, put the key in his pocket, and closed his eyes.

Ridgeway caught Cora looking. "He says it's the only way he can sleep."

Homer snored like a rich old man every night.

BOSEMAN, for his part, had been riding with Ridgeway for three years. He was a rambler out of South Carolina and found his way to slave catching after a hardscrabble sequence: dockhand, collection agent, gravedigger. Boseman was not the most intelligent fellow but had a knack for anticipating Ridgeway's wishes in a manner equal parts indispensable and eerie. Ridgeway's gang numbered five when Boseman joined, but his employees drifted off one by one. The reason was not immediately clear to Cora.

The previous owner of the ear necklace had been an Indian named Strong. Strong had promoted himself as a tracker, but the only creature he sniffed out reliably was whiskey. Boseman won the accessory in a wrestling contest, and when Strong disputed the terms of their match, Boseman clobbered the red man with a shovel. Strong lost his hearing and ditched the gang to work in a tannery in Canada, or so the rumor went. Even though the ears were dried and shriveled, they drew flies when it was hot. Boseman loved his souvenir, however, and the revulsion on a new client's face was too delectable. The flies hadn't harassed the Indian when he owned it, as Ridgeway reminded him from time to time.

Boseman stared at the hills between bites and had an uncharacteristically wistful air. He walked off to urinate and when he came back said, "My daddy passed through here, I think. He said it was forest then. When he came back, it had all been cleared by settlers."

"Now it's doubly cleared," Ridgeway responded. "It's true what you say. This road was a horse path. Next time you need to make a road, Boseman, make sure you have ten thousand starving Cherokee on hand to clear it for you. Saves time."

"Where did they go?" Cora asked. After her nights with Martin, she had a sense of when white men were on the brink of a story. It gave her time to consider her options.

Ridgeway was an ardent reader of gazettes. The fugitive bulletins made them a requirement in his line of work—Homer maintained a thorough collection—and current affairs generally upheld his theories about society and the human animal. The type of individuals in his employ had made him accustomed to explaining the most elementary facts and history. He could hardly expect a slave girl to know the significance of their environs.

They sat on what was once Cherokee land, he said, the land of their red fathers, until the president decided otherwise and ordered them removed. Settlers needed the land, and if the Indians hadn't learned by then that the white man's treaties were entirely worthless, Ridgeway said, they deserved what they got. Some of his friends had been with the army at that time. They rounded up the Indians in camps, the women and children and whatever they could carry on their backs, and marched them west of the Mississippi. The Trail of Tears and Death, as one Cherokee sage put it later, not without cause, not without that Indian flair for rhetoric. Disease and malnutrition, not to mention the biting winter that year, which Ridgeway himself remembered without fondness, claimed thousands. When they got to Oklahoma there were still more white people waiting for them, squatting on the land the Indians had been promised in the latest worthless treaty. Slow learners, the bunch. But here they were on this road today. The trip to Missouri was much more comfortable than it had been previously, tamped by little red feet.

"Progress," Ridgeway said. "My cousin got lucky and won some Indian land in the lottery, in the north part of Tennessee. Grows corn."

Cora cocked her head at the desolation. "Lucky," she said.

On their way in, Ridgeway told them that a lightning strike must have started the fire. The smoke filled the sky for hundreds of miles, tinting the sunset into gorgeous contusions of crimson and purple. This was Tennessee announcing itself: fantastic beasts twisting in a volcano. For the first time, she crossed into another state without using the underground railroad. The tunnels had protected her. The station master Lumbly had said that each state was a state of possibility, with its own customs. The red sky made her dread the rules of this next territory. As they rode toward the smoke, the sunsets inspired Jasper to share a suite of hymns whose central theme was the wrath of God and the mortifications awaiting the wicked. Boseman made frequent trips to the wagon.

The town at the edge of the fire line was overrun with escapees. "Runaways," Cora declared and Homer turned in his seat to wink. The white families swarmed in a camp off the main street, inconsolable and abject, the meager possessions they were able to save piled around their feet. Figures staggered through the street with demented expressions, wild-eyed, their clothes singed, rags tied around burns. Cora was well-accustomed to the screams of colored babies in torment, hungry, in pain, confused by the mania of those charged to protect them. Hearing the screams of so many little white babies was new. Her sympathies lay with the colored babies.

Empty shelves greeted Ridgeway and Boseman in the general store. The shopkeeper told Ridgeway that homesteaders had started the fire while trying to clear some scrub. The fire escaped them and ravaged the land with bottomless hunger until the rains came finally. Three million acres, the shopkeeper said. The government promised relief but no one could say when it would arrive. The biggest disaster in as long as anyone could remember.

The original residents had a more thorough list of wildfires and floods and tornadoes, Cora thought when Ridgeway shared the shopkeeper's words. But they were not here to contribute their knowledge. She didn't know which tribe had called this territory home, but knew it had been Indian land. What land hadn't been theirs? She had never learned history proper, but sometimes one's eyes are teacher enough.

"They must have done something to make God angry," Boseman said.

"Just a spark that got away is all," Ridgeway said.

They lingered by the road after their lunchtime meal, the white men smoking pipes by the horses and reminiscing an escapade. For all his talk of how long he had hunted her, Ridgeway displayed no urgency about delivering Cora to Terrance Randall. Not that she hurried toward that reunion. Cora stutter-stepped into the burned field. She'd learned to walk with irons. It was hard to believe it had taken this long. Cora had always pitied the downcast coffles marching in their pathetic line past the Randall place. Now look at her. The lesson was unclear. In one respect she had been spared an injury for many years. In another, misfortune had merely bided time: There was no escape. Sores puckered on her skin beneath the iron. The white men paid her no mind as she walked to the black trees.

By then she had run a few times. When they stopped for supplies, Boseman was distracted by a funeral procession rounding the corner and she made it a couple of yards before a boy tripped her. They added a neck collar, iron links dropping to her wrists like moss. It gave her the posture of a beggar or praying mantis. She ran when the men stopped to relieve themselves at the side of the trail and made it a little farther that time. She ran once at dusk, by a stream, the water making a promise of movement. The slick stones sent her tumbling into the water, and Ridgeway thrashed her. She stopped running.

THEY seldom spoke the first days after leaving North Carolina. She thought the confrontation with the mob had exhausted them as much as it had exhausted her, but silence was their policy in general—until Jasper came into their midst. Boseman whispered his rude suggestions and Homer turned back from the driver's seat to give her an unsettling grin on his inscrutable schedule, but the slave catcher kept his distance at the head of the line. Occasionally he whistled.

Cora caught on that they were heading west instead of south. She'd never paid attention to the sun's habits before Caesar. He told her it might aid their escape. They stopped in a town one morning, outside a bakery. Cora steeled herself and asked Ridgeway about his plans.

His eyes widened, as if he'd been waiting for her to approach. After this first conversation Ridgeway included her in their plans as if she had a vote. "You were a surprise," he said, "but don't worry, we'll get you home soon enough."

She was correct, he said. They were headed west. A Georgia planter named Hinton had commissioned Ridgeway to return one of his slaves. The negro in question was a wily and resourceful buck who had relatives in one of the colored settlements in Missouri; reliable information confirmed Nelson plied his trade as a trapper, in broad daylight, without concern of retribution. Hinton was a respected farmer with an enviable spread, a cousin of the governor. Regrettably, one of his overseers had gossiped with a slave wench and now Nelson's behavior made his owner an object of ridicule on his own land. Hinton had been grooming the boy to be a boss. He promised Ridgeway a generous bounty, going so far as to present a contract in a pretentious ceremony. An elderly darky served as witness, coughing into his hand the while.

Given Hinton's impatience, the most sensible course was to travel on to Missouri. "Once we have our man," Ridgeway said, "you can be reunited with your master. From what I've seen, he'll prepare a worthy welcome."

Ridgeway didn't hide his disdain for Terrance Randall; the man had what he called an "ornate" imagination when it came to nigger discipline. This much was plain from the moment his gang turned down the road to the big house and saw the three gallows. The young girl was installed in hers, hooked through her ribs by a large metal spike and dangling. The dirt below dark with her blood. The other two gallows stood waiting.

"If I hadn't been detained upstate," Ridgeway said, "I'm sure I'd have scooped up the three of you before the trail got cold. Lovey—was that its name?"

Cora covered her mouth to keep in her scream. She failed. Ridgeway waited ten minutes for her to regain her composure. The townspeople looked at the colored girl laying there collapsed on the ground and stepped over her into the bakery. The smell of the snacks filled the street, sweet and beguiling.

Boseman and Homer waited in the drive while he talked to the master of the house, Ridgeway said. The house had been lively and inviting when the father was alive—yes, he had been there before to search for Cora's mother and come up empty-handed. One minute with Terrance and the cause of the terrible atmosphere was evident. The son was mean, and it was the kind of meanness that infected everything around. The daylight was gray and sluggish from the thunderheads, the house niggers slow and glum.

The newspapers liked to impress the fantasy of the happy plantation and the contented slave who sang and danced and loved Massa. Folks enjoyed that sort of thing and it was politically useful given the combat with the northern states and the antislavery movement. Ridgeway knew that image to be false—he didn't need to dissemble about the business of slavery—but neither was the menace of the Randall plantation the truth. The place was haunted. Who could blame the slaves their sad comportment with that corpse twisting on a hook outside?

Terrance received Ridgeway into the parlor. He was drunk and had not bothered to dress himself, lounging on the sofa in a red robe. It was tragic, Ridgeway said, to see the degeneration that can happen in just one generation, but money does that to a family sometimes. Brings out the impurities. Terrance remembered Ridgeway from his earlier visit, when Mabel disappeared into the swamp, just like this latest trio. He told Ridgeway that his father had been touched that he came in person to apologize for his incompetence.

"I could have slapped the Randall boy twice across the face without losing the contract," Ridgeway said. "But in my mature years I decided to wait until I had you and the other one in hand. Something to look forward to." He assumed from Terrance's eagerness and the size of the bounty that Cora was her master's concubine.

Cora shook her head. She had stopped sobbing and stood now, her trembling under control, hands in fists.

Ridgeway paused. "Something else, then. At any rate, you exert a powerful influence." He resumed the story of his visit to Randall. Terrance briefed the slave catcher on the state of affairs since Lovey's capture. Just that morning his man Connelly had been informed that Caesar frequented the premises of a local shopkeeper—the man sold the nigger boy's woodwork, supposedly. Perhaps the slave catcher might visit this Mr. Fletcher and see what developed. Terrance wanted the girl alive but didn't care how the other one came back. Did Ridgeway know that the boy came from Virginia originally?

Ridgeway did not. This was some sort of jousting about his home state. The windows were closed and yet a disagreeable smell had moved into the room.

"That's where he learned his bad habits," Terrance had said. "They're soft up there. You make sure he learns how we do things in Georgia." He wanted the law kept out of it. The pair was wanted for the murder of a white boy and wouldn't make it back once the mob got wind. The bounty accounted for his discretion.

The slave catcher took his leave. The axle of his empty wagon complained, as it did when there was no weight to quiet it. Ridgeway promised himself it would not be empty when he returned. He wasn't going to apologize to another Randall, certainly not that whelp who ran the place now. He heard a sound and turned back to the house. It came from the girl, Lovey. Her arm fluttered. She was not dead after all. "Lingered another half day, from what I heard."

Fletcher's lies collapsed immediately—one of those weak religious specimens—and he relinquished the name of his associate on the railroad, a man named Lumbly. Of Lumbly there was no sign. He never returned after taking Cora and Caesar out of state. "To South Carolina was it?" Ridgeway asked. "Was he also the one who conveyed your mother north?"

Cora kept her tongue. It was not hard to envision Fletcher's fate, and perhaps his wife's as well. At least Lumbly made it out. And they hadn't discovered the tunnel beneath the barn. One day another desperate soul might use that route. To a better outcome, fortune willing.

Ridgeway nodded. "No matter. We have plenty of time to catch each other up. It's a long ride to Missouri." The law had caught up with a station master in southern Virginia, he said, who gave up the name of Martin's father. Donald was dead, but Ridgeway wanted to get a sense of the man's operation if he could, to understand the workings of the larger conspiracy. He hadn't expected to find Cora but had been utterly delighted.

Boseman chained her to the wagon. She knew the sound of the lock now. It hitched for a moment before falling into place. Jasper joined them the next day. His body shivered like that of a beaten dog. Cora tried to engage him, asking after the place he fled, the business of working cane, how he took flight. Jasper responded with hymns and devotions.

THAT was four days ago. Now she stood in a black pasture in bad-luck Tennessee, crunching burned wood beneath her feet.

The wind picked up, and the rain. Their stop was over. Homer cleaned after their meal. Ridgeway and Boseman tapped out their pipes and the younger man whistled for her to return. Tennessee hills and mountains rose around Cora like the sides of a black bowl. How awful the flames must have been, how fierce, to make such ruin. We're crawling in a bowl of ashes. What's left when everything worthwhile has been consumed, dark powder for the wind to take.

Boseman slid her chains through the ring in the floor and secured them. Ten rings were bolted to the wagon floor, two rows of five, enough for the occasional big haul. Enough for these two. Jasper claimed his favorite spot on the bench, crooning with vigor, as if he'd just gobbled down a Christmas feast. "When the Savior calls you up, you're going to lay the burden down, lay that burden down."

"Boseman," Ridgeway said softly.

"He's going to look in your soul and see what you done, sinner, He's going to look in your soul and see what you done."

Boseman said, "Oh."

The slave catcher got into the wagon for the first time since he picked up Cora. He held Boseman's pistol in his hand and shot Jasper in the face. The blood and the bone covered the inside of the canopy, splashing Cora's filthy shift.

Ridgeway wiped his face and explained his reasoning. Jasper's reward was fifty dollars, fifteen of that for the tinker who brought the fugitive to jail. Missouri, back east, Georgia—it would be weeks before they delivered the man to his owner. Divide thirty-five dollars by, say, three weeks, minus Boseman's share, and the lost bounty was a very small price to pay for silence and a restful mind.

Homer opened his notebook and checked his boss's figures. "He's right," he said.

Tennessee proceeded in a series of blights. The blaze had devoured the next two towns on the cindered road. In the morning the remains of a small settlement emerged around a hill, an arrangement of scorched timber and black stonework. First came the stumps of the houses that had once contained the dreams of pioneers, and then the town proper in a line of ruined structures. The town farther along was larger but its rival in destruction. The heart was a broad intersection where ravaged avenues had converged in enterprise, now gone. A baker's oven in the ruins of the shop like a grim totem, human remains bent behind the steel of a jail cell.

Cora couldn't tell what feature of the landscape had persuaded the homesteaders to plant their futures, fertile earth or water or vistas. Everything had been erased. If the survivors returned it would be to confirm the resolution to try again somewhere else, scurrying back east or ever west. No resurrection here.

Then they escaped the wildfire's reach. The birches and wild grasses vibrated with impossible color after their time in the burned land, Edenic and fortifying. In jest, Boseman imitated Jasper's singing, to mark the change in mood; the black scenery had worked on them more than they knew. The robust corn in the fields, already two feet high, pointed to an exuberant harvest; with equal force the ruined territory had advertised reckonings to come.

Ridgeway called for a stop shortly after noon. The slave

catcher stiffened as he read aloud the sign at the crossroads. The town up the road was overcome by yellow fever, he said. All travelers warned away. An alternative trail, smaller and uneven, led southwest.

The sign was new, Ridgeway observed. Most likely the sickness had not run its course.

"My two brothers passed of yellow fever," Boseman said. He grew up on the Mississippi, where the fever liked to visit when the weather turned warm. His younger brothers' skin turned jaundiced and waxen, they bled from their eyes and asses and seizures wracked their tiny bodies. Some men took away their corpses in a squeaky wheelbarrow. "It's a miserable death," he said, his jokes taken from him again.

Ridgeway knew the town. The mayor was a corrupt boor, the food turned your guts runny, but he held a good thought for them. Going around would add considerable time to their trip. "The fever comes on the boats," Ridgeway said. From the West Indies, all the way from the dark continent, following in the wake of trade. "It's a human tax on progress."

"Who's the taxman came to collect it?" Boseman said. "I never saw him." His fear made him skittish and petulant. He didn't want to linger, even this crossroads too close to the fever's embrace. Not waiting for Ridgeway's order—or obeying a signal shared only by the slave catcher and the boy secretary—Homer drove the wagon away from the doomed town.

Two more signs along the southwesterly course maintained the warning. The trails feeding into the quarantined towns displayed no sign of the danger ahead. Traveling through the handiwork of the fire for so long made an unseeable menace more terrifying. It was a long time, after dark, before they stopped again. Time enough for Cora to take stock of her journey from Randall and make a thick braid of her misfortunes.

List upon list crowded the ledger of slavery. The names gathered first on the African coast in tens of thousands of manifests. That human cargo. The names of the dead were as important as the names of the living, as every loss from disease and suicide—and the other mishaps labeled as such for accounting purposes—needed to be justified to employers. At the auction block they tallied the souls purchased at each auction, and on the plantations the overseers preserved the names of workers in rows of tight cursive. Every name an asset, breathing capital, profit made flesh.

The peculiar institution made Cora into a maker of lists as well. In her inventory of loss people were not reduced to sums but multiplied by their kindnesses. People she had loved, people who had helped her. The Hob women, Lovey, Martin and Ethel, Fletcher. The ones who disappeared: Caesar and Sam and Lumbly. Jasper was not her responsibility, but the stains of his blood on the wagon and her clothes might as well have represented her own dead.

Tennessee was cursed. Initially she assigned the devastation of Tennessee—the blaze and the disease—to justice. The whites got what they deserved. For enslaving her people, for massacring another race, for stealing the very land itself. Let them burn by flame or fever, let the destruction started here rove acre by acre until the dead have been avenged. But if people received their just portion of misfortune, what had she done to bring her troubles on herself? In another list, Cora marked the decisions that led her to this wagon and its iron rings. There was the boy Chester, and how she had shielded him. The whip was the standard punishment for disobedience. Running away was a transgression so large that the punishment enveloped every generous soul on her brief tour of freedom.

Bouncing on the wagon springs, she smelled the damp earth and the heaving trees. Why had this field escaped while another burned five miles back? Plantation justice was mean and constant, but the world was indiscriminate. Out in the world, the wicked escaped comeuppance and the decent stood in their stead at the whipping tree. Tennessee's disasters were the fruit of indifferent nature, without connection to the crimes of the homesteaders. To how the Cherokee had lived their lives.

Just a spark that got away.

No chains fastened Cora's misfortunes to her character or actions. Her skin was black and this was how the world treated black people. No more, no less. Every state is different, Lumbly said. If Tennessee had a temperament, it took after the dark personality of the world, with a taste for arbitrary punishment. No one was spared, regardless of the shape of their dreams or the color of their skin.

A young man with curly brown hair, pebbly eyes dark beneath his straw hat, drove a team of workhorses from the west. His cheeks were sunburned a painful red. He intercepted Ridgeway's gang. A big settlement lay ahead, the man said, with a reputation for a rambunctious spirit. Free of yellow fever as of that morning. Ridgeway told the man what lay ahead of him and gave his thanks.

Immediately the traffic on the road resumed, even the animals and insects contributing activity. The four travelers were returned to the sights and sounds and smells of civilization. On the outskirts of the town, lamps glowed in the farmhouses and shacks, the families settling in for the evening. The town rose into view, the biggest Cora had seen since North Carolina, if not as long established. The long main street, with its two banks and the loud row of taverns, was enough to bring her back to the days of the dormitory. The town gave no indication of quieting for the night, shops open, citizens a-prowl on the wooden sidewalks.

Boseman was adamant about not spending the night. If the fever was so close it might strike here next, perhaps it already churned in the bodies of the townspeople. Ridgeway was irritated but gave in, even though he missed a proper bed. They'd camp up the road after they resupplied.

Cora remained chained to the wagon as the men pursued errands. Strollers caught her face through the openings in the canvas and looked away. They had hard faces. Their clothes were coarse and homespun, less fine than the white people's clothes in the eastern towns. The clothes of settlers, not of the settled.

Homer climbed in the wagon whistling one of Jasper's more monotonous ditties. The dead slave still among them. The boy held a bundle wrapped in brown paper. "This is for you," he said.

The dress was dark blue with white buttons, soft cotton that gave off a medicinal smell. She held up the dress so that it blocked the blood stains on the canvas, which were stark on the fabric from the streetlamps outside.

"Put it on, Cora," Homer said.

Cora raised her hands, the chains making a noise.

He unlocked her ankles and wrists. As she did every time, Cora considered the chances of escape and came up with the dead result. A town like this, rough and wild, made good mobs, she figured. Had news of the boy in Georgia reached here? The accident she never thought about and which she didn't include in her list of transgressions. The boy belonged on his own list—but what were its terms?

Homer watched her as she dressed, like a valet who had waited on her since the cradle.

"I'm caught," Cora said. "You choose to be with him."

Homer looked puzzled. He took out his notebook, turned to the last page, and scribbled. When he was finished, the boy fixed her manacles again. He gave her ill-fitting wooden shoes. He was about to chain Cora to the wagon when Ridgeway said to bring her outside.

Boseman was still out after a barber and a bath. The slave catcher handed Homer the gazettes and the fugitive bulletins he'd collected from the deputy in the jail. "I'm taking Cora for some supper," Ridgeway said, and led her into the racket. Homer dropped her filthy shift into the gutter, the brown of the dried blood seeping into the mud.

The wooden shoes pinched. Ridgeway didn't alter his stride to accommodate Cora's hindered pace, walking ahead of her and unconcerned that she might run. Her chains were a cowbell. The white people of Tennessee took no notice of her. A young negro leaned against the wall of a stable, the only person to register her presence. A freeman from his appearance, dressed in striped gray trousers and a vest of cowhide. He watched her move as she had watched the coffles trudge past Randall. To see chains on another person and be glad they are not your own—such was the good fortune permitted colored people, defined by how much worse it could be any moment. If your eyes met, both parties looked away. But this man did not. He nodded before passersby took him from view.

Cora had peeked inside Sam's saloon in South Carolina but never crossed the threshold. If she was an odd vision in their midst, one look from Ridgeway made the patrons return to their own business. The fat man tending the bar rolled tobacco and stared at the back of Ridgeway's head.

Ridgeway led her to a wobbly table against the rear wall. The smell of stewed meat rose above that of the old beer soaked into the floorboards and the walls and the ceiling. The pigtailed maid was a broad-shouldered girl with the thick arms of a cotton loader. Ridgeway ordered their food.

"The shoes were not my first choice," he told Cora, "but the dress suits you."

"It's clean," Cora said.

"Now, well. Can't have our Cora looking like the floor of a butcher's shop."

He meant to elicit a reaction. Cora declined. From the saloon next door, a piano started up. It sounded as if a raccoon ran back and forth, mashing on the keys.

"All this time you haven't asked about your accomplice," Ridgeway said. "Caesar. Did it make the newspapers up in North Carolina?"

This was going to be a performance then, like one of the Friday-night pageants on the park. He had her dress up for night at the theater. She waited.

"It's so strange going to South Carolina," Ridgeway said, "now that they have their new system. Had many a caper there in the old days. But the old days aren't that far off. For all their talk of negro uplift and civilizing the savage, it's the same hungry place it always was."

The maid delivered bread heels and bowls full of beef and potato stew. Ridgeway whispered to her while looking at Cora, something she couldn't hear. The girl laughed. Cora realized he was drunk.

Ridgeway slurped. "We caught up with it at the factory at the end of its shift," he said. "These big colored bucks around it, finding their old fear again after thinking they'd put it behind them. At first, wasn't no big fuss. Another runaway caught. Then word spread that Caesar was wanted for the murder of a little boy—"

"Not little," Cora said.

Ridgeway shrugged. "They broke into the jail. The sheriff opened the door, to be honest, but that's not as dramatic. They broke into the jail and ripped its body to pieces. The decent people of South Carolina with their schoolhouses and Friday credit."

News of Lovey had broken her down in front of him. Not this time. She was prepared—his eyes brightened when he was on the verge of a cruelty. And she had known Caesar was dead for a long time now. No need to ask after his fate. It appeared before her one night in the attic like a spark, a small and simple truth: Caesar did not make it out. He was not up north wearing a new suit, new shoes, new smile. Sitting in the dark, nestled into the rafters, Cora understood that she was alone again. They had got him. She had finished mourning him by the time Ridgeway came knocking on Martin's door.

Ridgeway plucked gristle from his mouth. "I made a little silver for the capture at any rate, and returned another boy to its master along the way. Profit in the end."

"You scrape like an old darky for that Randall money," Cora said.

Ridgeway laid his big hands on the uneven table, tilting it to his side. Stew ran over the rim of the bowls. "They should fix this," he said.

The stew was lumpy with the thickening flour. Cora mashed the lumps with her tongue the way she did when one of Alice's helpers had prepared the meal and not the old cook herself. Through the wall the piano player bit into an upbeat ditty. A drunken couple dashed next door to dance.

"Jasper wasn't killed by no mob," Cora said.

"There are always unexpected expenses," Ridgeway said. "I'm not going to get reimbursed for all the food I fed it."

"You go on about reasons," Cora said. "Call things by other names as if it changes what they are. But that don't make them true. You killed Jasper in cold blood."

"That was more of a personal matter," Ridgeway conceded, "and not what I'm talking about here. You and your friend killed a boy. You have your justifications."

"I was going to escape."

"That's all I'm talking about, survival. Do you feel awful about it?"

The boy's death was a complication of her escape, like the absence of a full moon or losing the head start because Lovey had been discovered out of her cabin. But shutters swung out inside her and she saw the boy trembling on his sickbed, his mother weeping over his grave. Cora had been grieving for him, too, without knowing it. Another person caught in this enterprise that bound slave and master alike. She moved the boy from the lonely list in her head and logged him below Martin and Ethel, even though she did not know his name. X, as she signed herself before she learned her letters.

Nonetheless. She told Ridgeway, "No."

"Of course not—it's nothing. Better weep for one of those burned cornfields, or this steer swimming in our soup. You do what's required to survive." He wiped his lips. "It's true, though, your complaint. We come up with all sorts of fancy talk to hide things. Like in the newspapers nowadays, all the smart men talking about Manifest Destiny. Like it's a new idea. You don't know what I'm talking about, do you?" Ridgeway asked.

Cora sat back. "More words to pretty things up."

"It means taking what is yours, your property, whatever you deem it to be. And everyone else taking their assigned places to allow you to take it. Whether it's red men or Africans, giving up themselves, giving of themselves, so that we can have what's rightfully ours. The French setting aside their territorial claims. The British and the Spanish slinking away.

"My father liked his Indian talk about the Great Spirit," Ridgeway said. "All these years later, I prefer the American spirit, the one that called us from the Old World to the New, to conquer and build and civilize. And destroy that what needs to be destroyed.

To lift up the lesser races. If not lift up, subjugate. And if not subjugate, exterminate. Our destiny by divine prescription—the American imperative."

"I need to visit the outhouse," Cora said.

The corners of his mouth sank. He gestured for her to walk in front. The steps to the back alley were slippery with vomit and he grabbed her elbow to steady her. Closing the outhouse door, shutting him out, was the purest pleasure she'd had in a long while.

Ridgeway continued his address undeterred. "Take your mother," the slave catcher said. "Mabel. Stolen from her master by misguided whites and colored individuals in a criminal conspiracy. I kept an eye out all this time, turned Boston and New York upside down, all the colored settlements. Syracuse. Northampton. She's up in Canada, laughing at the Randalls and me. I take it as a personal injury. That's why I bought you that dress. To help me picture her wrapped like a present for her master."

He hated her mother as much as she did. That, and the fact they both had eyes in their head, meant they had two things in common.

Ridgeway paused—a drunk wanted to use the privy. He shooed him away. "You absconded for ten months," he said. "Insult enough. You and your mother are a line that needs to be extinguished. A week together, chained up, and you sass me without end, on your way to a bloody homecoming. The abolitionist lobby loves to trot out your kind, to give speeches to white people who have no idea how the world works."

The slave catcher was wrong. If she'd made it north she would have disappeared into a life outside their terms. Like her mother. One thing the woman had passed on to her.

"We do our part," Ridgeway said, "slave and slave catcher. Master and colored boss. The new arrivals streaming into the harbors and the politicians and sheriffs and newspapermen and the mothers raising strong sons. People like you and your mother are the best of your race. The weak of your tribe have been weeded out, they die in the slave ships, die of our European pox, in the fields working our cotton and indigo. You need to be strong to survive the labor and to make us greater. We fatten hogs, not because it pleases us but because we need hogs to survive. But we can't have you too clever. We can't have you so fit you outrun us."

She finished her business and picked out a fugitive bulletin from the stack of paper to wipe herself. Then she waited. A pitiful respite, but it was hers.

"You heard my name when you were a pickaninny," he said. "The name of punishment, dogging every fugitive step and every thought of running away. For every slave I bring home, twenty others abandon their full-moon schemes. I'm a notion of order. The slave that disappears—it's a notion, too. Of hope. Undoing what I do so that a slave the next plantation over gets an idea that it can run, too. If we allow that, we accept the flaw in the imperative. And I refuse."

The music from next door was slow now. Couples coming together to hold each other, to sway and twist. That was real conversation, dancing slow with another person, not all these words. She knew that, even though she had never danced like that with another person and had refused Caesar when he asked. The only person to ever extend a hand to her and say, Come closer. Maybe everything the slave catcher said was true, Cora thought, every justification, and the sons of Ham were cursed and the slave master performed the Lord's will. And maybe he was just a man talking to an outhouse door, waiting for someone to wipe her ass.

CORA and Ridgeway returned to the wagon to find Homer rubbing his small thumbs on the reins and Boseman sipping whiskey from a bottle. "This town is sick with it," Boseman said, slurring. "I can smell it." The younger man led the way out of town. He shared his disappointments. The shave and bath had gone well; with a fresh face the man looked almost innocent. But he had not been able to perform like a man at the brothel. "The madam was sweating like a pig and I knew they had the fever, her and her whores." Ridgeway let him decide how far was far enough to camp.

She had been asleep for a short time when Boseman crept in and put his hand over her mouth. She was ready.

Boseman put his fingers to his lips. Cora nodded as much as his grip permitted: She would not cry out. She could make a fuss now and wake Ridgeway; Boseman would give him some excuse and that would be the end of it. But she had thought about this moment for days, of when Boseman let his carnal desires get the best of him. It was the most drunk he'd been since North Carolina. He complimented her dress when they stopped for the night. She steeled herself. If she could persuade him to unshackle her, a dark night like this was made for running.

Homer snored loudly. Boseman slipped her chains from the wagon ring, careful not to let the links sound against each other. He undid her ankles and cinched her wrist chains to silence them. He descended first and helped Cora out. She could just make out the road a few yards away. Dark enough.

Ridgeway knocked him to the ground with a growl and started kicking him. Boseman started his defense and Ridgeway kicked him in the mouth. She almost ran. She almost did. But the quickness of the violence, the blade of it, arrested her. Ridgeway scared her. When Homer came to the back of the wagon with a lantern and revealed Ridgeway's face, the slave catcher was staring at her with untempered fury. She'd had her chance and missed it and at the look on his face was relieved.

"What are you going to do now, Ridgeway?" Boseman wept.

He was leaning against the wagon wheel for support. He looked at the blood on his hands. His necklace had snapped and the ears made it look like the dirt was listening. "Crazy Ridgeway, does as he pleases. I'm the last one left. Only Homer left to beat on when I'm gone," he said. "I think he'll like it."

Homer chuckled. He got Cora's ankle chains from the wagon. Ridgeway rubbed his knuckles, breathing heavily.

"It is a nice dress," Boseman said. He pulled out a tooth.

"There'll be more teeth if any of you fellows move," the man said. The three of them stepped into the light.

The speaker was the young negro from town, the one who nodded at her. He didn't look at her now, monitoring Ridgeway. His wire spectacles reflected the lantern's glow, as if the flame burned inside him. His pistol wavered between the two white men like a dowser's stick.

A second man held a rifle. He was tall and well-muscled, dressed in thick work clothes that struck her as a costume. He had a wide face and his long red-brown hair was combed up into a fan like a lion's mane. The man's posture said that he did not enjoy taking orders, and the insolence in his eyes was not slave insolence, an impotent pose, but a hard fact. The third man waved a bowie knife. His body shook with nerves, his quick breathing the night sound between his companion's talk. Cora recognized his bearing. It was that of a runaway, one unsure of the latest turn in the escape. She'd seen it in Caesar, in the bodies of the new arrivals to the dormitories, and knew she'd exhibited it many times. He extended the trembling knife in Homer's direction.

She had never seen colored men hold guns. The image shocked her, a new idea too big to fit into her mind.

"You boys are lost," Ridgeway said. He didn't have a weapon.

"Lost in that we don't like Tennessee much and would rather be home, yes," the leader said. "You seem lost yourself."

Boseman coughed and traded a glance with Ridgeway. He sat up and tensed. The two rifles turned to him.

Their leader said, "We're going to be on our way but we thought we'd ask the lady if she wanted to come with us. We're a better sort of traveling companion."

"Where you boys from?" Ridgeway said. He talked in a way that told Cora he was scheming.

"All over," the man said. The north lived in his voice, his accent from up there, like Caesar. "But we found each other and now we work together. You settle down, Mr. Ridgeway." He moved his head slightly. "I heard him call you Cora. Is that your name?"

She nodded.

"She's Cora," Ridgeway said. "You know me. That's Boseman, and that's Homer."

At his name, Homer threw the lantern at the man holding the knife. The glass didn't break until it hit the ground after bouncing off the man's chest. The fire splashed. The leader fired at Ridgeway and missed. The slave catcher tackled him and they both tumbled into the dirt. The red-headed rifleman was a better shot. Boseman flew back, a black flower blooming suddenly on his belly.

Homer ran to get a gun, followed by the rifleman. The boy's hat rolled into the fire. Ridgeway and his opponent scuffled in the dirt, grunting and hollering. They rolled over to the edge of the burning oil. Cora's fear from moments ago returned—Ridgeway had trained her well. The slave catcher got the upper hand, pinning the man to the ground.

She could run. She only had chains on her wrists now.

Cora jumped on Ridgeway's back and strangled him with her chains, twisting them tight against his flesh. Her scream came from deep inside her, a train whistle echoing in a tunnel. She yanked and squeezed. The slave catcher threw his body to smear her into the ground. By the time he shook her off, the man from town had his pistol again.

The runaway helped Cora to her feet. "Who's that boy?" he said.

Homer and the rifleman hadn't returned. The leader instructed the man with the knife to have a look, keeping the gun on Ridgeway.

The slave catcher rubbed his thick fingers into his ravaged neck. He did not look at Cora, which made her fearful again.

Boseman whimpered. He burbled, "He's going to look in your soul and see what you done, sinner . . ." The light from the burning oil was inconstant, but they had no trouble making out the widening puddle of blood.

"He's going to bleed to death," Ridgeway said.

"It's a free country," the man from town said.

"This is not your property," Ridgeway said.

"That's what the law says. White law. There are other ones." He addressed Cora in a gentler tone. "If you want, miss, I can shoot him for you." His face was calm.

She wanted every bad thing for Ridgeway and Boseman. And Homer? She didn't know what her heart wanted for the strange black boy, who seemed an emissary from a different country.

Before she could speak, the man said, "Though we'd prefer to put irons on them." Cora retrieved his spectacles from the dirt and cleaned them with her sleeve and the three of them waited. His companions returned empty-handed.

Ridgeway smiled as the men shackled his wrists through the wagon wheel.

"The boy is a devious sort," the leader said. "I can tell that. We have to go." He looked at Cora. "Will you come with us?"

Cora kicked Ridgeway in the face three times with her new

wooden shoes. She thought, If the world will not stir itself to punish the wicked. No one stopped her. Later she said it was three kicks for three murders, and told of Lovey, Caesar, and Jasper to let them live briefly again in her words. But that was not the truth of it. It was all for her.

Caesar

THE excitement over Jockey's birthday allowed Caesar to visit his only refuge on Randall. The dilapidated schoolhouse by the stables was generally empty. At night lovers sneaked in, but he never went there at night—he required light, and he was not going to risk lighting a candle. He went to the schoolhouse to read the book Fletcher gave him after much protest; he went when feeling low, to weep over his burdens; he went to watch the other slaves move about the plantation. From the window it was as if he were not one of their unlucky tribe but only observing their commerce, as one might watch strangers stroll past one's front door. In the schoolhouse it was as if he were not there at all.

Enslaved. In fear. Sentenced to death.

If his scheme came to fruition, this would be the last time he celebrated Jockey's birthday. God willing. Knowing him, the old man was apt to announce another one next month. The quarter was so jubilant over the tiny pleasures they scavenged together on Randall. A made-up birthday, a dance after toiling under the harvest moon. In Virginia the celebrations were spectacular. Caesar and his family rode in the widow's buggy to the farms of freemen, they visited relatives on estates for the Lord's holidays and New Year's Day. The pigs and venison steaks, ginger pies and cornbread cakes. The games went all day long, until Caesar and his companions fell in panting collapse. The masters in Virginia kept their distance those festival days. How could these Randall slaves truly enjoy themselves with that dumb menace waiting at the sidelines, poised to swoop? They didn't know their birthdays so had to invent them. Half these folks didn't know their mothers and fathers.

I was born on August 14th. My mother's name is Lily Jane. My father is Jerome. I don't know where they are.

Through the schoolhouse window, framed by two of the older cabins—their whitewash smeared to gray, worn down like those who slept inside them—Cora huddled with her favorite at the starting line. Chester, the boy who prowled the quarter with such enviable cheer. Obviously he'd never been beaten.

The boy turned his head shyly from something Cora said. She smiled—quickly. She smiled at Chester, and Lovey and the women from her cabin, with brevity and efficiency. Like when you see the shadow of a bird on the ground but look up and nothing's there. She subsisted on rations, in everything. Caesar had never spoken to her but had this figured out about her. It was sensible: She knew the preciousness of what little she called her own. Her joys, her plot, that block of sugar maple she perched on like a vulture.

He was drinking corn whiskey with Martin in the barn loft one night—the boy wouldn't say where he got the jug—when they started talking about the women of Randall. Who was most likely to mush your face into their titties, who'd scream so loud the whole quarter would know, and who would never tell. Caesar asked about Cora.

"Nigger don't fool with no Hob woman," Martin said. "They cut your thing off and make soup with it." He told him the old story of Cora and her garden and Blake's doghouse, and Caesar thought, That sounds about right. Then Martin said she liked to sneak out to fornicate with swamp animals, and Caesar realized the cotton picker was dumber than he thought.

None of the Randall men was that bright. The place had undone them. They joked and they picked fast when the bosses' eyes were on them and they acted big, but at night in the cabin after midnight they wept, they screamed from nightmares and wretched memories. In Caesar's cabin, in the next cabins over, and in every slave village near and far. When the work was done, and the day's punishments, the night waited as an arena for their true loneliness and despair.

Cheers and shouts—another race done. Cora set her hands on her hips, head tilted as if hunting after a tune hidden in the noise. How to capture that profile in wood, preserve her grace and strength—he didn't trust himself not to botch it. Picking had ruined his hands for delicate woodwork. The slope of a woman's cheek, lips in the midst of a whisper. His arms trembled at the end of the day, muscles throbbing.

How the old white bitch had lied! He should have been living with his mother and father in their cottage, rounding off barrels for the cooper or apprenticed to another of the town's craftsmen. His prospects were limited by his race, to be sure, but Caesar had grown up believing he was free to choose his own fate. "You can be whatever you want to be," his father said.

"Even go to Richmond?" From all reports, Richmond sounded far away and splendid.

"Even Richmond, if you like."

But the old woman had lied and now his crossroad was reduced to one destination, a slow death in Georgia. For him, for his entire family. His mother was slight and delicate and not made for field labor, she was too kind to endure the plantation's battery of cruelties. His father would hold out longer, donkey that he was, but not much. The old woman had destroyed his family so thoroughly it couldn't have been accidental. It wasn't her niece's greed—the old woman had played a trick on them the whole time. Tightening the knots every time she held Caesar in her lap and taught him a word.

Caesar pictured his father cutting cane in a Florida hell, burning his flesh as he stooped over the big kettles of molten sugar. The cat-o'-nine-tails biting into his mother's back when she failed to keep the pace with her sack. Stubborn breaks when it don't bend, and his family had spent too much time with the kindly white folks in the north. Kindly in that they didn't see fit to kill you fast. One thing about the south, it was not patient when it came to killing negroes.

In the old crippled men and women of the plantation he saw what lay in store for his mother and father. In time, what would become of him. At night, he was certain they were dead; in the daylight, merely maimed and half dead. Either way he was alone in the world.

Caesar approached her after the races. Of course she waved him away. She didn't know him. It could've been a prank, or a trap laid by the Randalls in a fit of boredom. Running was too big an idea—you had to let it set a while, turn it around in your head. It took Caesar months to permit it into his thoughts, and he needed Fletcher's encouragement to let it truly live. You need someone else to help you along. Even if she didn't know she'd say yes, he did. He'd told her he wanted her for good luck—her mother was the only one to ever make it out. Probably a mistake, if not an insult, to someone like her. She wasn't a rabbit's foot to carry with you on the voyage but the locomotive itself. He couldn't do it without her.

The terrible incident at the dance proved it. One of the house slaves told him the brothers were drinking at the big house. Caesar took it as a bad omen. When the boy carried the lantern down to the quarter, his masters following, violence was assured. Chester had never been beaten. Now he had been, and tomorrow he'd get his first hiding. No more children's games for him, races and hide-and-seek, but the grim trials of slave men. No one else in the village made a move to help the boy—how could they? They'd seen it a hundred times before, as victim or witness, and would see it a hundred times more until they died. But Cora did. She shielded the boy with her own body and took his blows for him. She was a stray through and through, so far off the path it was like she'd already run from the place long ago.

After the beating Caesar visited the schoolhouse at night for the first time. Just to hold the book in his hands. To make sure it was still there, a souvenir from a time when he had all the books he wanted, and all the time to read them.

What became of my companions in the boat, as well as those who escaped on the rock, or were left in the vessel, I cannot tell; but conclude they were all lost. The book will get him killed, Fletcher warned. Caesar hid *Travels into Several Remote Nations* in the dirt under the schoolhouse, wrapped in two swatches of burlap. Wait a little longer until we can make the preparations for your escape, the shopkeeper said. Then you can have any book you want. But if he didn't read, he was a slave. Before the book the only thing to read was what came written on a bag of rice. The name of the firm that manufactured their chains, imprinted in the metal like a promise of pain.

Now a page here and there, in the golden afternoon light, sustained him. Guile and pluck, guile and pluck. The white man in the book, Gulliver, roved from peril to peril, each new island a new predicament to solve before he could return home. That was the man's real trouble, not the savage and uncanny civilizations he encountered—he kept forgetting what he had. That was white people all over: Build a schoolhouse and let it rot, make a home then keep straying. If Caesar figured the route home, he'd never travel again. Otherwise he was liable to go from one troublesome island to the next, never recognizing where he was, until the world ran out. Unless she came with him. With Cora, he'd find the way home.

Indiana

50 **REWARD.**

LEFT my house on Friday evening the 26th about 10 o'clock P.M. (without provocation whatever) my negro girl SUKEY. She is about 28 years of age, of rather a light complexion, has high cheek bones, is slender in her person, and very neat in her appearance. Had on when she went away, a striped jean frock. Sukey was lately owned by L. B. Pearce, Esq. and formerly belonged to William M. Heritage, deceased. She is at present (from appearance) a strict member of the Methodist Church in this place, and is no doubt known to a majority of the members.

JAMES AYKROYD
OCTOBER 4

THEN she became the one lagging in her lessons, surrounded by impatient children. Cora was proud of the progress she made with her reading in South Carolina and the attic. The shaky footing of every new word, an unknown territory to struggle through letter by letter. She claimed each circuit through Donald's almanacs as a victory, then returned to the first page for another round.

Georgina's classroom revealed the smallness of her accomplishments. She didn't recognize the Declaration of Independence the day she joined them in the meeting house. The children's pronunciation was crisp and mature, so distant from Michael's stiff recitations back on Randall. Music lived in the words now, the melody asserting itself as each child took their turn, bold and confident. The boys and girls stood from the pews, turned over the paper where they'd copied the words, and sang the promises of the Founding Fathers.

With Cora, the class numbered twenty-five. The youngest— the six- and seven-year-olds—were exempt from the recital. They whispered and fussed in the pews until Georgina hushed them. Nor did Cora participate, being new to the class, the farm, their way of doing things. She felt conspicuous, older than all of them and so far behind. Cora understood why old Howard had wept, back in Miss Handler's schoolhouse. An interloper, like a rodent that had chewed through the wall.

One of the cooks rang the bell, drawing the lesson to a close. After the meal, the younger students would return to their lessons while the older ones took to their chores. On their way out of the meeting house, Cora stopped Georgina and said, "You taught these pickaninnies how to give a proper talk, that's for sure."

The teacher checked to make sure her students hadn't heard Cora. She said, "Here we call them children."

Cora's cheeks got hot. She'd never been able to make out what it meant, she added quickly. Did they know what was in all those big words?

Georgina hailed from Delaware and had that vexing way of Delaware ladies, delighting in puzzles. Cora had met a few of them on Valentine and didn't care for that regional peculiarity, even if they knew how to bake a good pie. Georgina said the children make of it what they can. What they don't understand today, they might tomorrow. "The Declaration is like a map. You trust that it's right, but you only know by going out and testing it yourself."

"You believe that?" Cora asked. From the teacher's face, she didn't know what to make of her.

Four months had passed since that first class. The harvest was done. Fresh arrivals to the Valentine farm made it so Cora was no longer the greenhorn, bumbling about. Two men Cora's age joined the lessons in the meeting house, eager runaways more ignorant than she was. They ran their fingers over the books as if the things were goofered, hopping with magic. Cora knew her way around. When to prepare her own meal because today's cook would muddle the soup, when to bring a shawl because Indiana nights were a shiver, colder than she'd ever known. The quiet places of shade to be alone.

Cora sat in the front of the class nowadays, and when Georgina corrected her—on her penmanship or arithmetic or speech— she no longer smarted. They were friends. Georgina was such a dedicated gossip that the lessons provided a reprieve from her constant reports on the farm's goings-on. *That strapping man from*

Virginia has a mischievous look, don't you think? Patricia ate all the pig's feet when we turned our backs. Delaware women liked to flap their gums, that was another thing.

This particular afternoon, Cora walked out with Molly once the bell sounded. She shared a cabin with the girl and her mother. Molly was ten years old, almond-eyed and reserved, careful with her affections. She had many friends but preferred to stand just outside the circle. The girl kept a green jar in her room for her treasures—marbles, arrowheads, a locket without a face—and got more pleasure from spreading them on the cabin floor, feeling the cool of blue quartz on her cheek, than playing outside.

Which was why their routine of late delighted Cora. Cora had started braiding the girl's hair on the mornings when her mother left for work early, and the last few days Molly had reached for her hand when school ended. A new thing between them. Molly tugged her along, squeezing hard, and Cora enjoyed being led. She hadn't been chosen by one of the little ones since Chester.

There was no noon meal on account of that night's big Saturday supper, the smell of which impelled the students to the barbecue pits. The barbecue men had been cooking the hogs since midnight, casting a spell property-wide. More than one of the residents had dreamed of gorging on a magnificent banquet, only to wake up devastated. Hours to go. Cora and Molly joined the hungry spectators.

Over the smoky greenwood coals, long sticks splayed out the two hogs. Jimmy was the pit master. His father had grown up in Jamaica and had passed down the fire secrets of the Maroons. Jimmy poked the roasting meat with his fingers and nudged the coals, prowling around the fire as if sizing up a grappling partner. He was one of the more wizened residents on the farm, late from North Carolina and the massacres, and preferred his meat melting soft. He only had two teeth.

One of his apprentices shook a jug of vinegar and pepper. He motioned to a little girl at the edge of the fire and guided her hands to mop the insides of the hog with the mixture. The drippings popped on the coals in the trenches. White plumes of smoke sent the crowd back and the girl squealed. It would be a fine meal.

CORA and Molly had an appointment at home. It was a short walk. Like most of the farm's work buildings, the older log cabins bunched on the eastern edge, put up in a hurry before they knew how big the community would become. Folks came from all over, plantations that had favored this or that arrangement of quarters, so the cabins came in various shapes. The newer ones—the latest additions the men put up now that the corn was picked—followed an identical style, with more spacious rooms, and were distributed on the property with more care.

Since Harriet had married and moved out, Cora, Molly, and Sybil were the only inhabitants of their cabin, sleeping in the two rooms off the main living area. In general, three families lived in each house. Newcomers and visitors shared Cora's room from time to time, but for the most part the other two beds were empty.

Her own room. Another unlikely gift from the Valentine farm after all her prisons.

Sybil and her daughter were proud of their house. They'd whitewashed the exterior with quicklime, tinted it pink. Yellow paint with white trim made the front room hum in the sunlight. Decorated with wildflowers in the warm season, the room remained pleasant in the autumn with wreaths of red and gold leaves. Purple curtains bunched in the windows. Two carpenters who lived on the farm lugged in furniture now and again—they were sweet on Sybil and kept their hands busy to distract from her indifference. Sybil had dyed some burlap sacks to make a carpet, which Cora laid on when she got one of her headaches. The front room had a nice breeze that took the bite out of the attacks.

Molly called after her mother when they reached the porch. Sarsaparilla boiled for one of Sybil's tonics, overpowering the aroma of the roasting meat. Cora headed straight to the rocking chair, which she'd claimed as hers on her first day. Molly and Sybil didn't mind. It creaked extravagantly, the handiwork of Sybil's less talented suitor. Sybil was of the mind that he'd made it loud on purpose, to remind her of his devotion.

Sybil emerged from the back, wringing her hands on her apron. "Jimmy working hard out there," she said, shaking her head in hunger.

"I can't wait," Molly said. The girl opened the pine chest by the hearth and removed their quilting. She was steadfast on finishing her latest project by supper.

They got to it. Cora hadn't picked up a needle apart from simple mending since Mabel left. Some of the Hob women tried to teach her to no avail. As she did in the classroom, Cora kept looking over at her companions for guidance. She cut out a bird, a cardinal; it came out looking like something dogs had fought over. Sybil and Molly encouraged her—they had badgered her into their pastime—but the quilt was botched. Fleas had found the batting, she insisted. The seams puckered, her corners unjoined. The quilt betrayed a crookedness in her thinking: run it up a pole as the flag of her wild country. She wanted to set it aside but Sybil forbid her. "You start something else when this one finished," Sybil said. "But this ain't finished yet."

Cora needed no advice on the virtues of perseverance. But she picked up the creature in her lap and picked at where she'd left off.

Sybil was twelve years her senior. Her dresses made her look slightly built, but Cora knew that it was merely her time away from the plantation working on the woman in the best way: Her new life required a different sort of strength. She was meticulous in her posture, a walking spear, in the manner of those who'd been made to bend and will bend no more. Her master had been a terror, Sybil told Cora, a tobacco man who competed with the neighboring planters every year over the biggest crop. His poor showing stirred him to malice. "He work us hard," she'd say, her thoughts lighting out to old miseries. Molly would come over from wherever she was and sit on her lap, nuzzling.

The three of them worked wordlessly for a while. A cheer went up over by the barbecue pit, as it did each time they turned the hogs. Cora was too distracted to reverse her mistakes in the quilt. The silent theater of Sybil and Molly's love moved her always. The way the child asked for assistance without speaking and the mother pointed, nodded, and pantomimed her child out of a fix. Cora wasn't accustomed to a quiet cabin—on Randall there was always a shriek or cry or sigh to break a moment—and certainly not accustomed to this type of maternal performance.

Sybil had absconded with Molly when her daughter was only two, toting her child all the way. Rumors from the big house held that their master meant to dispose of some property to cover debts from the disappointing crop. Sybil faced a public sale. She left that night—the full moon gave its blessing and guidance through the forest. "Molly didn't make no sound," Sybil said. "She knew what we were up to." Three miles over the Pennsylvania border they risked a visit to the cottage of a colored farmer. The man fed them, whittled toys for the little girl, and, through a line of intermediaries, contacted the railroad. After a spell in Worcester working for a milliner, Sybil and Molly made their way to Indiana. Word had spread of the farm.

So many fugitives had passed through Valentine—there was no telling who might have spent time there. Did Sybil happen to make the acquaintance of a woman from Georgia? Cora asked her one evening. Cora had been with them for a few weeks. Slept the night through once or twice, put back some of the weight she'd lost in the attic. The dry flies cut out their noise, leaving an opening in the night for a question. A woman from Georgia, maybe went by the name of Mabel, maybe not?

Sybil shook her head.

Of course she hadn't. A woman who leaves her daughter behind becomes someone else to hide the shame of it. But Cora asked everyone on the farm sooner or later, the farm being its own kind of depot, attracting people who were between places. She asked those who'd been on Valentine for years, she asked all the new people, pestered the visitors who came to the farm to see if what they'd heard was true. The free men and women of color, the fugitives who stayed and the ones who moved on. She asked them in the cornfield between a work song, rumbling in the back of a buggy on the way to town: gray eyes, scar across the back of her right hand from a burn, maybe went by the name of Mabel, maybe not?

"Maybe she in Canada," Lindsey answered when Cora decided it was her turn. Lindsey being a slim, hummingbird woman fresh out of Tennessee, who maintained a demented cheer that Cora couldn't understand. From what she saw, Tennessee was fire, disease, and violence. Even if it was there that Royal and them had rescued her. "Lot of folks, they fond of Canada now," Megan said. "Though it's awful cold."

Cold nights for the coldhearted.

Cora folded her quilt and retired to her room. She curled up, too distracted thinking on mothers and daughters. Fretting over Royal, three days overdue. Her headache approached like a thunderhead. She turned her face to the wall and did not move.

———

SUPPER was held outside the meeting house, the biggest building on the property. Legend had it that they put it up in a single day, before one of the first big gatherings, when they realized the assembled no longer fit inside Valentine's farmhouse. Most days it served as a schoolhouse. Sundays, a church. On Saturday evenings the farm got together for a common meal and diversions. Masons who worked on the courthouse downstate came back hungry, seamstresses returned from daywork for local white ladies and put on their nice dresses. Temperance was the rule except for Saturday night, when those with a taste for spirits partook and had something to think about at the next morning's sermon.

The hogs were the first order of business, chopped on the long pine table and covered in dipney sauce. Smoky collards, turnips, sweet potato pie, and the rest of the kitchen's concoctions sat in the Valentines' nice dishes. The residents were a reserved bunch, save for when Jimmy's barbecue came out—prim ladies used their elbows. The pit master lowered his head at every compliment, already thinking of improvements for the next roast. In a deft maneuver Cora tugged off a crispy ear, Molly's favorite, and presented it to the girl.

Valentine no longer kept count of how many families lived on his land. One hundred souls was a sturdy number to stop at—a fantastic figure by any measure—and that didn't account for the colored farmers who'd purchased adjacent land and got their own operations going. Of the fifty or so children, most were under the age of five. "Liberty make a body fertile," Georgina said. That, and the knowledge they will not be sold, Cora added. The women in the colored dormitories of South Carolina believed they knew liberty, but the surgeons' knives cut them to prove otherwise.

Once the hogs disappeared, Georgina and some of the younger women took the children to the barn for games and sing-alongs.

The children didn't sit still for all the talk at the meetings. Their absence placed the stakes of the discussions into relief; ultimately, it was for the young ones that they schemed. Even if the adults were free of the shackles that had held them fast, bondage had stolen too much time. Only the children could take full advantage of their dreaming. If white men let them.

The meeting house filled. Cora joined Sybil in a pew. Tonight was to be a subdued affair. Next month after the shucking bee, the farm would host the most important gathering yet, to address the recent debates about picking up stakes. In advance, the Valentines had reduced the Saturday-night entertainments. The pleasant weather—and the warnings of the coming Indiana winter, which scared those who'd never seen snow—kept them occupied. Trips to town turned into dallying expeditions. Social calls stretched into the evening now that so many colored settlers had put down roots, the advance guard of a great migration.

Many of the farm's leaders were out of town. Valentine himself was in Chicago meeting with the banks, his two sons in tow now that they were old enough to help with the farm's accounts. Lander traveled with one of the new abolitionist societies in New York, on a speaking tour of New England; they kept him busy. What he learned during this latest excursion into the country would doubtless shape his contribution to the big meeting.

Cora studied her neighbors. She'd held out hope that Jimmy's hogs would lure Royal back in time, but he and his partners were still engaged in their mission for the underground railroad. There was no word from their party. Gruesome reports reached the farm concerning a posse that had strung up some colored troublemakers the previous night. It had happened thirty miles downstate, and the victims supposedly worked for the railroad, but nothing specific on top of that. A freckled woman unfamiliar to Cora—so many strangers these days—carried on about the lynchings in a loud voice. Sybil turned and shushed her, then gave Cora a quick hug as Gloria Valentine stepped to the lectern.

Gloria had been working in the laundry of an indigo plantation when John Valentine met her. "The most delicious vision these eyes ever beheld," Valentine liked to tell the new arrivals, drawing out *delicious* as if ladling hot caramel. Valentine didn't make a habit of visiting slavers in those days, but he'd gone in on a shipment of feed with Gloria's owner. By the end of the week he had purchased her freedom. A week after that they wed.

She was still delicious, and as graceful and composed as if she'd gone to a finishing school for white ladies. She protested that she didn't enjoy filling in for her husband, but her ease in front of a crowd argued otherwise. Gloria worked hard on eliminating her plantation inflections—Cora heard her slip when conversation took a folksy turn—but she was naturally impressive, whether she spoke colored or white. When Valentine's addresses took a stern tone, his practical disposition overcoming his generosity, Gloria stepped in to smooth matters.

"Did you all have a pleasant day?" Gloria said when the room quieted. "I was down in the root cellar all day and then I come up to see what a gift God gave us today. That sky. And them hogs . . ."

She apologized for her husband's absence. John Valentine wanted to take advantage of the big harvest to renegotiate their loan. "Lord knows, there's so much in the offing, it's nice to have a little peace of mind." She bowed at Mingo, who sat in front, next to the empty space usually reserved for Valentine. Mingo was a stoutly made man of middle stature, with a West Indian complexion that was livened by his red checkered suit tonight. He gave an amen and turned to nod at his allies in the meeting house.

Sybil nudged Cora at this acknowledgment of the farm's political arguments, an acknowledgment that legitimized Mingo's position. There was frequent talk now of lighting out west, where colored towns sprouted up on the other side of the Arkansas River. To places that didn't share a border with slave states, had never countenanced the abomination of slavery. Mingo advocated staying in Indiana, but with a severe reduction in those they sheltered: the runaways, the lost. People like Cora. The parade of famous visitors spreading the farm's renown made the place into a symbol of colored uplift—and a target. After all, the specter of colored rebellion, all those angry dark faces surrounding them, had stirred white settlers to leave the south. They come to Indiana, and right next door is a black nation rising. It always ended in violence.

Sybil scorned Mingo, his greasy personality and constant jockeying; an imperious nature lurked beneath his gregariousness. Yes, the man wore an honorable legend: After he hired himself out from his master for weekend labor, he had purchased the freedom of his wife, then his children, and finally himself. Sybil dismissed this prodigious feat—the man got lucky with regards to his master is all. Mingo would never be more than an opportunist, harassing the farm with his own notions about colored advancement. With Lander, he would take the lectern at next month's gathering to decide their future.

Cora declined to join her friend in her derision. Mingo had been distant to her on account of the attention that runaways brought to the farm, and when he heard she was wanted for murder, shunned Cora altogether. Still, the man had saved his family and could've died before completing his task—it was a mighty thing. Her first day in the schoolhouse his two girls, Amanda and Marie, had delivered the Declaration with poise. They were admirable girls. But no, Cora didn't like his smart talk. Something in his smile reminded her of Blake, that preening buck from the old days. Mingo didn't need a place to put his doghouse, but surely he was on the lookout to expand his domain.

They'd get to the music in short order, Gloria reassured them. There weren't what Valentine called "dignitaries" among them tonight—in fancy clothes, with Yankee accents—although some guests from the county had come down the road. Gloria asked them to stand up and identify themselves for a welcome. Then it was time for the diversions. "While you digest that fine meal, we have a sweet treat," she said. "You may recognize his face from his earlier visit to Valentine, a most distinguished young man of the arts."

The previous Saturday, it had been a pregnant opera singer from Montreal. The Saturday before that, a violinist from Connecticut who made half the women weep, so overcome were they with feeling. Tonight belonged to the poet. Rumsey Brooks was solemn and slim, dressed in a black suit with a black bow tie. He looked like a traveling preacher.

HE'D been there three months prior with a delegation out of Ohio. Did the Valentine farm deserve its reputation? An old white lady devoted to the cause of negro uplift had organized the expedition. The widow of a big Boston lawyer, she collected funds for various ventures, the publication and dissemination of colored literature a particular concern. After hearing one of Lander's orations, she arranged for the distribution of his autobiography; the printer had previously put out a line of Shakespeare's tragedies. The volume's first run sold out in days, a handsome edition with Elijah Lander's name in gold leaf. Rumsey's own manuscript was forthcoming next month, Gloria said.

The poet kissed his host's hand and asked permission to share some of his poetry. He was not without charisma, Cora had to admit. According to Georgina, Rumsey courted one of the milk-house girls, but was so liberal with flattery that he was obviously a young man open to the sweet mysteries of fate. "Who knows what destiny has in store for us," he asked Cora on his first visit, "and what kind of people we will have the pleasure to know?" Royal suddenly appeared at her side and pulled her away from the poet's honey words.

She should have recognized Royal's intentions. If she'd known how out of sorts his disappearances made her, she would have rebuffed him.

With Gloria's blessing, the poet cleared his throat. " 'Ere I saw a dappled wonder," he recited, his voice rising and dipping as if battling a headwind. "Settling 'cross the fields, hovering on angel wings and brandishing a blazing shield . . ."

The meeting house amened and sighed. Rumsey tried not to smile at their reaction, the effect of his performance. Cora couldn't make much out of his poems: a visitation of a magnificent presence, a seeker awaiting a message. A conversation between an acorn, a sapling, and a powerful oak. Also a tribute to Benjamin Franklin and his ingenuity. Versifying left her cold. Poems were too close to prayer, rousing regrettable passions. Waiting for God to rescue you when it was up to you. Poetry and prayer put ideas in people's heads that got them killed, distracting them from the ruthless mechanism of the world.

After the poetry the musicians were set to perform, some players who had just joined the farm. The poet prepared the dancing circles well, intoxicating them with visions of flight and release. If it made them happy, who was Cora to belittle them? They put bits of themselves into his characters, grafting their faces onto the figures in his rhymes. Did they see themselves in Benjamin Franklin or his inventions? Slaves were tools, so maybe the latter, but no one here was a slave. Counted as property by someone far away, perhaps, but not here.

The entire farm was something beyond her imagination. The Valentines had performed a miracle. She sat among the proof of it; more than that, she was part of that miracle. She had given herself too easily to the false promises of South Carolina. Now a bitter part of her refused the treasures of the Valentine farm, even as every day some blessing part came into bloom. In a young girl taking her hand. In her fears for a man she'd come to feel for.

Rumsey closed with an appeal for nurturing the artistic temperament in young and old alike, "to stoke that Apollonian ember in all mortal beings." One of the newcomers shoved the lectern across the stage. A cue for the musicians, and a cue for Cora. Sybil knew her friend's ways by now and kissed her farewell. The hall stifled; outside it was cold and dark. Cora left to the sound of the large pews scraping to make room to dance. She passed someone on the path who declared, "You going the wrong way, girl!"

When she got home, Royal was leaning against a post of her porch. His silhouette, even in the dark. "I thought you'd be along once that banjo got on," he said.

Cora lit the lamp and saw his black eye, the yellow-purple lump. "Oh," she said, hugging him, putting her face into his neck.

"A scuffle is all," he said. "We got away." Cora shuddered and he whispered, "I know you were worried. I didn't feel like mixing with folks tonight, reckoned I'd wait here."

On the porch, they sat on the lovelorn carpenters' chairs and took in the night. He moved over so their shoulders touched.

She told him what he'd missed, the poet and the meal.

"There'll be more," he said. "I got you something." He rummaged in his leather satchel. "It's this year's edition, but I thought you'd appreciate it even though it's October. When I get to a place where they got next year's, I'll pick it up."

She grabbed his hand. The almanac had a strange, soapy smell and made a cracking noise like fire as she turned the pages. She'd never been the first person to open a book.

Royal took her to the ghost tunnel after a month on the farm.

Cora started working her second day, thoughts in a knot over Valentine's motto: "Stay, and contribute." A request, and a cure. She contributed first in the washhouse. The head of the laundry was a woman named Amelia who'd known the Valentines in Virginia and followed two years later. Gently she warned Cora against "abusing the garments." Cora was quick with her labor on Randall. Working with her hands stirred her old, fearful industry. She and Amelia decided that she might prefer another chore. She helped in the milk house for a week and did a stint with Aunty, watching the babies while their parents worked. After that, she spread manure in the fields when the leaves of the Indian corn turned yellow. As Cora bent in the rows she looked out for an overseer, haunted.

"You look weary," Royal told her one August evening after Lander delivered one of his speeches. Lander's talk verged on a sermon, concerning the dilemma of finding your purpose once you've slipped the yoke of slavery. The manifold frustrations of liberty. Like the rest of the farm, Cora regarded the man with awe. He was an exotic prince, traveling from a far land to teach them how people conducted themselves in decent places. Places so far away they eluded all maps.

Elijah Lander's father was a rich white lawyer in Boston who lived openly with his colored wife. They suffered the rebukes of their circle and in midnight whispers characterized their offspring as the union of an African goddess and a pale mortal. A demigod. To hear the white dignitaries tell it in their long-winded introductions to his speeches, Lander demonstrated his brilliance from an early age. A sickly child, he made the family library his playground, poring over volumes he struggled to lift from the shelves. At the age of six, he played the piano like a European master. He performed concerts to the empty parlor, bowing to silent applause.

Family friends interceded to make him the first colored student at one of the prestigious white colleges. "They gave me a slave pass," as he described it, "and I used it for mischief." Lander lived in a broom closet; no one would room with him. After four years his fellows elected him valedictorian. He skittered between obstacles like a primeval creature who had outwitted the modern world. Lander could have been anything he wanted. A surgeon, a judge. Brahmins urged him to go to the nation's capital to make his mark in politics. He'd broken through into a small corner of American success where his race did not curse him. Some might have lived in that space happily, rising alone. Lander wanted to make room for others. People were wonderful company sometimes.

In the end, he chose to give speeches. In his parents' parlor to an audience of distinguished Bostonians, then in the homes of those distinguished Bostonians, in colored meeting houses and Methodist churches and lecture halls throughout New England. Sometimes he was the first colored person to set foot in the buildings apart from the men who built them, the women who cleaned them.

Red-faced sheriffs arrested him for sedition. He was jailed for inciting riots that weren't riots but peaceful gatherings. The Honorable Judge Edmund Harrison of Maryland issued a warrant for his arrest, accusing him of "promulgating an infernal orthodoxy that imperils the fabric of good society." A white mob beat him before he was rescued by those who had come to hear him read from his "Declarations of the Rights of the American Negro." From Florida to Maine his pamphlets, and later his autobiography, were burned in bonfires along with his effigy. "Better in effigy than in person," he said.

What private aches nagged him beneath that placid demeanor, none could say. He remained imperturbable and strange. "I'm what the botanists call a hybrid," he said the first time Cora heard him speak. "A mixture of two different families. In flowers, such a concoction pleases the eye. When that amalgamation takes its shape in flesh and blood, some take great offense. In this room we recognize it for what it is—a new beauty come into the world, and it is in bloom all around us."

WHEN Lander finished his address that August night, Cora and Royal sat on the meeting-house steps. The other residents streamed past them. Lander's words had set Cora in a melancholy place. "I don't want them to put me out," she said.

Royal turned over her palm and slid a thumb across her fresh calluses. No need to fret about that, he said. He proposed a trip to see more of Indiana, as a break from her labors.

The next day they set out in a buggy pulled by two piebald horses. With her wages she had bought a new dress and bonnet. The bonnet covered the scar on her temple, for the most part. The scar made her nervous lately. She'd never thought overlong about brands before, the Xs and Ts and clovers slave masters burned into their chattel. A horseshoe puckered on Sybil's neck, ugly and purple—her first owner had raised draft horses. Cora thanked the Lord that her skin had never been burned in such a way. But we have all been branded even if you can't see it, inside if not without—and the wound from Randall's cane was the very same thing, marking her as his.

Cora had been to town plenty, even climbed the steps of the

white bakery to buy a cake. Royal took them in the opposite direction. The sky was a sheet of slate but it was still warm, an August afternoon that let you know its kind was running out. They stopped for a picnic at the side of a meadow, under a crab apple tree. He'd packed some bread, jam, and sausage. She let him put his head in her lap. She considered running her hands through the soft black curls by his ears but refrained when a memory of old violence reared up.

On the way back Royal turned the buggy down an overgrown path. Cora wouldn't have seen it otherwise. Cottonwood swallowed the entrance. He said he wanted to show her something. She thought it might be a pond or a quiet place no one knew about. Instead they rounded a turn and stopped at a forlorn, ramshackle cottage, gray like chewed-up meat. Shutters slanted off, wild grasses bowing from the roof. Weather-beaten was the word—the house was a whipped mutt. She hesitated at the threshold. The grime and moss gave her a lonesome feeling, even with Royal there.

Weeds pushed out of the floor of the main room as well. She covered her nose from the stench. "It makes that manure smell sweet," she said. Royal laughed and said he'd always thought manure smelled sweet. He uncovered the trapdoor to the cellar and lit a candle. The stairs creaked. Animals scurried in the cellar, outraged over the intrusion. Royal counted off six paces and started digging. He stopped when he had exposed the second trapdoor, and they descended to the station. He warned her about the steps, which were slick with a gray slime.

It was the sorriest, saddest station yet. There was no drop to the tracks—the rails started at the end of the steps and jetted into the dark tunnel. A small handcar rested on the tracks, its iron pump waiting for a human touch to animate it. As in the mica mine in North Carolina, long wooden planks and struts buttressed the walls and ceiling.

"It's not made for a locomotive," Royal said. "The tunnel is too small, see. It doesn't connect to the rest of the line."

No one had been there in a long time. Cora asked where it went.

Royal grinned. "It's from before my time. The conductor I replaced showed me when I took over this section. I took that handcar a few miles in, but it was too unsettling. The walls hugging and coming close." Cora knew better than to ask who built it. All the railroad men, from Lumbly to Royal, countered with a variation of "Who do you think made it? Who makes everything?" She'd get him to tell her one day, she decided.

The ghost tunnel had never been used, Royal said, as far as anyone knew. No one knew when it was dug, or who had lived above. Some engineers told him the house had been built by one of the old surveyors, like Lewis and Clark, who had explored and mapped the American wilderness. "If you saw the entire country," Royal said, "from the Atlantic to the Pacific, the great Niagara Falls and the Rio Grande, would you make a home here, in the woods of Indiana?" An old station master offered that it had been the home of a major general in the Revolutionary War, a man who had witnessed much bloodshed and had withdrawn from the young nation after helping to bring it into existence.

A recluse story contained more sense, but Royal thought the army part was claptrap. Did Cora notice that there was no sign that someone had lived there, not even an old toothpick or a nail in the wall?

A notion crept over her like a shadow: that this station was not the start of the line but its terminus. Construction hadn't started beneath the house but at the other end of the black hole. As if in the world there were no places to escape to, only places to flee.

In the cellar above, the scavengers roused to activity, scraping. Such a dank little hole. Any trip with this point of origin could only be ill-fated. The last time she'd been in one of the railroad's departure stations it had been brightly lit, generous in its comforts, and had delivered her to the bounty of Valentine. That was in Tennessee, when they waited to be carried away from the dangerous escapade with Ridgeway. The events of that night still made her heart quicken.

ONCE they left the slave catcher and his wagon, her rescuers gave their names. Royal was the man who'd spied her in town; his partner was Red, owing to the rusty color of his curly hair. The timid one was Justin, a fugitive like her and unaccustomed to waving bowie knives at white men.

After Cora agreed to go with them—never had an inevitability been so politely proposed—the three men made haste to hide the signs of the altercation. Homer's looming presence, somewhere in the dark, magnified the urgency. Red kept watch with his rifle as Royal and Justin chained first Boseman and then Ridgeway to the wagon. The slave catcher did not speak, sneering at Cora with his bloody mouth the while.

"That one," she said, pointing, and Red chained him to the ring her captors had used for Jasper.

They drove the slave catcher's wagon to the far edge of the pasture, hiding it from the road. Red shackled Ridgeway five times over, using every chain in the wagon's boot. He tossed the keys into the grass. They chased away the horses. Of Homer, there was no sound; perhaps the boy skulked just outside the lantern light. Whatever head start these measures gave would have to suffice. Boseman let out a mortifying gasp as they departed, which Cora took as his death rattle.

Her rescuers' cart was a short walk down the road from Ridgeway's camp. She and Justin hid under a thick blanket in the back and they charged off, at dangerous velocity given the darkness and the uniformly poor quality of Tennessee roads. So agitated by the fight were Royal and Red that they forgot to blindfold their cargo for several miles. Royal was bashful about it. "It's for the safety of the depot, miss."

That third trip on the underground railroad began beneath a stable. By now a station meant a descent down impossibly deep steps and the revelation of the next station's character. The owner of the premises was away on business, Royal told them as he untied the rags from their eyes, a ruse to hide his part in their enterprise. Cora never got his name, nor that of the town of departure. Just that he was another person of subterranean inclinations—and a taste for imported white tile. The walls of the station were covered with it.

"Every time we come down here, there's something new," Royal said. The four of them waited for the train at a table covered with a white tablecloth, sitting in heavy chairs upholstered in crimson. Fresh flowers jutted from a vase and paintings of farmland hung on the walls. There was a cut-crystal pitcher full of water, a basket of fruit, and a big loaf of pumpernickel for them to eat.

"This is a rich folk's house," Justin said.

"He likes to maintain a mood," Royal answered.

Red said he liked the white tiles, which were an improvement over the pine boards that had been there formerly. "I don't know how he put them up himself," he added.

Royal said he hoped the help had a still tongue.

"You killed that man," Justin said. He was numb. They had discovered a jug of wine inside a cupboard and the fugitive drank with abandon.

"Ask the girl if he had it coming," Red said.

Royal grabbed Red's forearm to stop the man's trembling. His friend had never taken a man's life before. The premise of their misadventure was enough to get them hanged, but the murder ensured grim abuse before they swung. Royal was taken aback when Cora told him later that she was wanted for murder in Georgia. He recovered and said, "Then our course was already set from the moment I laid eyes on you, on that dirty street."

Royal was the first freeborn man Cora had ever met. There were many freemen in South Carolina who'd relocated for the so-called opportunities, but they'd served their time as chattel. Royal took in liberty with his first breath.

He was raised in Connecticut; his father was a barber and his mother a midwife. They were freeborn as well, hailing from New York City. On their orders, Royal apprenticed with a printer as soon as he was old enough to labor. His parents believed in the dignity of the honest trades, envisioning the generations of their family branching into the future, each more accomplished than the last. If the north had eliminated slavery, one day the abominable institution would fall everywhere. The negro's story may have started in this country with degradation, but triumph and prosperity would be his one day.

Had his parents realized the power of their reminiscences on the boy, they might have been more reserved in their stories of their native city. Royal lit out for Manhattan at eighteen, and his first sight of the majestic city from the rail of the ferry confirmed his fate. He took a room with three other men in a colored boardinghouse in Five Points and hung a shingle as a barber until he met the famous Eugene Wheeler. The white man started a conversation with Royal at an antislavery meeting; impressed, Wheeler told him to come to his office the next day. Royal had read of the man's exploits in the newspaper—lawyer, abolitionist crusader, bane of slavers and those who did their dirty work. Royal scouted the city jail for runaways the lawyer might defend, ran messages between enigmatic persons, and distributed funds from antislavery societies to relocated fugitives. By his official induction into the underground railroad, he had been its instrument for some time.

"I oil the pistons," he liked to say. Royal placed the coded messages in the classifieds that informed runaways and conductors of departures. He bribed ship captains and constables, rowed shivering pregnant women across rivers in leaky skiffs, and delivered judges' release orders to frowning deputies. In general he was paired with a white ally, but Royal's quick wits and proud bearing made it clear the color of his skin was no impediment. "A free black walks different than a slave," he said. "White people recognize it immediately, even if they don't know it. Walks different, talks different, carries himself different. It's in the bones." Constables never detained him and kidnappers kept their distance.

His association with Red began with the Indiana posting. Red was from North Carolina, absconding after the regulators strung up his wife and child. He walked the Freedom Trail for miles, searching for their bodies to say goodbye. He failed—the trail of corpses went on forever it seemed, in every direction. When Red made it north, he took up with the railroad and dedicated himself to the cause with a sinister resourcefulness. On hearing of Cora's accidental killing of the boy in Georgia, he smiled and said, "Good."

The Justin mission was unusual from the start. Tennessee lay outside Royal's posting, but the railroad's local representative had been out of contact since the wildfire. To cancel the train would be disastrous. With no one else available, Royal's superiors reluctantly sent the two colored agents deep into the Tennessee badlands.

The guns were Red's idea. Royal had never held one before.

"It fits in your hand," Royal said, "but it's as heavy as a cannon."

"You looked fearsome," Cora said.

"I was shaking, but inside," he told her.

Justin's master often hired him out for masonry work and a sympathetic employer made arrangements with the railroad on his behalf. There was one condition—that Justin hold off on making tracks until he finished the stone wall around the man's property. They agreed that a gap of three stones was acceptable, if Justin left thorough instructions for completion.

On the appointed day, Justin set off for work one last time. His absence wouldn't be noticed until nightfall; his employer insisted that Justin never showed up that morning. He was in the back of Royal and Red's cart by ten o'clock. The plan changed when they came upon Cora in town.

The train pulled into the Tennessee station. It was the most splendid locomotive yet, its shiny red paint returning the light even through the shroud of soot. The engineer was a jolly character with a booming voice, opening the door to the passenger car with no little ceremony. Cora suspected a kind of tunnel madness afflicted railroad engineers, to a man.

After the rickety boxcar and then the cargo platform that had conveyed her to North Carolina, to step into a proper passenger car—well-appointed and comfortable like the ones she'd read about in her almanacs—was a spectacular pleasure. There were seats enough for thirty, lavish and soft, and brass fixtures gleamed where the candlelight fell. The smell of fresh varnish made her feel like the inaugural passenger of a magical, maiden voyage. Cora slept across three seats, free from chains and attic gloom for the first time in months.

The iron horse still rumbled through the tunnel when she woke. Lumbly's words returned to her: *If you want to see what this nation is all about, you have to ride the rails. Look outside as you speed through, and you'll find the true face of America.* It was a joke, then, from the start. There was only darkness outside the windows on her journeys, and only ever would be darkness.

Justin talked in the seat in front of her. He said that his brother and three nieces he'd never met lived up in Canada. He'd spend a few days at the farm and then head north.

Royal assured the fugitive that the railroad was at his disposal. Cora sat up and he repeated what he'd just told her fellow fugitive. She could continue on to a connection in Indiana, or stay on the Valentine farm.

White people took John Valentine as one of theirs, Royal said. His skin was very light. Any person of color recognized his Ethiopian heritage immediately. That nose, those lips, good hair or no. His mother was a seamstress, his father a white peddler who passed through every few months. When the man died, he left his estate to his son, the first time he acknowledged the boy outside of the walls of their house.

Valentine tried his hand at potato farming. He employed six freemen to work his land. He never claimed to be that which he was not, but did not disabuse people of their assumptions. When Valentine purchased Gloria, no one thought twice. One way of keeping a woman was to keep her in bondage, especially if, like John Valentine, you were new to romantic liaisons. Only John, Gloria, and a judge on the other side of the state knew she was free. He was fond of books and taught his wife her letters. They raised two sons. The neighbors thought it broad-minded, if wasteful, that he set them free.

When his eldest boy was five, one of Valentine's teamsters was strung up and burned for reckless eyeballing. Joe's friends maintained that he hadn't been to town that day; a bank clerk friendly with Valentine shared the rumor that the woman was trying to make a paramour jealous. As the years pass, Valentine observed, racial violence only becomes more vicious in its expression. It will not abate or disappear, not anytime soon, and not in the south. He and his wife decided that Virginia was an unfit place to raise a family. They sold the farm and picked up stakes. Land was cheap in Indiana. There were white people there, too, but not so close.

Valentine learned the temperament of Indian corn. Three lucky seasons in a row. When he visited relations back in Virginia, he promoted the advantages of his new home. He hired old cronies. They could even live on his property until they found their footing; he'd expanded his acreage.

Those were the guests he invited. The farm as Cora discovered it originated one winter night after a blur of slow, heavy snow. The woman at the door was an awful sight, frozen half to death. Margaret was a runaway from Delaware. Her journey to the Valentine farm had been fraught—a troupe of hard characters took her on a zigzag route away from her master. A trapper, the pitchman of a medicine show. She roamed from town to town with a traveling dentist until he turned violent. The storm caught her between places. Margaret prayed to God for deliverance, promised an end to the wickedness and moral shortcomings she had expressed in her flight. The lights of Valentine emerged in the gloom.

Gloria tended to her visitor the best she could; the doctor came around on his pony. Margaret's chills never subsided. She expired a few days later.

The next time Valentine went east on business, a broadsheet promoting an antislavery meeting stopped him in his tracks. The woman in the snow was the emissary of a dispossessed tribe. He bent himself to their service.

By that autumn, his farm was the latest office of the underground railroad, busy with fugitives and conductors. Some runaways lingered; if they contributed, they could stay as long as they liked. They planted the corn. In an overgrown patch, a former plantation bricklayer built a forge for a former plantation black-smith. The forge spat out nails at a remarkable rate. The men cross-cut trees and erected cabins. A prominent abolitionist stopped for a day en route to Chicago and stayed for a week. Luminaries, ora-tors, and artists started attending the Saturday-night discussions on the negro question. One freewoman had a sister in Delaware who'd gotten into difficulties; the sister came out west for a new start. Valentine and the farm's parents paid her to teach their chil-dren, and there were always more children.

With his white face, Royal said, Valentine went down to the county seat and bought parcels for his friends with black faces, the former field hands who had come west, the fugitives who had found a haven on his farm. Found a purpose. When the Valen-tines arrived, that neck of Indiana was unpopulated. As the towns erupted into being, quickened by the relentless American thirst, the black farm was there as a natural feature of the landscape, a mountain or a creek. Half the white stores depended on its patron-age; Valentine residents filled the squares and Sunday markets to sell their crafts. "It's a place of healing," Royal told Cora on the train north. "Where you can take stock and make preparations for the next leg of the journey."

The previous night in Tennessee, Ridgeway had called Cora and her mother a flaw in the American scheme. If two women were a flaw, what was a community?

ROYAL didn't mention the philosophical disputes that domi-nated the weekly meetings. Mingo, with his schemes for the next stage in the progress of the colored tribe, and Lander, whose ele-gant but opaque appeals offered no easy remedy. The conductor also avoided the very real matter of the white settlers' mounting resentment of the negro outpost. The divisions would make them-selves known by and by.

As they hurtled through the underground passage, a tiny ship on this impossible sea, Royal's endorsement achieved its purpose. Cora slapped her hands on the cushions of the parlor car and said the farm suited her just fine.

Justin stayed two days, filled his belly, and joined his relations in the north. He later sent a letter describing his welcome, his new position at a building company. His nieces had signed their names in different-colored ink, frisky and naïve. Once Valentine lay before her in its seductive plenty, there was no question of Cora leaving. She contributed to the life of the farm. This was labor she recognized, she understood the elemental rhythms of planting and harvest, the lessons and imperatives of the shifting seasons. Her visions of city life clouded—what did she know about places like New York City and Boston? She'd grown up with her hands in the dirt.

One month after her arrival, at the mouth of the ghost tunnel, Cora remained certain of her decision. She and Royal were about to return to the farm when a gust swept out of the tunnel's murky depths. As if something moved toward them, old and dark. She reached for Royal's arm.

"Why did you bring me here?" Cora said.

"We're not supposed to talk about what we do down here," Royal said. "And our passengers aren't supposed to talk about how the railroad operates—it'd put a lot of good people in danger. They could talk if they wanted to, but they don't."

It was true. When she told of her escape, she omitted the tunnels and kept to the main contours. It was private, a secret about yourself it never occurred to you to share. Not a bad secret, but an intimacy so much a part of who you were that it could not be made separate. It would die in the sharing.

"I showed you because you've seen more of the railroad than

most," Royal continued. "I wanted you to see this—how it fits together. Or doesn't."

"I'm just a passenger."

"That's why," he said. He rubbed his spectacles with his shirt-tail. "The underground railroad is bigger than its operators—it's all of you, too. The small spurs, the big trunk lines. We have the newest locomotives and the obsolete engines, and we have hand-cars like that one. It goes everywhere, to places we know and those we don't. We got this tunnel right here, running beneath us, and no one knows where it leads. If we keep the railroad running, and none of us can figure it out, maybe you can."

She told him she didn't know why it was there, or what it meant. All she knew is that she didn't want to run anymore.

November sapped them with Indiana cold, but two events made Cora forget about the weather. The first was Sam's appearance on the farm. When he knocked on her cabin, she hugged him tight until he pleaded for her to stop. They wept. Sybil brewed cups of root tea while they composed themselves.

His coarse beard was entwined with gray and his belly had grown large, but he was the same garrulous fellow who'd taken in her and Caesar those long months past. The night the slave catcher came to town had cleaved him from his old life. Ridgeway snatched Caesar at the factory before Sam could warn him. Sam's voice faltered as he told her how their friend was beaten in the jail. He kept mum about his comrades, but one man said he'd seen the nigger talking to Sam on more than one occasion. That Sam abandoned the saloon in the middle of his shift—and the fact some in town had known Sam since they were children and disliked his self-satisfied nature—sufficed to get his house burned to the ground.

"My grandfather's house. My house. Everything that was mine." By the time the mob tore Caesar from the jail and mortally assaulted him, Sam was well on his way north. He paid a peddler for a ride and was on a ship bound for Delaware the next day.

A month later under cover of night, operatives filled in the entrance to the tunnel beneath his house, per railroad policy. Lumbly's station had been dealt with in similar fashion. "They don't like to take chances," he said. The men brought him back a

souvenir, a copper mug warped from the fire. He didn't recognize
it but kept it anyway.

"I was a station agent. They found me different things to do."
Sam drove runaways to Boston and New York, hunkered over the
latest surveys to devise escape routes, and took care of the final
arrangements that would save a fugitive's life. He even posed as a
slave catcher named "James Olney," prying slaves from jail on the
pretext of delivering them to their masters. The stupid constables
and deputies. Racial prejudice rotted one's faculties, he said. He
demonstrated his slave-catcher voice and swagger, to Cora's and
Sybil's amusement.

He had just brought his latest cargo to the Valentine farm, a
family of three who'd been hiding out in New Jersey. They had
insinuated themselves into the colored community there, Sam
said, but a slave catcher nosed around and it was time to flee. It
was his final mission for the underground railroad. He was western bound. "Every pioneer I meet, they like their whiskey. They'll
be needing barkeeps in California."

It heartened her to see her friend happy and fat. So many of
those who had helped Cora had come to awful fates. She had not
got him killed.

Then he gave her the news from her plantation, the second
item that took the sting out of the Indiana cold.

Terrance Randall was dead.

From all accounts, the slave master's preoccupation with Cora
and her escape only deepened over time. He neglected the plantation's affairs. His day to day on the estate consisted of conduct-
ing sordid parties in the big house and putting his slaves to bleak
amusements, forcing them to serve as his victims in Cora's stead.
Terrance continued to advertise for her capture, filling the classifieds in far-off states with her description and details of her crime.
He upped the considerable reward more than once—Sam had seen

the bulletins himself, astounded—and hosted any slave catcher who passed through, to provide a fuller portrait of Cora's villainy and also to shame the incompetent Ridgeway, who had failed first his father and then him.

Terrance died in New Orleans, in a chamber of a Creole brothel. His heart relented, weakened by months of dissipation.

"Or even his heart was tired of his wickedness," Cora said. As Sam's information settled, she asked about Ridgeway.

Sam waved his hand dismissively. "He's the butt of humor now. He'd been at the end of his career even before"—here he paused—"the incident in Tennessee."

Cora nodded. Red's act of murder was not spoken of. The railroad discharged him once they got the full story. Red wasn't bothered. He had new ideas about how to break the stranglehold of slavery and refused to give up his guns. "Once he lays his hand to the plow," Royal said, "he is not one to turn back." Royal was sad to see his friend ride off, but there was no bringing their methods into convergence, not after Tennessee. Cora's own act of murder he excused as a matter of self-protection, but Red's naked bloodthirstiness was another matter.

Ridgeway's penchant for violence and odd fixations had made it hard to find men willing to ride with him. His soiled reputation, coupled with Boseman's death and the humiliation of being bested by nigger outlaws, turned him into a pariah among his cohort. The Tennessee sheriffs still searched for the murderers, of course, but Ridgeway was out of the hunt. He had not been heard of since the summer.

"What about the boy, Homer?"

Sam had heard about the strange little creature. It was he who eventually brought help to the slave catcher, out in the forest. Homer's bizarre manner did nothing for Ridgeway's standing—

their arrangement fed unseemly speculations. At any rate, the two disappeared together, their bond unbroken by the assault. "To a dank cave," Sam said, "as befits those worthless shits."

Sam stayed on the farm for three days, pursuing the affections of Georgina to no avail. Long enough to mix it up with the shucking bee.

THE competition unfolded on the first night of the full moon. The children spent all day arranging the corn into two mammoth piles, inside a border of red leaves. Mingo captained one team—the second year in a row, Sybil observed with distaste. He picked a team full of allies, heedless of representing the breadth of farm society. Valentine's eldest son, Oliver, gathered a diverse group of newcomers and old hands. "And our distinguished guest, of course," Oliver said finally, beckoning Sam.

A little boy blew the whistle and the shucking began in a frenzy. This year's prize was a large silver mirror Valentine had picked up in Chicago. The mirror stood between the piles, tied with a blue ribbon, reflecting the orange flicker of the jack-o'-lanterns. The captains shouted orders to their men while the audience hooted and clapped. The fiddler played a fast and comical accompaniment. The smaller children raced around the piles, snatching the husks, sometimes before they even touched the ground.

"Get that corn!"

"You best hurry up over there!"

Cora watched from the side, Royal's hand resting on her hip. She had permitted him to kiss her the night before, which he took, not without reason, as an indication Cora was finally allowing him to step up his pursuit. She'd made him wait. He'd wait more. But Sam's report on Terrance's demise had softened her, even as it bred spiteful visions. She envisioned her former master tangled in linens, purple tongue poking from his lips. Calling for help that never arrived. Melting to a gory pulp in his casket, and then torments in a hell out of Revelation. Cora believed in that part of the holy book, at least. It described the slave plantation in code.

"This wasn't harvest on Randall," Cora said. "It was full moon when we picked, but there was always blood."

"You're not on Randall anymore," Royal said. "You're free."

She kept ahold of her temper and whispered, "How so? Land is property. Tools is property. Somebody's going to auction the Randall plantation, the slaves, too. Relations always coming out when someone dies. I'm still property, even in Indiana."

"He's dead. No cousin is going to bother over getting you back, not like he did." He said, "You're free."

Royal joined the singing to change the subject and to remind her that there were things a body could feel good about. A community that had come together, from seeding to harvest to the bee. But the song was a work song Cora knew from the cotton rows, drawing her back to the Randall cruelties and making her heart thud. Connelly used to start the song as a signal to go back to picking after a whipping.

How could such a bitter thing become a means of pleasure? Everything on Valentine was the opposite. Work needn't be suffering, it could unite folks. A bright child like Chester might thrive and prosper, as Molly and her friends did. A mother raise her daughter with love and kindness. A beautiful soul like Caesar could be anything he wanted here, all of them could be: own a spread, be a schoolteacher, fight for colored rights. Even be a poet. In her Georgia misery she had pictured freedom, and it had not looked like this. Freedom was a community laboring for something lovely and rare.

Mingo won. His men chaired him around the piles of naked cobs, hoarse with cheers. Jimmy said he'd never seen a white man work so hard and Sam beamed with pleasure. Georgina remained unswayed, however.

On the day of Sam's departure, Cora embraced him and kissed his whiskered cheek. He said he'd send a note when he settled, wherever that was.

They were in the time of short days and long nights. Cora visited the library frequently as the weather turned. She brought Molly when she could coax the girl. They sat next to each other, Cora with a history or a romance, and Molly turning the pages of a fairy tale. A teamster stopped them one day as they were about to enter. "Master said the only thing more dangerous than a nigger with a gun," he told them, "was a nigger with a book. That must be a big pile of black powder, then!"

When some of the grateful residents proposed building an addition to Valentine's house for his books, Gloria suggested a separate structure. "That way, anyone with a mind to pick up a book can do so at their leisure." It also gave the family more privacy. They were generous, but there was a limit.

They put up the library next to the smokehouse. The room smelled pleasantly of smoke when Cora sat down in one of the big chairs with Valentine's books. Royal said it was the biggest collection of negro literature this side of Chicago. Cora didn't know if that was true, but she certainly didn't lack for reading material. Apart from the treatises on farming and the cultivation of various crops, there were rows and rows of histories. The ambitions of the Romans and the victories of the Moors, the royal feuds of Europe. Oversize volumes contained maps of lands Cora had never heard of, the outlines of the unconquered world.

And the disparate literature of the colored tribes. Accounts of African empires and the miracles of the Egyptian slaves who had erected pyramids. The farm's carpenters were true artisans—they had to be to keep all those books from jumping off the shelves, so many wonders did they contain. Pamphlets of verse by negro poets, autobiographies of colored orators. Phillis Wheatley and Jupiter Hammon. There was a man named Benjamin Banneker who composed almanacs—almanacs! she devoured them all—and served as a confidant to Thomas Jefferson, who composed the Declaration. Cora read the accounts of slaves who had been born in chains and learned their letters. Of Africans who had been stolen, torn from their homes and families, and described the miseries of their bondage and then their hair-raising escapes. She recognized their stories as her own. They were the stories of all the colored people she had ever known, the stories of black people yet to be born, the foundations of their triumphs.

People had put all that down on paper in tiny rooms. Some of them even had dark skin like her. It put her head in a fog each time she opened the door. She'd have to get started if she was going to read them all.

Valentine joined her one afternoon. Cora was friendly with Gloria, who called Cora "the Adventuress," owing to the many complications of her journey, but she hadn't spoken to Gloria's husband beyond greetings. The enormity of her debt was inexpressible, so she avoided him altogether.

He regarded the cover of her book, a romance about a Moorish boy who becomes the scourge of the Seven Seas. The language was simple and she was making quick work of it. "I never did read that," Valentine said. "I heard you like to spend time here. You're the one from Georgia?"

She nodded.

"Never been there—the stories are so dismal, I'm liable to lose my temper and make my wife a widow."

Cora returned his smile. He'd been a presence in the summer months, looking after the Indian corn. The field hands knew indigo, tobacco—cotton, of course—but corn was its own beast. He was pleasant and patient in his instructions. With the changing of the season he was scarce. Feeling poorly, people said. He spent most of his time in the farmhouse, squaring the farm's accounts.

He wandered to the shelves of maps. Now that they were in the same room, Cora was compelled to rectify her months of silence. She asked after the preparations for the gathering.

"Yes, that," Valentine said. "Do you think it will happen?"

"It has to," Cora said.

The meeting had been postponed twice on account of Lander's speaking engagements. Valentine's kitchen table started the culture of debate on the farm, when Valentine and his friends— and later, visiting scholars and noted abolitionists—stayed up past midnight arguing over the colored question. The need for trade schools, colored medical schools. For a voice in Congress, if not a representative then a strong alliance with liberal-minded whites. How to undo slavery's injury to the mental faculties—so many freed men continued to be enslaved by the horrors they'd endured.

The supper conversations became ritual, outgrowing the house and migrating to the meeting house, whereupon Gloria stopped serving food and drink and let them fend for themselves. Those favoring a more gradual view of colored progress traded barbs with those on a more pressing schedule. When Lander arrived— the most dignified and eloquent colored man any of them had seen—the discussions adopted a more local character. The direction of the nation was one matter; the future of the farm, another.

"Mingo promises it will be a memorable occasion," Valentine said. "A spectacle of rhetoric. These days, I hope they get the spectacle done early so I can retire at a decent hour." Worn down by Mingo's lobbying, Valentine had ceded organization of the debate.

Mingo had lived on the farm for a long time, and when it came to addressing Lander's appeals, it was good to have a native voice. He was not as accomplished a speaker, but as a former slave spoke for a large segment of the farm.

Mingo had taken advantage of the delay to press for improved relations with the white towns. He swayed a few from Lander's camp—not that it was clear exactly what Lander had in mind. Lander was plainspoken but opaque.

"What if they decide that we should leave?" Cora was surprised at her difficulty in mustering the words.

"They? You're one of us." Valentine took the chair that Molly favored on her visits. Up close, it was plain the burden of so many souls had exacted its toll. The man was weariness itself. "It may be out of our hands," he said. "What we built here . . . there are too many white people who don't want us to have it. Even if they didn't suspect our alliance with the railroad. Look around. If they kill a slave for learning his letters, how do you think they feel about a library? We're in a room brimming with ideas. Too many ideas for a colored man. Or woman."

Cora had come to cherish the impossible treasures of the Valentine farm so completely that she'd forgotten how impossible they were. The farm and the adjacent ones operated by colored interests were too big, too prosperous. A pocket of blackness in the young state. Valentine's negro heritage became known years before. Some felt tricked that they'd treated a nigger as an equal—and then to have that uppity nigger shame them with his success.

She told Valentine of an incident the previous week, when she'd been walking up the road and was almost trampled by a wagon. The driver yelled disgusting epithets as he passed. Cora was not the only victim of abuse. The new arrivals to the nearby towns, the rowdies and low whites, started fights when residents came for supplies. Harassed the young women. Last week a feed store hung a shingle saying WHITES ONLY—a nightmare reaching up from the south to claim them.

Valentine said, "We have a legal right as American citizens to be here." But the Fugitive Slave Law was a legal fact as well. Their collaborations with the underground railroad complicated things. Slave catchers didn't show their faces often, but it wasn't unheard of. Last spring, two catchers appeared with a warrant to search every house on the farm. Their quarry was long gone, but the reminder of the slave patrols exposed the precarious nature of the residents' lives. One of the cooks urinated in their canteens as they ransacked the cabins.

"Indiana was a slave state," Valentine continued. "That evil soaks into the soil. Some say it steeps and gets stronger. Maybe this isn't the place. Maybe Gloria and I should have kept going after Virginia."

"I feel it when I go to town now," Cora said. "See that look in their eyes I know." It wasn't just Terrance and Connelly and Ridgeway she recognized, the savage ones. She'd watched the faces in the park in North Carolina during the daytime, and at night when they gathered for atrocities. Round white faces like an endless field of cotton bolls, all the same material.

Taking in Cora's downcast expression, Valentine told her, "I'm proud of what we've built here, but we started over once. We can do it again. I have two strong sons to help now, and we'll get a nice sum for the land. Gloria has always wanted to see Oklahoma, although for the life of me I don't know why. I try to make her happy."

"If we stay," Cora said, "Mingo wouldn't allow people like me. The runaways. Those with nowhere to go."

"Talk is good," Valentine said. "Talk clears the air and makes it so you can see what's what. We'll see what the mood of the farm is. It's mine, but it's everybody's, too. Yours. I'll abide by the decision of the people."

Cora saw the discussion had depleted him. "Why do all this," she asked. "For all of us?"

"I thought you were one of the smart ones," Valentine said. "Don't you know? White man ain't going to do it. We have to do it ourselves."

If the farmer had come in for a specific book, he left empty-handed. The wind whistled through the open door and Cora pulled her shawl tight. If she kept reading, she might start another book by suppertime.

The final gathering on Valentine farm took place on a brisk December night. In the years to come, the survivors shared their versions of what happened that evening, and why. Until the day she died, Sybil insisted Mingo was the informer. She was an old lady then, living on a Michigan lake with a gang of grandchildren who had to listen to her familiar stories. According to Sybil, Mingo told the constables that the farm harbored fugitives and provided the particulars for a successful ambush. A dramatic raid would put an end to relations with the railroad, the endless stream of needy negroes, and ensure the longevity of the farm. When asked if he anticipated the violence, she pressed her lips into a line and said no more.

Another survivor—Tom the blacksmith—observed that the law had hunted Lander for months. He was the intended target. Lander's rhetoric inflamed passions; he fomented rebellion; he was too uppity to allow to run free. Tom never learned to read but liked to show off his volume of Lander's *Appeal*, which the great orator had signed to him.

Joan Watson was born on the farm. She was six years old that night. In the aftermath of the attack she wandered the forest for three days, chewing acorns, until a wagon train discovered her. When she got older, she described herself as a student of American history, attuned to the inevitable. She said that white towns had simply banded together to rid themselves of the black stronghold in their midst. That is how the European tribes operate, she said. If they can't control it, they destroy it.

If anyone on the farm knew what was to come, they gave no sign. Saturday proceeded in lazy calm. Cora spent most of the day in her bedroom with the latest almanac Royal had given her. He'd picked it up in Chicago. He knocked on her door 'round midnight to give it to her; he knew she was awake. It was late and she didn't want to disturb Sybil and Molly. Cora took him into her room for the first time.

She broke down at the sight of next year's almanac. Thick as a book of prayer. Cora had told Royal about the attic days in North Carolina, but seeing the year on the cover—an object conjured from the future—spurred Cora to her own magic. She told him about her childhood on Randall where she had picked cotton, tugging a sack. About her grandmother Ajarry who'd been kidnapped from her family in Africa and tilled a small corner of land, the only thing to call her own. Cora spoke of her mother, Mabel, who absconded one day and left her to the inconstant mercy of the world. About Blake and the doghouse and how she had faced him down with a hatchet. When she told Royal about the night they took her behind the smokehouse and she apologized to him for letting it happen, he told her to hush. She was the one due an apology for all her hurts, he said. He told her that every one of her enemies, all the masters and overseers of her suffering, would be punished, if not in this world then the next, for justice may be slow and invisible, but it always renders its true verdict in the end. He folded his body into hers to quiet her shaking and sobs and they fell asleep like that, in the back room of a cabin on the Valentine farm.

She didn't believe what he said about justice, but it was nice to hear him say it.

Then she woke up the next morning and felt better, and had to admit that she did believe it, maybe just a little.

Thinking Cora was laid up with one of her headaches, Sybil brought her some food around noon. She teased Cora about Royal staying the night. She was mending the dress she'd wear to the gathering when he "come sneaking out of here holding his boots in his hand and looking like a dog that'd stolen some scraps." Cora just smiled.

"Your man ain't the only one come around last night," Sybil said. Lander had returned.

That accounted for Sybil's playfulness. Lander impressed her mightily, every one of his visits fortifying her for days after. Those honeyed words of his. Now he had finally come back to Valentine. The gathering would happen, to an unknowable outcome. Sybil didn't want to move west and leave her home, which everyone assumed to be Lander's solution. She'd been adamant about staying ever since the talk of resettling started. But she wouldn't abide Mingo's conditions, that they stop providing shelter to those in need. "There ain't no place like here, not anywhere. He wants to kill it."

"Valentine won't let him spoil it," Cora said, though after talking with the man in the library it seemed he'd already packed up in his mind.

"We'll see," Sybil said. "I may have to give a speech my own self, and tell these people what they need to hear."

That night Royal and Cora sat in the front row next to Mingo and his family, the wife and children he had rescued from slavery. His wife, Angela, was silent, as always; to hear her speak, you had to hide under the window of their cabin as she counseled her man in private. Mingo's daughters wore bright blue dresses, their long pigtails entwined with white ribbons. Lander played guessing games with the youngest one as the residents filled the meeting hall. Her name was Amanda. She held a bouquet of cloth flowers; he made a joke about them and they laughed. When Cora caught

Lander at a moment such as this, in a brief lapse between performances, he reminded her of Molly. For all his friendly talk, she thought he'd prefer to be home by himself, playing concerts in empty rooms.

He had long, dainty fingers. How curious that one who'd never picked a boll or dug a trench or experienced the cat-o'-nine-tails had come to speak for those who had been defined by those things. He was lean in build, with glowing skin that announced his mixed parentage. She had never seen him rush or hurry. The man moved with exquisite calm, like a leaf drifting on the surface of a pond, making its own way on gentle currents. Then he opened his mouth, and you saw that the forces steering him to your presence were not gentle at all.

There were no white visitors this night. Everyone who lived and worked on the farm was in attendance, as well as the families from the neighboring colored farms. Seeing them all in one room, Cora got an idea of how large they were for the first time. There were people she'd never seen before, like the mischievous little boy who winked at her when their eyes met. Strangers but family, cousins but never introduced. She was surrounded by men and women who'd been born in Africa, or born in chains, who had freed themselves or escaped. Branded, beaten, raped. Now they were here. They were free and black and stewards of their own fates. It made her shiver.

Valentine gripped the lectern for support. "I didn't grow up the way you did," he said. "My mother never feared for my safety. No trader was going to snatch me in the night and sell me south. The whites saw the color of my skin, and that sufficed to let me be. I told myself I was doing nothing wrong, but I conducted myself in ignorance all my days. Until you came here and made a life with us."

He left Virginia, he said, to spare his children the ravages of prejudice and its bully partner, violence. But saving two children is not enough when God has gifted you with so much. "A woman came to us out of the bitter winter—sick and desperate. We could not save her." Valentine's voice rasped. "I neglected my duty. As long as one of our family endured the torments of bondage, I was a freeman in name only. I want to express my gratitude to everyone here for helping me to put things right. Whether you have been among us for years or just a few hours, you have saved my life."

He faltered. Gloria joined him and gathered his body in hers. "Now some of our family have things they want to share with you," Valentine said, clearing his throat. "I hope you'll listen to them like you listen to me. There's room enough for different notions when it comes to charting our path through the wilderness. When the night is dark and full of treacherous footing."

The farm's patriarch withdrew from the lectern and Mingo replaced him. Mingo's children trailed him, kissing his hands for good luck before returning to the pews.

Mingo opened with the story of his journey, the nights he spent begging the Lord for guidance, the long years it took to purchase his family's freedom. "With my honest labor, one by one, just as you saved yourselves." He rubbed a knuckle in his eye.

Then he changed course. "We accomplished the impossible," Mingo said, "but not everyone has the character we do. We're not all going to make it. Some of us are too far gone. Slavery has twisted their minds, an imp filling their minds with foul ideas. They have given themselves over to whiskey and its false comforts. To hopelessness and its constant devils. You've seen these lost ones on the plantations, on the streets of the towns and cities—those who will not, cannot respect themselves. You've seen them here, receiving the gift of this place but unable to fit in. They always disappear in the night because deep in their hearts they know they are unworthy. It is too late for them."

Some of his cronies in the back of the room amened. There are realities we have to face, Mingo explained. White people aren't going to change overnight. The farm's dreams are worthy and true, but require a gradual approach. "We can't save everyone, and acting as if we can will doom us all. You think the white folks— just a few miles from here—are going to endure our impudence forever? We flaunt their weakness. Harboring runaways. Underground railroad agents with guns coming and going. People who are wanted for murder. Criminals." Cora made fists as Mingo's gaze fell on her.

The Valentine farm had taken glorious steps into the future, he said. White benefactors supplied schoolbooks for their children— why not ask them to pass the hat for entire schools? And not just one or two, but dozens more? By proving the negro's thrift and intelligence, Mingo argued, he will enter into American society as a productive member with full rights. Why jeopardize that? We need to slow things down. Reach an accommodation with our neighbors and, most of all, stop activities that will force their wrath upon us. "We've built something astounding here," he concluded. "But it is a precious thing, and it needs to be protected, nourished, or else it will wither, like a rose in a sudden frost."

During the applause, Lander whispered to Mingo's daughter and they giggled again. She removed one of the cloth flowers from her bouquet and twisted it into the top buttonhole of his green suit. Lander pretended to sniff its fragrance and mock-swooned.

"It's time," Royal said as Lander shook Mingo's hand and assumed his place at the lectern. Royal had spent the day with him, walking the grounds and talking. Royal didn't share what Lander would speak on that night, but he had an optimistic air. Formerly, when the subject of relocating came up, Royal told Cora he favored Canada over the west. "They know how to treat free negroes there," he said. And his work with the railroad? Have to

settle down sometime, Royal said. Can't raise a family while running around on railroad errands. Cora changed the subject when
he engaged in such talk.

Now she'd see for herself—they'd all see—what the man from
Boston had in mind.

"Brother Mingo made some good points," Lander said. "We
can't save everyone. But that doesn't mean we can't try. Sometimes
a useful delusion is better than a useless truth. Nothing's going to
grow in this mean cold, but we can still have flowers.

"Here's one delusion: that we can escape slavery. We can't. Its
scars will never fade. When you saw your mother sold off, your
father beaten, your sister abused by some boss or master, did you
ever think you would sit here today, without chains, without the
yoke, among a new family? Everything you ever knew told you
that freedom was a trick—yet here you are. Still we run, tracking
by the good full moon to sanctuary.

"Valentine farm is a delusion. Who told you the negro deserved
a place of refuge? Who told you that you had that right? Every
minute of your life's suffering has argued otherwise. By every fact
of history, it can't exist. This place must be a delusion, too. Yet
here we are.

"And America, too, is a delusion, the grandest one of all. The
white race believes—believes with all its heart—that it is their right
to take the land. To kill Indians. Make war. Enslave their brothers.
This nation shouldn't exist, if there is any justice in the world, for
its foundations are murder, theft, and cruelty. Yet here we are.

"I'm supposed to answer Mingo's call for gradual progress,
for closing our doors to those in need. I'm supposed to answer
those who think this place is too close to the grievous influence
of slavery, and that we should move west. I don't have an answer
for you. I don't know what we should do. The word *we*. In some
ways, the only thing we have in common is the color of our skin.

Our ancestors came from all over the African continent. It's quite large. Brother Valentine has the maps of the world in his splendid library, you can look for yourself. They had different ways of subsistence, different customs, spoke a hundred different languages. And that great mixture was brought to America in the holds of slave ships. To the north, the south. Their sons and daughters picked tobacco, cultivated cotton, worked on the largest estates and smallest farms. We are craftsmen and midwives and preachers and peddlers. Black hands built the White House, the seat of our nation's government. The word *we*. We are not one people but many different people. How can one person speak for this great, beautiful race—which is not one race but many, with a million desires and hopes and wishes for ourselves and our children?

"For we are Africans in America. Something new in the history of the world, without models for what we will become.

"Color must suffice. It has brought us to this night, this discussion, and it will take us into the future. All I truly know is that we rise and fall as one, one colored family living next door to one white family. We may not know the way through the forest, but we can pick each other up when we fall, and we will arrive together."

WHEN the former residents of the Valentine farm recalled that moment, when they told strangers and grandchildren of how they used to live and how it came to an end, their voices still trembled years later. In Philadelphia, in San Francisco, in the cow towns and ranches where they eventually made a home, they mourned those who died that day. The air in the room turned prickly, they told their families, quickened by an unseen power. Whether they had been born free or in chains, they inhabited that moment as one: the moment when you aim yourself at the north star and decide to run. Perhaps they were on the verge of some new order, on the verge of clasping reason to disorder, of putting all the lessons of their history to bear on the future. Or perhaps time, as it will, lent the occasion a gravity that it did not possess, and everything was as Lander insisted: They were deluded.

But that didn't mean it wasn't true.

The shot hit Lander in the chest. He fell back, dragging down the lectern. Royal was the first one to his feet. As he ran to the fallen man, three bullets bit into his back. He jerked like one of Saint Vitus's dancers and dropped. Then came a chorus of rifle fire, screams, and broken glass, and a mad scramble overtook the meeting hall.

The white men outside whooped and howled over the carnage. Pell-mell the residents hastened to the exits, squeezing between pews, climbing over them, climbing over one another. Once the main entrance bottlenecked, people crawled over the windowsills. More rifles crackled. Valentine's sons helped their father to the door. To the left of the stage, Gloria crouched over Lander. She saw there was nothing to be done and followed her family out.

Cora held Royal's head in her lap, just as she had the afternoon of the picnic. She ran her fingers through his curls and rocked him and wept. Royal smiled through the blood that bubbled on his lips. He told her not to be afraid, the tunnel would save her again. "Go to the house in the woods. You can tell me where it goes." His body went slack.

Two men grabbed her and removed her from Royal's body. It's not safe here, they said. One of them was Oliver Valentine, come back to help others escape the meeting house. He cried and shouted. Cora broke from her rescuers once they got her outside and down the steps. The farm was a commotion. The white posse dragged men and women into the dark, their hideous faces awash with delight. A musket cut down one of Sybil's carpenters—he held a baby in his arms and they both crashed to the ground. No one knew where best to run, and no reasonable voice could be heard above the clamor. Each person on their own, as they ever had been.

Mingo's daughter Amanda shook on her knees, her family absent. Desolate in the dirt. Her bouquet had shed its petals. She gripped the naked stems, the iron wires the blacksmith had drawn out on the anvil last week, just for her. The wires cut her palms, she gripped them so tight. More blood in the dirt. As an old woman she would read about the Great War in Europe and recall this night. She lived on Long Island then, after roaming all over the country, in a small house with a Shinnecock sailor who doted on her to excess. She'd spent time in Louisiana and Virginia, where her father opened colored institutions of learning, and California. A spell in Oklahoma, where the Valentines resettled. The conflict in Europe was terrible and violent, she told her sailor, but she took exception to the name. The Great War had always been between the white and the black. It always would be.

Cora called for Molly. She didn't see anyone she recognized; their faces had been transformed by fear. The heat from the fires washed over her. Valentine's house was ablaze. A jar of oil exploded against the second floor and John and Gloria's bedroom caught. The windows of the library shattered and Cora saw the books burning on the shelves inside. She made two steps toward it before Ridgeway grabbed her. They struggled and his big arms encircled her, her feet kicking against the air like those of one hanging from a tree.

Homer was at his side—he was the boy she'd seen in the pews, winking at her. He wore suspenders and a white blouse, looking like the innocent child he would have been in a different world. At the sight of him, Cora added her voice to the chorus of lamentation that echoed across the farm.

"There's a tunnel, sir," Homer said. "I heard him say it."

Mabel

THE first and last things she gave to her daughter were apologies. Cora slept in her stomach, the size of a fist, when Mabel apologized for what she was bringing her into. Cora slept next to her in the loft, ten years later, when Mabel apologized for making her a stray. Cora didn't hear either one.

At the first clearing Mabel found the north star and reoriented. She gathered herself and resumed her escape through the black water. Kept her eyes forward because when she looked back she saw the faces of those she left behind.

She saw Moses's face. She remembered Moses when he was little. A twitching bundle so frail no one expected him to survive until he was old enough for pickaninny work, the trash gang, or offering a ladle of water in the cotton. Not when most children on Randall died before their first steps. His mother used the witch-woman cures, the poultices and root potions, and sang to him every night, crooning in their cabin. Lullabies and work tunes and her own maternal wishes in singsong: Keep the food in your stomach, break the fever, breathe until morning. He outlived most of the boys born that year. Everybody knew it was his mother, Kate, who saved him from affliction and the early winnowing that is every plantation slave's first trial.

Mabel remembered when Old Randall sold off Kate once her arm went numb and wasn't fit for labor. Moses's first whipping for stealing a potato, and his second whipping for idleness, when Connelly had the boy's wounds washed out with hot pepper until he howled. None of that made Moses mean. It made him silent and strong and fast, faster than any other picker in his gang. He wasn't mean until Connelly made him a boss, the master's eyes and ears over his own kind. That's when he became Moses the monster, Moses who made the other slaves quake, black terror of the rows.

When he told her to come to the schoolhouse she scratched his face and spat at him and he just smiled and said if you're not game I'll find someone else—how old is your Cora now? Cora was eight. Mabel didn't fight him after that. He was quick and he wasn't rough after that first time. Women and animals, you only have to break them in once, he said. They stay broke.

All those faces, living and dead. Ajarry twitching in the cotton, bloody foam on her lips. She saw Polly swinging on a rope, sweet Polly, who she'd come up with in the quarter, born the same month. Connelly transferred them from the yard to the cotton fields the same day. Always in tandem until Cora lived but Polly's baby didn't—the young women delivered within two weeks of each other, with one baby girl crying when the midwife pulled her out and the other making no sound at all. Stillborn and stone. When Polly hung herself in the barn with a loop of hemp, Old Jockey said, You did everything together. Like Mabel was supposed to hang herself now, too.

She started to see Cora's face and she looked away. She ran.

Men start off good and then the world makes them mean. The world is mean from the start and gets meaner every day. It uses you up until you only dream of death. Mabel wasn't going to die on Randall, even if she'd never been a mile away from the grounds in her life. One midnight she decided, up in the sweltering loft, *I am going to survive*—and the next midnight she was in the swamp, tracking after the moon in stolen shoes. She turned her escape over in her head all day, let no other thought intrude or dissuade.

There were islands in the swamp—follow them to the continent of freedom. She took the vegetables she raised, flint and tinder, a machete. Everything else she left behind, including her girl.

Cora, sleeping back in the cabin she was born in, that Mabel was born in. Still a girl, before the worst of it, before she learns the size and heft of a woman's burdens. If Cora's father had lived, would Mabel be here now, tramping through the marsh? Mabel was fourteen when Grayson arrived on the southern half, sold down south by a drunken indigo farmer in North Carolina. Tall and black, sweet-tempered with a laughing eye. Swaggering even after the hardest toil. They couldn't touch him.

She picked him out that first day and decided: him. When he grinned it was the moon shining down on her, a presence in the sky blessing her. He scooped her up and twirled her when they danced. I'm going to buy our freedom, he said, hay in his hair from where they lay down. Old Randall didn't go in for that, but he'd convince him. Work hard, be the best hand on the plantation— he'd earn his way out of bondage and take her, too. She said, You promise? Half believing he could do it. Grayson the Sweet, dead of fever before she knew she carried their child. His name never again crossed her lips.

Mabel tripped over a cypress root and went sprawling into the water. She staggered through the reeds to the island ahead and flattened on the ground. Didn't know how long she had been running. Panting and tuckered out.

She took a turnip from her sack. It was young and tender-soft, and she took a bite. The sweetest crop she'd ever raised in Ajarry's plot, even with the taste of marsh water. Her mother had left that in her inheritance, at least, a tidy plot to watch over. You're supposed to pass on something useful to your children. The better parts of Ajarry never took root in Mabel. Her indomitability, her perseverance. But there was a plot three yards square and the hearty stuff that sprouted from it. Her mother had protected it with all her heart. The most valuable land in all of Georgia.

She lay on her back and ate another turnip. Without the sound of her splashing and huffing, the noises of the swamp resumed. The spadefoot toads and turtles and slithering creatures, the chattering of black insects. Above—through the leaves and branches of the black-water trees—the sky scrolled before her, new constellations wheeling in the darkness as she relaxed. No patrollers, no bosses, no cries of anguish to induct her into another's despair. No cabin walls shuttling her through the night seas like the hold of a slave ship. Sandhill cranes and warblers, otters splashing. On the bed of damp earth, her breathing slowed and that which separated herself from the swamp disappeared. She was free.

This moment.

She had to go back. The girl was waiting on her. This would have to do for now. Her hopelessness had gotten the best of her, speaking under her thoughts like a demon. She would keep this moment close, her own treasure. When she found the words to share it with Cora, the girl would understand there was something beyond the plantation, past all that she knew. That one day if she stayed strong, the girl could have it for herself.

The world may be mean, but people don't have to be, not if they refuse.

Mabel picked up her sack and got her bearings. If she kept a good pace, she'd be back well before first light and the earliest risers on the plantation. Her escape had been a preposterous idea, but even a sliver of it amounted to the best adventure of her life.

Mabel pulled out another turnip and took a bite. It really was sweet.

The snake found her not long into her return. She was wending through a cluster of stiff reeds when she disturbed its rest. The cottonmouth bit her twice, in the calf and deep in the meat of her thigh. No sound but pain. Mabel refused to believe it. It was a water snake, it had to be. Ornery but harmless. When her mouth went minty and her leg tingled, she knew. She made it another mile. She had dropped her sack along the way, lost her course in the black water. She could have made it farther—working Randall land had made her strong, strong in body if nothing else—but she stumbled onto a bed of soft moss and it felt right. She said, Here, and the swamp swallowed her up.

The North

——◆——

RAN AWAY

from her legal but not rightful master fifteen
months past, a slave girl called CORA; of ordinary
height and dark brown complexion; has a star-shape
mark on her temple from an injury; possessed of
a spirited nature and devious method. Possibly
answering to the name BESSIE.

Last seen in Indiana among the outlaws of John
Valentine Farm.

She has stopped running.

Reward remains unclaimed.

SHE WAS NEVER PROPERTY.

DECEMBER 23

——◆——

HER point of departure that final voyage on the underground railroad was a tiny station beneath an abandoned house. The ghost station.

Cora led them there after her capture. The posse of bloodthirsty whites still rampaged across the Valentine farm when they left. The gunfire and screams came from farther away, deeper in the property. The newer cabins, the mill. Perhaps as far as the Livingston spread, the mayhem encompassing the neighboring farms. The whites meant to rout the entirety of colored settlers.

Cora fought and kicked as Ridgeway carried her to the wagon. The burning library and farmhouse illuminated the grounds. After a barrage to his face, Homer finally gathered her feet together and they got her inside, chaining her wrists to her old ring in the wagon floor. One of the young white men watching the horses cheered and asked for a turn when they were done. Ridgeway clopped him in the face.

She relinquished the location to the house in the woods when the slave catcher put his pistol to her eye. Cora lay down on the bench, seized by one of her headaches. How to snuff her thoughts like a candle? Royal and Lander dead. The others who were cut down.

"One of the deputies said it reminded him of the old days of proper Indian raids," Ridgeway said. "Bitter Creek and Blue Falls. I think he was too young to remember that. Maybe his daddy." He sat in the back with her on the bench opposite, his outfit reduced to the wagon and the two skinny horses that pulled it. The fire danced outside, showing the holes and long tears in the canvas.

Ridgeway coughed. He had been diminished since Tennessee. The slave catcher was completely gray, unkempt, skin gone sallow. His speech was different, less commanding. Dentures replaced the teeth Cora ruined in their last encounter. "They buried Boseman in one of the plague cemeteries," he said. "He would have been appalled, but he didn't have much of a say. The one bleeding on the floor—that was the uppity bastard who ambushed us, yes? I recognized his spectacles."

Why had she put Royal off for so long? She thought they had time enough. Another thing that might have been, snipped at the roots as if by one of Dr. Stevens's surgical blades. She let the farm convince her the world is other than what it will always be. He must have known she loved him even if she hadn't told him. He had to.

Night birds screeched. After a time Ridgeway told her to keep a lookout for the path. Homer slowed the horses. She missed it twice, the fork in the road signaling they'd gone too far. Ridgeway slapped her across the face and told her to mind him. "It took me awhile to find my footing after Tennessee," he said. "You and your friends did me a bad turn. But that's done. You're going home, Cora. At last. Once I get a look-see at the famous underground railroad." He slapped her again. On the next circuit she found the cottonwoods that marked the turn.

Homer lit a lantern and they entered the mournful old house. He had changed out of his costume and back into his black suit and stovepipe hat. "Below the cellar," Cora said. Ridgeway was wary. He pulled up the door and jumped back, as if a host of black outlaws waited in a trap. The slave catcher handed her a candle and told her to go down first.

"Most people think it's a figure of speech," he said. "The underground. I always knew better. The secret beneath us, the entire time. We'll uncover them all after tonight. Every line, every one."

Whatever animals lived in the cellar were quiet this night. Homer checked the corners of the cellar. The boy came up with the spade and gave it to Cora.

She held out her chains. Ridgeway nodded. "Otherwise we'll be here all night." Homer undid the shackles. The white man was giddy, his former authority easing into his voice. In North Carolina, Martin had thought he was onto his father's buried treasure in the mine and discovered a tunnel instead. For the slave catcher the tunnel was all the gold in the world.

"Your master is dead," Ridgeway said as Cora dug. "I wasn't surprised to hear the news—he had a degenerate nature. I don't know if the current master of Randall will pay your reward. I don't rightly care." He was surprised at his words. "It wasn't going to be easy, I should have seen that. You're your mother's daughter through and through."

The spade struck the trapdoor. She cleared out a square. Cora had stopped listening to him, to Homer's unwholesome snickering. She and Royal and Red may have diminished the slave catcher when they last met, but it was Mabel who first laid him low. It flowed from her mother, his mania over their family. If not for her, the slave catcher wouldn't have obsessed so over Cora's capture. The one who escaped. After all it cost her, Cora didn't know if it made her proud or more spiteful toward the woman.

This time Homer lifted the trapdoor. The moldy smell gusted up.

"This is it?" Ridgeway asked.

"Yes, sir," Homer said.

Ridgeway waved Cora on with his pistol.

He would not be the first white man to see the underground railroad, but the first enemy. After all that had befallen her, the shame of betraying those who made possible her escape. She hesitated on the top step. On Randall, on Valentine, Cora never joined the dancing circles. She shrank from the spinning bodies, afraid of another person so close, so uncontrolled. Men had put a fear in her, those years ago. Tonight, she told herself. Tonight I will hold him close, as if in a slow dance. As if it were just the two of them in the lonesome world, bound to each other until the end of the song. She waited until the slave catcher was on the third step. She spun and locked her arms around him like a chain of iron. The candle dropped. He attempted to keep his footing with her weight on him, reaching out for leverage against the wall, but she held him close like a lover and the pair tumbled down the stone steps into the darkness.

They fought and grappled in the violence of their fall. In the jumble of collisions, Cora's head knocked across the stone. Her leg was ripped one way, and her arm twisted under her at the bottom of the steps. Ridgeway took the brunt. Homer yelped at the sounds his employer made as he fell. The boy descended slowly, the lantern light shakily drawing the station from shadow. Cora untwined herself from Ridgeway and crawled toward the handcar, left leg in agony. The slave catcher didn't make a sound. She looked for a weapon and came up empty.

Homer crouched next to his boss. His hand covered in blood from the back of Ridgeway's head. The big bone in the man's thigh stuck out of his trousers and his other leg bent in a gruesome arrangement. Homer leaned his face in and Ridgeway groaned.

"Are you there, my boy?"

"Yes, sir."

"That's good." Ridgeway sat up and howled in anguish. He looked over the station's gloom, recognizing nothing. His gaze passed over Cora without interest. "Where are we?"

"On the hunt," Homer said.

"Always more niggers to hunt. Do you have your journal?"

"Yes, sir."

"I have a thought."

Homer removed his notes from the satchel and opened to a fresh page.

"The imperative is . . . no, no. That's not it. The American imperative is a splendid thing . . . a beacon . . . a shining beacon." He coughed and a spasm overtook his body. "Born of necessity and virtue, between the hammer . . . and the anvil . . . Are you there, Homer?"

"Yes, sir."

"Let me start again . . ."

Cora leaned into the pump of the handcar. It didn't move, no matter how much weight she heaved on it. At her feet on the wooden platform was a small metal buckle. She snapped it and the pump squeaked. She tried the lever again and the handcar crawled forward. Cora looked back at Ridgeway and Homer. The slave catcher whispered his address and the black boy recorded his words. She pumped and pumped and rolled out of the light. Into the tunnel that no one had made, that led nowhere.

She discovered a rhythm, pumping her arms, throwing all of herself into movement. Into northness. Was she traveling through the tunnel or digging it? Each time she brought her arms down on the lever, she drove a pickax into the rock, swung a sledge onto a railroad spike. She never got Royal to tell her about the men and women who made the underground railroad. The ones who excavated a million tons of rock and dirt, toiled in the belly of the earth for the deliverance of slaves like her. Who stood with all those other souls who took runaways into their homes, fed them, carried them north on their backs, died for them. The station masters and conductors and sympathizers. Who are you after you finish something this magnificent—in constructing it you have also journeyed through it, to the other side. On one end there was who you were before you went underground, and on the other end a new person steps out into the light. The up-top world must be so ordinary compared to the miracle beneath, the miracle you made with your sweat and blood. The secret triumph you keep in your heart.

She put miles behind her, put behind her the counterfeit sanctuaries and endless chains, the murder of Valentine farm. There was only the darkness of the tunnel, and somewhere ahead, an exit. Or a dead end, if that's what fate decreed—nothing but a blank, pitiless wall. The last bitter joke. Finally spent, she curled on the handcar and dozed, aloft in the darkness as if nestled in the deepest recess of the night sky.

When she woke, she decided to go the rest of the way on foot—her arms were empty. Limping, tripping over crossties. Cora ran her hand along the wall of the tunnel, the ridges and pockets. Her fingers danced over valleys, rivers, the peaks of mountains, the contours of a new nation hidden beneath the old. *Look outside as you speed through, and you'll find the true face of America.* She could not see it but she felt it, moved through its heart. She feared she'd gotten turned around in her sleep. Was she going deeper in or back from where she came? She trusted the slave's choice to guide her—anywhere, anywhere but where you are escaping from. It had gotten her this far. She'd find the terminus or die on the tracks.

She slept twice more, dreaming of her and Royal in her cabin. She told him of her old life and he held her, then turned her around so they faced each other. He pulled her dress over her head and took off his trousers and shirt. Cora kissed him and ran her hands over the territory of his body. When he spread her legs she was wet and he slid inside her, saying her name as no one had ever said it and as no one ever would, sugary and tender. She awoke each time to the void of the tunnel and when she was done weeping over him she stood and walked.

The mouth of the tunnel started as a tiny hole in the dark. Her strides made it a circle, and then the mouth of a cave, hidden by brush and vines. She pushed aside the brambles and entered the air.

It was warm. Still that stingy winter light but warmer than Indiana, the sun almost overhead. The crevice burst open into a forest of scrub pine and fir. She didn't know what Michigan or Illinois or Canada looked like. Perhaps she wasn't in America anymore but had pushed beyond it. She kneeled to drink from the creek when she stumbled on it. Cool clear water. She washed the soot and grime from her arms and face. "From the mountains," she said, after an article in one of the dusty almanacs. "Snowmelt." Hunger made her head light. The sun told her which way was north.

It was getting dark when she came upon the trail, worthless and pocked rut that it was. She heard the wagons after she'd been sitting on the rock awhile. There were three of them, packed for a long journey, laden with gear, inventories lashed to the sides. They were headed west.

The first driver was a tall white man with a straw hat, gray-whiskered and as impassive as a wall of rock. His wife sat beside him on the driver's box, pink face and neck poking out of a plaid blanket. They regarded her neutrally and passed on. Cora made no acknowledgment of their presence. A young man drove the second wagon, a redheaded fellow with Irish features. His blue eyes took her in. He stopped.

"You're a sight," he said. High in pitch, like a bird's chirping. "You need something?"

Cora shook her head.

"I said, do you need anything?"

Cora shook her head again and rubbed her arms from the chill.

The third wagon was commanded by an older negro man. He was thickset and grizzled, dressed in a heavy rancher's coat that had seen its share of labor. His eyes were kind, she decided. Familiar though she couldn't place it. The smoke from his pipe smelled like potatoes and Cora's stomach made a noise.

"You hungry?" the man asked. He was from the south, from his voice.

"I'm very hungry," Cora said.

"Come up and take something for yourself," he said.

Cora clambered to the driver's box. He opened the basket. She tore off some bread and gobbled it down.

"There's plenty," he said. He had a horseshoe brand on his neck and pulled up his collar to hide it when Cora's eyes lingered. "Shall we catch up?"

"That's good," she said.

He barked at the horses and they proceeded on the rut.

"Where you going?" Cora said.

"St. Louis. From there the trail to California. Us, and some people we going to meet in Missouri." When she didn't respond he said, "You come from down south?"

"I was in Georgia. I ran away." She said her name was Cora. She unfolded the blanket at her feet and wrapped herself in it.

"I go by Ollie," he said. The other two wagons came into view around the bend.

The blanket was stiff and raspy under her chin but she didn't mind. She wondered where he escaped from, how bad it was, and how far he traveled before he put it behind him.

ACKNOWLEDGMENTS

Thanks to Nicole Aragi, Bill Thomas, Rose Courteau, Michael Goldsmith, Duvall Osteen, and Alison Rich (still) for getting this book into your hands. At Hanser over the years: Anna Leube, Christina Knecht, and Piero Salabe. Also: Franklin D. Roosevelt for funding the Federal Writers' Project, which collected the life stories of former slaves in the 1930s. Frederick Douglass and Harriet Jacobs, obviously. The work of Nathan Huggins, Stephen Jay Gould, Edward E. Baptist, Eric Foner, Fergus Bordewich, and James H. Jones was very helpful. Josiah Nott's theories of "amalgamation." *The Diary of a Resurrectionist.* Runaway slave advertisements come from the digital collections of the University of North Carolina at Greensboro. The first one hundred pages were fueled by early Misfits ("Where Eagles Dare [fast version]," "Horror Business," "Hybrid Moments") and Blanck Mass ("Dead Format"). David Bowie is in every book, and I always put on *Purple Rain* and *Daydream Nation* when I write the final pages; so thanks to him and Prince and Sonic Youth. And finally, Julie, Maddie, and Beckett for all the love and support.